WESTMAR COLLEGE LIBRARY

P9-CMO-323

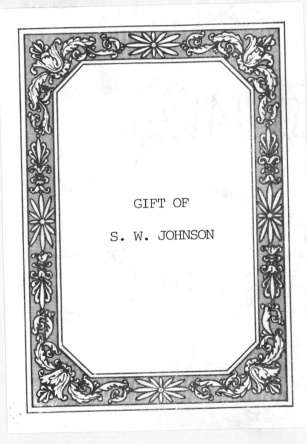

GIFT OF

S. W. JOHNSON

Understanding Educational Measurement and Evaluation

Understanding Educational Measurement and Evaluation

JERRY BERGMAN
Bowling Green State University, Ohio

Houghton Mifflin Company   **Boston**
Dallas   Geneva, Illinois   Hopewell, New Jersey   Palo Alto   London

Copyright © 1981 by Houghton Mifflin Company. All rights reserved. No part of this work may be reproduced in any form or by any means, electronic or mechanical, including photocopying and recording, or by any information storage or retrieval system, without permission in writing from the publisher.

Printed in the U.S.A.

Library of Congress Catalog Card Number: 79-7417

ISBN: 0-395-30782-1

Contents

Preface

Understanding Educational Measurement and Evaluation is a basic text that can be used in introductory testing-and-measurement courses at both the undergraduate and graduate levels. The standard topics of testing and measurement as they apply to both standardized and teacher-made tests are treated simply and directly. Special effort is given to making fundamental information interesting and readily understandable without sacrificing technical accuracy and completeness. Numerous examples and case studies are used to relate theoretical concepts to everyday classroom situations. This practical, down-to-earth approach will make this book equally useful to prospective and practicing elementary- and secondary-school teachers, counselors, administrators, and concerned parents.

The approach of the text is also very humanistic: its focus is on the construction and use of tests as diagnostic tools to help students learn and grow. Much emphasis is placed on the positive role tests can play in the teaching-learning process when there is open communication between teachers and students about tests and their results. To help teachers maximize test benefits, extensive practical guidelines for test construction, administration, analysis, improvement, and feedback are offered and amply illustrated. Statistical concepts are included when critical to understanding, but the emphasis is on interpretation and use—not on computation.

The book is divided into four major sections. Part I introduces the subject of measurement and evaluation through a look at history and a survey of current issues. Special attention is given to ways in which feedback can be used to help students overcome negative attitudes and begin to appreciate tests as important, and even enjoyable, learning experiences.

Part II contains a highly practical examination of the many forms of tests and test questions. Here the major emphasis is on the how-to of testing. Detailed, step-by-step guidelines are given for developing teacher-made tests; helping students take tests; writing specific test items, such as true-or-false statements, essay questions, and the like; improving tests through item analysis; scoring tests; evaluating and using tests; and choosing, administering, and interpreting standardized tests. Numerous examples, as well as frank discussion of the strengths and weaknesses of testing techniques and question types, make this section easily understandable and readily applicable to any classroom situation.

Part III focuses on grading, rating, and social measurement. It begins by examining the pros and cons of the most commonly used grading systems and addresses the issues of validity and reliability. Following an overview of rating-scale formats, the administration and applications of such social measurement tools as personal interviews, interest surveys, and self-expressive devices are examined. The section closes with a discussion of sociograms and the very important issue of invasion of student privacy.

Elementary statistical concepts are introduced in Part IV. Although familiarity with basic statistics is crucial to the understanding of measurement and evaluation, it is an aspect that many students resist. For this reason, emphasis is placed more on comprehension and interpretation than on computation. After having completed this section, students should be well-equipped to understand and discuss the full spectrum of standardized-test reporting mechanisms, even though they may not be prepared to produce complex statistical data themselves.

I am indebted to Dr. Clare Erwin, Dr. Ronald Marcott, and Dr. William Reitz for their instruction and guidance during my graduate studies in evaluation and research at Wayne State University in Detroit. I also extend heartfelt thanks to the reviewers, whose discerning critiques led to a better product: Professor Alan F. Patrick, Towson State University; Professor B. O. Smith, University of South Florida; Professor William R. Guilfoile, Thomas More College. A special note of appreciation is due my willing and patient editors, Trisha Nealon and Cynthia Fostle, who made this book a reality. Finally, of all the people who contributed to this project, I'm most grateful to Marie, who not only typed most of the original manuscript, but constantly offered invaluable advice on content and style, thus ensuring that the book would be both practical and readable.

Understanding Educational Measurement and Evaluation

Part I
Introduction

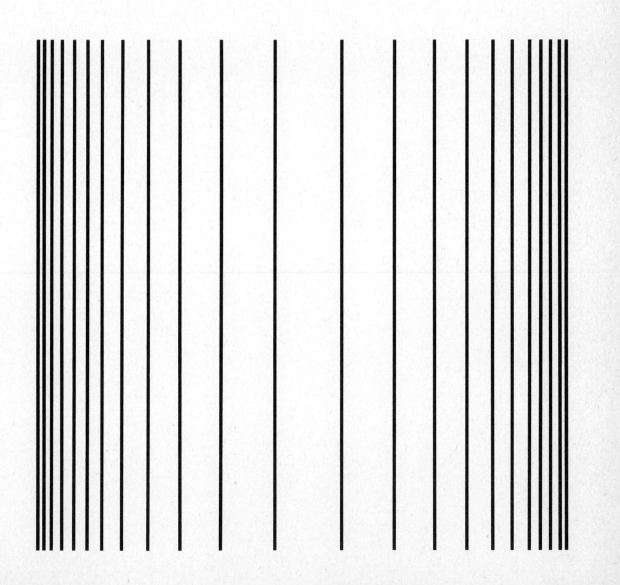

1 Measurement and Evaluation: A Background

Our earliest written records show that as long as people have been people, they have evaluated and judged each other. Parents have evaluated their children in the hopeful attempt to respond to their best interests. Employers have evaluated their employees and responded to what information they received from the evaluation process. Likewise, in a teaching situation, where the teacher is responsible for helping the student grow intellectually and emotionally, evaluation has always played an important role. Writings by the philosophers Socrates, Aristotle, and Plato show that evaluation took place during classical times, although not necessarily through written testing. For centuries, personal observation, oral questioning, and subjective judgment have been the methods commonly used to evaluate students.

Introduction: Looking Back

In many early schools, from the American Revolution through the early 1900s, it had been customary for lay committees (non-teachers) to be partially responsible for evaluating local schools. Our present-day school boards have evolved from such committees (Noll et al., 1972: 20). The lay committees usually visited the schools at least once a year for "inspection" purposes. During their visits, committee members commonly questioned the students in order to evaluate their progress. (Movies about the schools in the early 1900s often showed this procedure.) This method has become increasingly rare, but there is a growing faction of educators and parents who feel that there are many advantages to a system where an outside body evaluates the progress of students (Hill et al. 1978).

Gerberich et al. (1962) conclude from their review of educational literature that measurement of performance in the schools and elsewhere may be divided into three periods. In the first period, from the beginning of historical records to about the nineteenth century, "measurement in education was naturally quite crude" (Gerberich et al. 1962, 19). Although elaborate written examinations were used by the Chinese as early as 2200 B.C. in their selection of public officials, most evaluation elsewhere was rather informal, and evidently few attempts were made to standardize evaluation or base it on what we today call objective criteria. Physical prowess and stoicism were judged with formal tests as early as 500 B.C. in Sparta. At this time in Greece proficiency tests in athletic games, language, and the fine arts were also used. Instead of formal evaluation, often committees would simply discuss the performances of candidates, students, or those seeking work or public office and vote on decisions about promotion, retention, or employment.

Gerberich's study concludes that historically most people have not felt the need for extensive evaluation. Instead people have believed themselves able to adequately evaluate individuals informally—at least for positions in the military, in the schools, or for some social and political positions. Systematic evaluation did not occur until people, in an organized way, began to research the world. Throughout history intuition and, in essence, common sense were heavily relied upon. Through socialization, people were taught a certain set of beliefs and often accepted these as being fully true. Many ancients, such as Socrates, felt that humans are born knowing everything—and teaching simply *draws this knowledge out* through the questioning process. According to such a philosophy, there is therefore no need to evaluate learning, because teaching can only draw out what students already know.

The ancients were much more confident about their set of beliefs than we are about ours today. Most people then were not exposed to different cultures and to a large body of knowledge as we are today, but instead they simply accepted the small world around them. It could be said that evaluation was not seen as important because there was not that much data to evaluate! Today's knowledge explosion has changed all that. Most of what is known was discovered during the past few years, and almost all of history's most significant scientists have lived during the past few years. Until recently evaluation techniques were primarily subjective. Our present preoccupation with measurement and evaluation is *a major result* of the scientific revolution begun by Bacon, Galileo, and others who introduced a new way of knowing called **scientific research** and the **experimental method**. These concepts will be discussed later.

Formal testing eventually was to express itself in written testing. In more modern times, the first written tests were probably developed and used at the University of Bologna and at the University of Paris during the thirteenth century and improved at Cambridge in the early 1900s. Although much of the testing done at these universities was still oral, the written testing taking place was at least somewhat similar to the type of written testing used today.

European history shows that most people's occupations were determined primarily by the social class into which they were born. Unfortunately, it was rare for a person's abilities and interests to be deciding factors in occupational choice. As a result of the belief prevalent in the early American colonies that advancement should be based upon abilities and interests and *not* upon the social class one is born into, and with early America's disdain for and rejection of the British system in which one's social and occupational role in life is largely ascribed and not achieved, came the idea of **universal education**. This system was based on the belief that *every* child should be able to attend school, and at the state's expense, until he or she reaches adulthood. With universal education came the opportunity for each individual to fulfill his or her own level of ability; theoretically, the individual is limited only by innate factors—not by social class.

And significantly, as a tie-in to this belief, tests began to become more and more important in America. One could not fairly place individuals in occupations according to social class, but rather one had to evaluate innate abilities. It is true that social class did play an important role in early America, as it today still does, but more and more individuals from lower social classes began to be able to scale the occupational and social hierarchy based at least somewhat on their own achievements. In Europe, where for generations only the children of the upper social classes usually went very far in school, there seemed to be more similarity in students' intellectual and other measurable learning abilities than was apparent in the American system. Because children of many social classes and intellectual levels began to attend school in America, more than ever before a need grew to measure and evaluate these students, both in grading them and in developing programs to help them.

It is not hard to imagine why many of the first examinations were oral—a major reason was the unavailability and expense of paper and writing implements. With the development of inexpensive paper and writing tools (such as pencils in the late 1880s, the ballpoint pen after World War II, and even the popular felt-tip pen in the early 1960s), it became increasingly feasible to use written forms of tests. It also became increasingly *practical* to use written testing, for the reason that enrollments became so large in the 1800s that school committees could not easily examine all pupils orally.

The Contributions of Horace Mann

A forerunner for the development of modern written testing was Horace Mann. In 1845, the Boston school system developed written examinations in arithmetic, Scripture knowledge, geography, grammar, history, astronomy, and natural philosophy. Partially because of increased enrollments, Mann and others argued that written examinations were better. These assumptions could be questioned, but Mann argued on the following grounds:

1. they are more impartial, and less biased
2. they are more thorough than older forms of examination
3. they determine more accurately whether pupils have been competently taught
4. they reduce the possibility of favoritism.

Mann felt that without written evaluation the schools could not adequately evaluate the progress of their students. To test Mann's contention that the students were not learning nearly as much as the schools felt they were learning, a total of 154 questions were prepared and administered to 530 pupils who were "the flowers of the Boston Public Schools," selected from a total of 7,526 students. The committee scored the papers and tabulated the answers.

The eagerly awaited results proved Mann's criticisms to be correct. The findings "revealed great inequalities among schools and startling ignorance on the part of many pupils" (Noll et al. 1972, 21). Unfortunately, though, this experiment did not result in effective schoolwide testing.

More Efforts to Standardize

There were other periodic efforts to develop standardized testing programs. For example Reverend George Fisher devised what were probably the first objective measures of achievement. Called "scale books," because they measured or "scaled" knowledge, these tests evaluated student skills and accomplishments in subject areas including handwriting, spelling, mathematics, navigation, Scripture knowledge, and grammar and composition. In this way they were somewhat similar to modern achievement tests.

He thus provided examinations by which students could be evaluated and therefore compared to each other, not only in each subject area, but also on the whole. Teachers could begin to identify those students who needed help in specific areas. Again, though, the work of Fisher made little immediate impact on the schools. There was still a great deal of resistance to what was in essence standardized testing. This resistance has re-emerged in the past two decades, at least partially because of the evidence that socially and economically disadvantaged groups, such as blacks and other minorities, as a whole do not tend to do as well on standardized tests compared to more advantaged groups.

Remember that into the late 1800s teachers and school officials did not appreciate the extent or effect of individual differences as we do today. The tremendous amount of psychological, sociological, and general scientific research on human beings that verified the clear differences between persons on thousands of traits and abilities was yet to come. Many people strongly felt that most individual differences could be explained in such terms as "laziness" and that the way to cure this problem was use of corporal punishment. If people could acknowledge a "reason," it was often gender—boys typically did poorer because they were boys. Today we are aware of conditions such as dyslexia, dysgraphia, aphasia, alexia, anomia, agnosia, and apraxia—all of which produce difficulty in a student's handling of schoolwork, and all of which at one time probably produced what was called "laziness."

Sir Francis Galton (1822-1911) was one of the first to sense the many real implications of the fact that individuals seemed to differ intellectually and emotionally and not just physically. Of course one can say that even today we do not fully appreciate the importance of individual differences. In spite of the fact that colleges of education repeatedly stress the importance of individualizing (teaching students according to their individual needs, talents, abilities, shortcomings, handicaps, etc.), there is still a tendency to attribute poor performance in school to innate or personality faults.

Galton researched individual differences using a number of methods, demonstrating that individuals "differ in physical, sensory-motor, and personality traits" (Noll 1972, 22). He found through his early experiments that people display consistent differences in, for example, the speed with which they are able to press down a telegraph key in reaction to a flashing light (i.e., this experiment measured differences in **sensory motor response**). Although early researchers hoped to find relationships in the speed of human response to certain stimuli and intelligence, the results were often disappointing. A good explanation for this is related to the growing evidence that the interrelationships between different characteristics are much more complicated than the early scientists first expected them to be. These relationships are still being researched. Nonetheless, early psychologists were able to determine that there *were* distinct differences between people in virtually every imaginable human trait—the ability to run through mazes, assemble blocks, put together picture puzzles, memorize lists of adjectives (likewise there were differences between memorizing lists of *nouns* and lists of *verbs*). To study relationships between these differences, psychologists have developed many elaborate tools such as memory drums, various mazes, response boards, and other psychological tests. Importantly, it has been found that these differences are only partly amenable to learning and practice.

In one of the most fascinating early experiments, M. J. Rice developed a research design to test the common assumption that increased study almost always improves learning and raises the **level of mastery**. A commonly held belief of the past (and even the present) has been that one who studies more or longer will do better in school, and conversely, poor school performance is the result of not studying enough. Rich found that those who studied spelling 30 minutes a day for eight years were "not better spellers than children who studied the subject 15 minutes a day for eight years" (Gerberich 1962, 23). (There are several reasons for this that we know of—one is that spelling ability is largely a result of memory, and memory function tends to be at least to a degree innate.) Ironically, when the results of experimental research goes against commonly accepted assumptions, we often reject, or at least seriously question, the results of the research. This was the early experience in research and testing, and it is still the experience today. And there is good reason for being skeptical; we cannot afford to accept data as fact without serious challenge—that's the scientific method. But when one examines a subject in close detail, he or she often finds that things which "seem to be so" simply are not true.

Rice was trying to determine what the schoolteachers were actually accomplishing. As do researchers today, Rice utilized a number of techniques to separate, or isolate, some of the factors he felt could influence spelling in order to discover the more important ones and the amount of influence each had. A list of fifty spelling words was given as a test to more than 16,000 students in grades four to eight. In an effort to reduce some of the variation that he anticipated with this test, Rice devised a test in which the spelling words were used in sentences. With this technique, Rice personally directed the examination of more than 13,000 children. The last test Rice used was that in which a story, accompanied by a picture, was read to the class, after which they were asked to write a composition about the story and picture. The papers were checked for spelling errors. Rice found that spelling abilities varied from city to city, school to school, and even class to class. Rice also tried to control such factors as time devoted to study, location of the school, and efficiency of the teacher. As studies today are also showing, Rice found that spelling ability is due to a wide variety of factors, all influenced by many different elements. Today we are still trying to isolate the many factors which influence skills such as spelling. Elaborate statistical and research techniques (such as **multivariate analyses**, for one example) have been developed to separate the influence of various factors, but there is still much progress that needs to be made.

Alfred Binet and the Development of I.Q. Tests

No history of evaluation is complete without a discussion of Alfred Binet's work. At the turn of the century, Binet was a fairly well-known French psychologist. He had become interested in mental measurement through his work with the school children in Paris. At this time, the Paris educational authorities noticed that there were clear individual differences in the abilities of students to profit from school instruction. The authorities wanted a quick, simple way to isolate those students who needed special help, most notably those who we today classify as mentally handicapped (EMR). When the authorities requested this information from teachers, teachers often gave the names of "problem" (i.e. discipline problem) students, and not those of students who were academically or mentally disadvantaged. Binet was interested in the question of how individual mental differences could be sorted out, and so began working on developing a test.

His "test," which became the famous "intelligence quotient" (I.Q.) test, was originally developed primarily as an attempt at finding an effective way to determine whether or not a student could benefit from standard school instruction. Since then the I.Q. test has often been seen by the public as a measure similar in precision to the measurement of height or weight. Many people, however, also believe it is very accurate and yields results that cannot be changed.

After years of study and experimenting, Binet and his associate Theodore Simon published an article in 1905 in which they presented a series of tests, or a scale, to measure the level of mental development in children. The article aroused worldwide interest, most notably the interest of Lewis Terman, then of Stanford University in California. In

1908 Binet and Simon published an improved version of their scale, and in 1911, Binet published another revised version. The work of perfecting the intelligence test was largely taken up by Terman when Binet died soon after the second revision. The version that Terman developed was known as the Stanford Binet. Noll (1972, 26) stated that Binet's work "constituted one of the most important milestones in the development of mental tests. His was the first successful method for measuring intelligence and expressing individual differences in accurate, quantitative terms. Indeed, Binet's method in materials for the measurement of intelligence forms the basis of the approach still generally used today." Although there is currently a tremendous amount of criticism of the I.Q. test, much of which is justified, many researchers feel that the I.Q. test is probably the most successful, the most valid, and the most reliable psychological test ever developed.

The Development of Modern Standardized Tests

Today there is much criticism of tests, especially standardized tests. Many feel that standardized tests are useless or even harmful. Among a cast of others, the critics of tests on the whole include Van Allen (1976), Gross (1962) and Fine (1975).

Gerberich et al. (1962, 23) note that "attempts during the last decade of the nineteenth century by Cattell and others to measure intelligence by means of physical characteristics, sensory acuity, and motor skills tests, gave, for the most part, negative results." Comparatively, then, Binet's test was by far the most successful; it spurred on the development of an entire testing industry and a new profession called **psychometrics**. It was felt that if intelligence could be successfully measured, so could traits such as memory, attention, comprehension, suggestibility, imagination, or aesthetic appreciation. As noted, however, success in measuring these areas often falls far below that achieved in measuring "intelligence," at least intelligence for school-related activities.

With increasing stress on the scientific method, empirical investigation, and experimental psychological research, psychological laboratories such as those begun by Wundt in 1879 in Leipsic, Germany, spurred on the development of various types of tests which attempted to accurately measure personality. Thus, behavior, thinking, and emotions began to be studied more and more scientifically; they were looked at according to basic "psychological" laws. Many of these laws were later assumed under the title "behaviorism," a theory which proposed that all behavior and personality characteristics could be directly measured by some type of physiological or psychological test. There was much optimism at the turn of the century, and many scientists believed it was at least *possible* to measure these traits. Although repeated efforts have produced controversial or disappointing results, and even with the I.Q. test under serious challenge, many today still believe measurement in these areas is possible.

How the Stanford-Binet Test Works

Basically, the scale that Binet and Simon developed compares *mental* age with chronological age. If one has a mental age of 10 and a chrono- logical age of 10, one would have a 1.00 relationship, or an I.Q. of 100 (Binet multiplied by 100 to eliminate decimal points to the second place). If one had a mental age of 5, and a chronological age of 10, one's I.Q. would be .50 times 100, or 50. The simple equation:

$$5 \div 10 = .50; .50 \times 100 = 50$$

If one had a mental age of 10 and a chronological age of 5, one would have an I.Q. of 2.00, times 100, or 200. Again:

$$10 \div 5 = 2 \times 100 = 200$$

Although this concept is useful with school children; it loses its validity to some extent when it is used with adults. Mental growth does not continue in adults at the same rate as in children. To say that a certain 5-year-old is "mentally like a 10-year-old" has meaning, but to say that a certain 40-year-old is "mentally like an 80-year-old" borders on the ridiculous, even though under the I.Q. concept both persons would have an I.Q. of 200. Nonetheless, systems have been developed which enable the I.Q. concept to remain in use. The I.Q. concept con- siders around 80 or below mentally retarded and 90-110 "normal" (about 70 percent of the population have I.Q.s that fall between 85 and 115). On the other hand, "gifted" is usually defined as 130 or above. Because there is no firm dividing line, a school may consider gifted 115 or 120 or above, especially if it is committed to gifted education or has funds for larger classes and thus can include more potentially gifted children.

Entering World War I and World War II

The two world wars, probably more than any other factor, encouraged the development and use of various types of tests, first outside the field of education then, when technology became more advanced, both inside the field of education and in the business world and other segments of society. The Army had a need to quickly evaluate draftees and volunteers, partly in order to determine for which jobs which people should be trained. It was obviously expensive for the Army to train someone to be, for example, a flyer when he or she did not show the potential. Time was also important, and the Army hired scores of psychologists to develop tests.

The Army Alpha and the Army Beta

Around 1917 Dr. Arthur S. Otis and others developed an important test, the *Army Alpha*, which came to be used for measuring and placing U.S. Army recruits and draftees during World War I. The Alpha was the first **group intelligence test** (an I.Q. test given to a group of persons at one time) to be published (Greene et al. 1953, 30). Up to this point all other intelligence tests were **individual intelligence tests**, or those that were given to one person at a time. (See Chapter 11.) And because a significant number of inductees could not read English, the *Army Beta*, a non-language test, was developed for use with illiterates. All in all, nearly two million men were tested by either the *Army Alpha* or the *Army Beta* in 1917 and 1918 (Noll et al. 1972, 29).

The *Army Alpha* and *Beta* were picked up and widely used by educators, even after the close of the war. Public schools used the tests on thousands of high school students. Almost immediately following World War I, group intelligence tests on the whole became more and more common. The *Army Alpha*, as a forerunner for group tests, proved itself far faster and less costly than were individual intelligence tests and led to the wide acceptance and popularity of the group intelligence test format in the field of education.

And A Variety of Other Tests

Another test developed for World War I, a personality test, one of the first known as a **personal data sheet**, was devised by R. S. Woodworth (Noll 1972, 29). Woodworth's *Personal Data Sheet* was developed for use on Army soldiers during World War I. The test consists of a list of questions designed to determine whether or not the testee has any of the common neurotic symptoms such as "I have a hard time sleeping" or "I often think people are out to get me." Aside from obtaining information about intelligence or personality, the Army also developed tests which were useful in determining, to some degree, mechanical, clerical, and various other aptitudes. These tests, although they were not evidentally as successful, were likewise important.

The basic Army Alpha was later revised and other tests were developed including *Otis Group Intelligence* Scale, the *Miller Mental Abilities Test,* and *Terman Group Tests.*

The Survey Test Shortly after World War I, the "survey test," an example of which is the Stanford Achievement Test, was developed. This test is designed primarily for use at the elementary level in order to survey *a wide variety of abilities* such as spelling, reading, comprehension, grammar, punctuation, etc. This type of test is still in wide use today. One of the most useful is the *Wide Range Achievement Test* (WRAT), which surveys first grade through college in the basic subject areas.

Broadened Subject Areas Once the testing industry began, psychometricians and researchers broadened the subject areas into other fields, such as music, art, and physical education. For example, one of the earliest tests in music, the *Seashore Test,* tried to measure such things as pitch discrimination, intensity or loudness of sound tones, and rhythm, because these qualities were thought to be the main components of musical ability. Stenquist developed a test of mechanical aptitude, and Thurstone developed a test of clerical aptitude. Today, there are standardized tests which purport to measure virtually every quality exhibited by humans—and a few which purport to measure qualities many people question that humans exhibit.

It should be noted here that, although there are a number of different *types* of tests—aptitude tests, achievement tests, I.Q. tests—these labels may distort somewhat in that, for example, there is not always a clear difference between an aptitude test and an I.Q. test. Most of these tests, to some degree, actually measure achievement rather than aptitude or intelligence. We will discuss this in more detail later.

Measures of Personality: Projective Tests

One of the best known early measures of personality was developed in 1921 by Herman Rorschach and is known today as the *Rorschach Ink Blot Test.* This test was the first of what is known as **projective tests** in which, instead of being asked for the "right answer," the student "projects" his or her personality in response to the test. It was not until some 15 years later, however, that projective techniques employing such unstructured situations as ink blots and pictures came into wide use in the study of personality (Watson 1938, 369).

Projective, personality, psychological, I.Q., and other tests in time contributed to the creation of an entire new industry, that of psychological testing. Much psychological research utilizes various standardized and questionnaire type tests. These tests have enabled us to explore many facets of personality previously not amenable to exploration. Among the first to research personality by using tests (actually questionnaires) in order to understand human beings better were Hartshorne and May, who carried out the *Character Education Inquiry* research, from which they learned a great deal about character education, cheating, dishonesty, and the effectiveness of various religious and moral educational programs as they relate to the "character," or personality. Hartshorne and May were not primarily concerned with the educational institutions but with religious indoctrination and moral teaching programs in the church, Sunday school, and, at that time, in public schools. Nonetheless, most of the research was done in public and private schools, and much of it is applicable to the school situation. For the first time *extensive* research was done on various personality factors, and the development of dozens of psychological tests and other written feedback forms enabled us to research in this area.

A Proliferation of Literature

About this time, the early twentieth century, partially due to the development of such research tools as tests, dozens of new scientific journals and professional societies in the field of education as well as psychology and other areas appeared. Many of the larger and more well-known scientific journals were already established around the turn of the century or shortly thereafter. There was also an incredible proliferation of professional journals during World War II. Today the journal population is still growing, and there are thousands of journals in any one general field and a dozen or more in each specific field. Of those journals established in the area of education during World War II, many were devoted at least in part to problems of measurement in education. Likewise, the professional societies in education and psychology that were established included many persons interested in the field of measurement in general, educational testing, and psychological testing as well.

Questions for the New Field

By 1930 most *types* of educational and psychological tests still used today were fairly well established. After the 1930s, however, began a period of questioning and doubt in the field of educational measurement. As more and more tests were developed, unfavorable reactions were inevitable. One concern was that all of the tests relied too heavily upon learning, especially on the type of learning that more commonly took place in the upper middle social class. There was also strong feeling at this time that the tests measured specific and limited ability—and did not measure some of the most fundamental educational objectives (Noll et al. 1972, 33). Both concerns are still with us today. **Gestalt psychology**, a school of psychology that emphasizes the interrelatedness of the parts of a whole, i.e., the integration of the individual promotes growth and, ultimately, maturity, had a marked influence on measurement and evaluation during this period.

Thus, the concept of "the whole child" and an effort to try to understand test scores in terms of this concept—as only a small part of the total child—were viewed as important. A child may have a low I.Q. but a high level of motivation and a fairly high level of creativity. Consequently, that child may perform better than many children with much higher I.Q.s. The fact that a child's I.Q. is relatively low does *not* mean a great deal in itself, it only has meaning in relation to understanding the myriad aspects of a child's personality. Each person is a unique individual with many facets and aspects of his or her personality, all of which in some way contribute to make him or her the person he or she is. Although this "uniqueness" factor has been used to criticize tests, it could equally well be argued that Gestalt psychology argues for *more* and not fewer tests. The more tests we are able to utilize (and the more different kinds of tests such as personality, performance, etc.), the more we are able to understand the total person. Although it is true that tests can often hurt people (and we will stress this throughout this presentation), nonetheless tests *can be used to help people.* And, if individuals are trained properly, one could say that it is possible that tests can, *in most cases,* be used to help people.

Major Growth in the Field of Testing

During the Second World War testing became more widespread, partly because of the need for people to work in the new specialties such as radio, radar, and tank repair, all of which emerged due to the increased technology of World War II compared to that of World War I. Again, a situation in which it was important to determine which people were best for specific kinds of defense duty was in the national foreground. It is extremely expensive for the Army to train a person to repair heavy equipment when he or she is simply not suited for that kind of work and could instead work more effectively for the Armed Services as a mathematician, for example. In addition, the large amount of research on the nature of human abilities that took place *between* World War I and World War II was utilized in developing even better tests, tests that became available for use during the war years.

Yet another factor that spurred on the use of tests in the schools was the increased concern over mental health and the increased emphasis on the work of psychiatrists, psychologists, and other mental health professionals. For most of history, unfortunately people have tended to blame emotional problems on the person who has them (i.e., blaming the victim). Likewise many people tended to feel emotional problems could be best dealt with by a priest, minister, rabbi, or other clergymen. With time, though, for various reasons more and more people began to put their faith on the growing mental health professions in the hope of curing mental illness. In an effort to improve their techniques, psychiatrists were strongly interested in the development of psychological tests. Thus, there was a market for the psychological test and much interest in the field. These two factors together spurred on the huge modern psychological test industry.

High school curriculum literally exploded beginning with the 30s, as more and more individuals went to high school. At one time considered a luxury, high school became a necessity. Federally aided vocational programs in the schools as well as record high school enrollment stimulated the **guidance movement**, and both increased use of and development of various kinds of tests to help students both academically and in guidance.

The guidance movement especially encouraged the development of specialized standardized tests. More and more schools, in the 20s and 30s and after, began hiring counselors. The schools increasingly began to realize that one of the main impediments to learning was the existence of psychological and emotional problems, however minor or "normal." The schools thus began to realize that in order to teach students effectively, they must, in a sense, enter the psychology business. Thus, individuals were trained specifically to help students with these types of problems. Although most schools today have counselors, more and more schools are hiring psychologists and psychiatrists. In the 50s, the latter were often called visiting teachers, social workers, and other less "fearful" names. There now seems to be increased reliance on the work of professional people and their use of the scientific method—and this means an inclination toward measurement and evaluation to specify and quantify. All this means the progressive acceptance and effective use of various standardized tests.

After World War II, one of the major developments in the field of tests was *improvement* rather than radical *new* test types. An important development in the correction of tests is the use of high speed electronic computers. Before this tests had to be corrected by hand, and statistical manipulations were difficult. With computers, a large battery of tests are able to be corrected in a matter of minutes. The computer can also calculate norms, perform item analysis, and make other statistical manipulations to help the teacher understand both the students' performances and the accuracy and effectiveness of the test itself.

Over the past decade the government has increasingly had indirect influence on school policy. In several ways, Government funds have encouraged much research about testing and the use of standardized testing as a whole. Allocation of government monies depends to some degree on the results of standardized tests, whether for grade placement, job placement, or simply the identification of abilities or lack of abilities.

To illustrate the large amount of standardized testing used in the middle 1900s, the Education Records Bureau estimated that, in 1944, appropriately 60 million tests were administered to around 20 million persons. In addition, Woodruff and Pitchard (1949, 105-8) found that, in 1948, their tests files included some 1,080 tests, representing the output of about 74 test publishers. Since then, standardized testing has mushroomed considerably. We will discuss standardized testing in detail in Chapter 15.

Summary

Our earliest records show that people evaluate and judge each other. Systematic evaluation occurred when people began a more organized research of the world. Tests became significant in America largely as a result of the idea of *universal education*. Due to the economic factor, many of the first tests were oral. Written tests began to be developed with the emergence of inexpensive paper and writing tools. Horace Mann, Reverend George Fisher, Sir Francis Galton, M.J. Rice, and Albert Binet are some of the names to remember in the early development of testing. The two world wars were largely responsible for the development of testing outside of education. Once the testing industry began, researchers broadened the subject areas into other fields. One of the first *projective tests* was the Rorschach Ink Blot Test (1921). A whole new industry, psychological testing, developed. The guidance movement in schools encouraged the development of standardized tests. Most types of tests used today were developed by 1930, but there began a period of controversy as to the validity of testing. After World War II, the thrust was to improve upon already developed tests. Government funds have encouraged much research in the field of testing.

Suggested Readings

Aiken, Lewis R. *Psychological Testing and Assessment*. 3d rev. ed. Boston: Allyn and Bacon, 1979. Chapter 1.

Gerberich, J. Raymond, Harry A. Greene and Albert N. Jorgensen. *Measurement and Evaluation in the Modern School*. New York: David McKay Company, 1962. Chapter 2.

Michaels, William J. and M. Ray Karnes. *Measuring Educational Achievement*. New York: McGraw-Hill, 1950. Chapter 1.

Noll, Victor A. and Dale P. Scannell. *Introduction to Educational Measurement*. Boston: Houghton Mifflin, 1972. Chapter 2.

Ross, Clay Campbell and Julian C. Stanley. *Measurement in Today's Schools*. 3d rev. ed. Englewood Cliffs, N. J.: Prentice Hall, 1954. Chapters 1, 2.

Sax, Gilbert. *Principles of Educational Measurement and Evaluation*. Belmont, Calif.: Wadsworth Publishing Company, 1974. Chapters 1, 2.

Thorndike, Robert Ladd and Elizabeth Hagen. *Measurement and Evaluation in Psychology and Education*. 4th rev. ed. New York: John Wiley and Sons, 1977. Chapter 1.

2 Feedback: A Look at Its Importance and Uses

Recently a friend of mine took a short trip alone in an automobile. A common occurrence? Yes, except for the fact that my friend it totally blind. Since driving requires an awareness of where your car is in relation to the road and other vehicles, feedback in such a situation is of course imperative, and my sightless friend obviously must have had some kind of feedback. What kind did he have?* Let's first examine the general process of feedback.

Feedback is more or less continuous report about an ongoing process that is given to the person controlling the process. Feedback is necessary for the completion of most human activities, especially those involving learning. The following dialogue between a father and son as the son learns to hold a baseball bat illustrates the role of feedback in the learning process. Notice that most of the father's statements are almost pure feedback.

SON: Is this how you hold the bat?

FATHER: Not quite. Move your hands toward the small end and put them together like this.

SON: Like this?

FATHER: Yes, now you have it, except that you should put your fingers a little closer together.

(The son puts his fingers together and looks questioningly at his father.)

---

*My friend was able to drive a car even though he was blind because he was participating in an experiment. A TV camera picked up feedback from the road and converted it into sensory impressions that were conveyed to him on his back. Research in this area is still experimental, but promising. The point of this illustration, it should be stressed, is that feedback is *imperative* in an ongoing process such as driving. It is hard for us to imagine a successful, ongoing process without feedback. And the better the feedback, the easier the ongoing process. You knew he could not drive the car without some form of feedback, didn't you!

Key Concepts
Feedback
Learning analysis
Information-gathering tools
Diagnostic test
Labeling
Tracking

FATHER: There we go! Now when you swing, be sure to keep the bat level.

SON: What do you mean by level?

FATHER: Parallel with the ground, so that each part of the bat is about the same distance away from the ground, like this. If the end points toward the ground (*he tilts one end toward the ground*), the bat is no longer level. Now try to hold the bat this way when you swing.

SON: But Dad, this way seems harder.

FATHER: It may at first, but it helps you line up the bat with the path of the moving ball. If the bat is always level, all you have to worry about is the height of your hands.

SON: Oh, I see. Let me try it.

Notice that the child learned primarily from the feedback he received from his father. While he could learn how to bat without some of the feedback his father gave him, he would *still* need feedback. Without his father, he would learn from his own experience, using the information he received from his successes and failures to modify his batting style. The trial-and-error method is often much slower and more difficult.

The usefulness of feedback is not limited to the refinement of motor activities such as batting. It is important when learning almost anything. Three examples of academic feedback are:

1. comparing the procedure used to solve a problem with the steps in the textbook's examples,
2. looking up an answer to see if the correct solution was obtained,
3. receiving corrections and comments on a term paper.

Besides being an important component of the learning process, feedback plays an important role in decision making. Usually the more feedback (or information) we have, the more certain we can be that our decision is the best one. Should the tutor spend more time helping Leon with his math or does he understand the concepts adequately? Will the class be sufficiently interested in oceanography to spend two weeks on it? Do these students have enough algebra to be able to balance chemical equations? Teachers must constantly make educational decisions for which often they lack adequate background information. Usually, the more data they can gather, the better their decisions will be. Similar needs for data can be found in students. The more appropriate the feedback their teachers provide, the more effectively they are likely to learn. To be successful in the classroom, a teacher must know how to provide, gather, and interpret feedback.

Feedback: The Key to Effective Teaching

After videotaping thousands of hours of teachers at work, researchers at Wayne State University were able to identify a relatively small number of factors that separated the teachers judged "successful" from those judged "unsuccessful." One of these qualities was the ability to be keenly aware of where each child was—physically, emotionally, mentally, and academically. Teachers who are sensitive to their students' needs are more likely to spot individuals who are having difficulty and take remedial action. This is an especially important attribute because many youngsters either fear asking for help or do not realize they need it.

The Need for Tests as Feedback Tools

Testing is merely one of many forms of feedback—a way of monitoring a student's progress and conveying the results in order to reward achievement and redirect future learning. The main problem with tests as feedback, however, is that they are usually not given often enough. Effective teaching depends on almost constant monitoring of all students' progress, which requires many samples of students' work. Tests, quizzes, and homework can be effective feedback tools only if they form the basis for discussions between teachers, students, and parents about study habits, interests, and concerns. By spending time working directly with students as they complete their schoolwork, talking with students and their peers, using questionnaires, and involving students in projects that require application of what has been studied, teachers can learn more about their students and thus ensure that they provide adequate and appropriate feedback.

Developing Awareness

One way in which a teacher can obtain feedback is by circulating through the class as students work, observing each child's progress and noting areas of misunderstanding. The teacher is then able to give appropriate feedback, either individually or to the whole class. By paying attention to facial expressions, degree of involvement, and similar cues, a teacher can determine whether a student is totally lost, just confused, or fully understands an assignment. He or she can then decide whether or not intervention would be appropriate.

This is just one technique teachers can use to gather information that will enable them to help their students. To be optimally effective, most teachers utilize *many* information-gathering tools. And, they recognize that gathering information is actually half of the total feedback process; the other half is using this information appropriately to help the student.

Of course, other important feedback tools are the various teacher-made tests, but formal tests are another tool teachers can use to keep track of how well they are teaching and how well their students are learning. In this textbook we will cover a wide range of feedback tools. Ideally, teachers should use tests primarily to indicate areas in which their students need additional work and adjust their teaching accordingly.

Present Attitudes Towards Tests

When a test is announced, students usually react with mixed emotions, many of which are negative. Actually, many students' objections are not really against testing, but against the way tests have been used. Unfortunately, since one common reason for giving tests is to assign grades, students often see tests as roadblocks to A's. Tests, grades, and learning thus become intertwined, even though grades do not necessarily reflect learning. Is it any wonder that so many students dislike tests? A few examples will illustrate the degree of fear some students have developed towards tests.

Case 1 A bright, nineteen-year-old college student asked his professor to be excused from taking tests with the rest of the class because testing situations made him so tense that he literally could not read the questions. He stated that tests had always upset him, but that in the sixth grade a particular test, which was to count as a large percent of his grade, was the breaking point. He became hysterical during the test and his parents felt it best that he consult a doctor. Since then, his instructors have either waived tests or given him oral, take-home or similar substitute examinations on which he usually does well.

Case 2 An eighteen-year-old high school dropout seeking employment counseling was given an individual I.Q. test and found to be in the superior intellectual range. When questioned about his educational background, he replied that although he had very poor grades, he had always enjoyed studying. Nonetheless, no matter how hard he tried he said, he never could do well on tests. Continual poor perform-ance caused him to quit school in the tenth grade.

Although he was extremely bright according to I.Q. tests and other data, he lacked school test-taking skills, and his memory and writing skills were both substandard. Consistently doing poorly had increased his anxiety level to the point where it seriously interfered with his self-confidence. Although he developed very negative attitudes towards school and academic activities, he did a great deal of reading and drawing outside of school. Nonetheless, he interpreted his poor grades as indicating that he had a low intelligence and minimal academic ability.

Case 3 A highly motivated student of average ability experienced con-tinual difficulties in school, at least according to her report card. She hoped to become a research scientist and, although self-confident and capable, was discouraged by the fact that she couldn't earn higher grades. According to her own report, she enjoyed school, especially reading and science.

When she was in seventh grade, her school program had been cut to half-days in a drive to economize. She was assigned to the afternoon session, but elected to attend the morning session, too. During this time, she worked with the science teacher in the school laboratory, did experiments for other classes, tutored fellow students, and studied in the library. She also studied conscientiously each evening and inde-pendently pursued academic subjects that piqued her curiosity. Despite her great motivation, however, she rarely received grades higher than C throughout junior high and high school.

She was eventually accepted on probation by a community college, but was forced to withdraw due to poor grades. Her second attempt at college was more successful because she chose an innovative school that was more responsive to her individual needs. With her associate's degree, she was able to enter a conventional university and complete her bachelor's degree. Three years later she received her Ph.D. in biol-ogy and is now very active in scientific research, specializing in genetics.

These cases illustrate that some students who seem to be failing in school may really be failing only in achieving grades. And since grades are almost totally a result of performance on tests, a poor academic rec-ord may stem primarily from poor performance on tests. As the major-ity of teacher-made tests tend mostly to tap memory, it may even be said that poor academic performance is often the result of a deficiency in only one area—memory. While memory is important, success in life and in most professions usually depends on a diversity of factors, such as personality traits, ability to think abstractly, motivation level, and manual dexterity. Most tests, of course, do not tap these skills. This is indicated by the large percentage of highly successful individuals who have not done well in school. Goertzel and Goertzel (1962, p. 241) found that fully three-fifths of their sample of individuals who achieved high prominence in their respective fields had serious school problems. Among the many famous people who have had difficulties in school are Thomas Edison, Edgar Allan Poe, Nicholas Copernicus, J. Paul Getty, John Locke, Isaac Newton, Leo Tolstoy, Winston Churchill, Frederic Chopin, Albert Einstein, Enrico Fermi, Pablo Picasso, John Steinbeck, Louis Pasteur, Charles Darwin, Dwight Eisenhower, Franklin Roosevelt, and Carl Sandburg.

Fear of tests is very widespread. In one survey of college students (Bergman 1976b), 97 percent of the respondents used negative adjectives to describe their feelings just before taking a test. If tests are intended primarily to help students, and if students understand that tests are tools to help them achieve their goals, most students should have more positive feelings toward them. A surprising discovery was that despite their negative experiences, many students want to take tests, especially if they feel capable of doing well. Although anxiety may be associated with tests, many students see exams as challenging and enjoyable aspects of the learning experience.

For example, a graduate class in counseling, prepared to take their final exam, was told during the final exam class that there would be no exam; they would be graded only on their midterm and the four projects they already had completed. After hearing this information, the class was *visibly upset*! In a class discussion afterward, it was found that the three main reasons for disappointment were:

1. They wanted to "show off" what they knew.
2. They were counting on the test to pull up their grade.
3. They were upset that they "had studied for nothing."

The writer (1978) told one educational psychology class to prepare for a midterm exam on a given date. On the date of the midterm, the class was told that they would not have a midterm, but that the final would be cumulative and count twice as much as before. When discussing their feelings about this "new idea," most students strongly objected, feeling that the midterm would give them an idea of "where they were at" and point out problem areas so that they could be better prepared for the final exam. The students, in other words, wanted feedback so they could determine how they were doing in the class, and what type of test they could expect for the final. Most students also wanted to avoid the pressure of taking a single exam that would be the primary basis of their grade. Thus, although there are often mixed feelings, students generally *want* tests for feedback—especially when their grades depend on them.

These examples illustrate the reactions of highly grade-oriented students who become disoriented when the academic system doesn't work in ways they have come to expect. Would most students want to take tests if the test results had no bearing whatsoever on their grades? The same study indicates that better students often fear tests even more than other students. Many teachers have noted that the students who are most concerned about their test results tend to be better performers. While most students express concern, better students worry just as much or more than average students in spite of consistently high past performance.

Attempting to Reduce Negative Feelings About Tests

Many of the negative consequences of testing could be avoided if tests were actually used to help students rather than to grade them, as is presently the case. If teachers clearly used tests to help children from the earliest grades on, they could prevent many negative feelings from ever developing. Diagnostic tests can serve this purpose particularly well. Such tests can be used to help students to find out what they already know so they can concentrate on the specific material that they have not yet mastered. Ideally, all testing should be diagnostic to some extent. When a teacher finds a student has not yet mastered certain material, which is what almost any low score indicates, help should be given before the student progresses to other subject matter. Tests can be used to help students in at least twelve other ways:

1. **Learning analysis**
   Through learning analysis, we try to find out why a student didn't learn and what can be done to help him or her. A math test should tell us, for example, not only that Mike doesn't know how to divide fractions, but also why he doesn't know how to divide fractions. Perhaps he doesn't understand that when dividing fractions, the second fraction (the divisor) should be inverted and the resultant set multiplied. A good test should be designed to find out what students don't know and why so that the teacher can take appropriate action.

2. **Improvement of curriculum**
   Many students doing poorly in a specific area may indicate one or more of the following problems:

1. The teacher is not explaining the material clearly.
2. The textbook is not clear.
3. The students are not properly prepared to learn the concept.
4. The students do not see the importance of the material.

If only a few students have difficulty, the teacher can meet with them separately and extend special help. Often however, an entire class may misunderstand or fail to comprehend. This often means the curriculum needs to be revised or special units need to be developed in order for the class to continue.

3. **Improvement of teacher**

   Test results yield as much information about teacher performance as they do about student performance. When an entire class does well on an effective test, it is highly probable that the teacher presented the material well. When an entire class does poorly, its teacher should try to find out why by looking carefully at his or her methods and attitudes towards each subject area. It has been said that when a standardized grading system is used, the *class average* is actually also the *grade the teacher has earned.*

4. **Improvement of films, textbooks, realia, classroom design, bulletin boards, and other teaching media and tools**

   If a teacher uses a film or other teaching tool to present a series of new ideas and most students do poorly when tested on this material, the teacher should find out *why* the tool was ineffective. At the same time, it should be remembered that a test may not tap some changes that have occurred. For example, a test that requires recall of facts may not uncover important attitude changes. Therefore, a teacher should try to develop questions that assess the effects of the media on the students' beliefs, values, and attitudes.

5. **Individualization**

   Effective tests always indicate differences in students' learning that can serve as a basis for individual help. Optimal use of test results almost always requires individualization. When a test clearly indicates that a student has mastered only a small amount of required material, he or she cannot be expected to continue at the same pace as the rest of the class. But, with well-planned special remedial help from the teacher, the youngster may be able to catch up quickly.

6. **Placement**

   Standardized tests almost always yield several sets of scores that can be used to develop general groups. Although much attention is often given to placing students in the "correct" group, great exactness is not crucial. If based on tests that accurately measure *general levels of knowledge,* individualization can be achieved by placing students in *fluid* groups, either homogeneous or heterogeneous, depending on the purpose of the group. Then, if a student is improving, he or she can be put into a higher-level group, or, if doing poorly, moved to a lower-level group.

7. **Selection**

When enrollment opportunities are limited, tests can be used to select the best from among the contenders. In such programs, teachers understandably want to select those most able to contribute to and benefit from the goals of the group. An example of this type of test is one used to select players for sport teams. Obviously the coach wants the players to optimize the chances of the team winning.

8. **Counseling and guidance**

Results from appropriate tests can help teachers and counselors guide students in assessing courses to take and future academic and career possibilities. In such cases, standardized test scores may actually be more reliable than course grades. Rugg (1965) typically found a low correlation between grades in specific courses and success in occupations for which those courses were purportedly designed to prepare students. This is true partially because past school testing has been both inadequate and inappropriate. Encouraging results have been obtained when tests of performance, application, and learning are used instead of memory tests.

9. **Research**

Formal research is necessary to help teachers find better individual and group teaching methods. Every classroom teacher should be engaged in *some form of research*, the simplest level of which can be finding out if the class prefers film A or film B, textbook A or textbook B, a demonstration or a lecture, and similar practical information. Feedback tools can also be used to find effective methods of teaching and to learn more about students, their interests, goals, and achievements. We will discuss this in more detail under the *weak link* method of improving teaching.

10. **Selling and interpreting the schools to the community**

Effective tests help the community to understand just what the students are learning. Since tests are representative of content covered in a class, parents or community members interested in such information could review a year's tests in a given subject to obtain a general idea of what was studied. Tests can also be used to diagnose general schoolwide weaknesses and strengths that require community support. Billions of dollars are spent on education and the taxpayers who provide this money at times demand evidence of what the schools are accomplishing. One good form of evidence is test results—both teacher-made and standardized. Although such data can be abused, they are generally more effective than either an outsider's or insider's subjective evaluation.

11. **Identification of exceptional children**
    It is often difficult to evaluate a child's level of academic achievement or special abilities merely by working with him or her. Many teachers are able, in time, to assess much of this information, but tests are often helpful in reaching a quicker judgment. When trying to identify exceptional children, one should assess not only I.Q. scores but all handicaps and special abilities, no matter how minor. When in the development stage, in fact, most abilities, even those of persons who have high potential, could probably be seen as close to average; therefore every child should be encouraged to maximize his or her personal capacities. This includes very talented children as well as those with average and even limited abilities. Students with high I.Q.s, though, tend to be overlooked, ignored, and mistreated (as will be discussed later) when in actuality they too need to be identified and given special help. A student with an extremely high I.Q. may have just as much (or even more) trouble in school as a student with a very low I.Q. The more teachers know about their students, the better their position to help.

12. **Evaluation of the total learning program**
    Teacher-made tests are often developed to obtain a blanket evaluation of the total learning environment rather than to diagnose specific learning and teaching difficulties. Ideally, tests should also evaluate the effectiveness of each element in the learning program. To use tests to evaluate a program, teachers must understand the uses, abuses, and serious limitations of feedback tools in general, but especially those of teacher-made tests.

Unproductive Uses of Tests: Avoiding Them

There are specific purposes that tests should *not* be used for, including the following:

Grading. A test may be *one piece of data in a set of data* used to evaluate a student but should not be the *sole* or *primary* determinant of this evaluation. Most tests do not accurately reflect total student performance or true abilities because they depend heavily on reading and writing ability and memory. If students are deficient in these skills, no matter how developed their other skills, they will more than likely do poorly on tests. This point will be discussed in greater detail later.

Labeling. It is often a serious disservice to label a student, whether the label be backward, slow, inferior, or extremely bright, genius, superior. If a student is called slow often enough, he or she may well come to believe the label and act accordingly. His or her performance level drops so that, in time, a self-fulfilling prophecy occurs. Ironically, students categorized as genius or extremely bright may suffer from their labels too. Such youngsters may underproduce to avoid standing out as different, or they may become overconfident and not put forth much effort.

Labels can be useful, and given the great amount of information that teachers must convey to each other, labels are probably necessary abbreviations. Unfortunately, like all summaries, they tend to distort reality. Labeling itself rarely helps anyone, even though it can serve as a tool to begin the process of specific remediation. As such, labels rarely need to be conveyed to students or their parents and should probably be communicated to other professionals only with extreme caution. Educators who understand the limitations of labels use them merely as starting points to help the students avoid much potential damage.

Threatening. Teachers may often be tempted to use tests as threats. A comment such as "You kids better buckle down and study hard—I plan to make the test this Friday extremely difficult" may seem at first to be a good disciplinary tactic. But following through on such a threat is not likely to yield positive results. Giving a difficult test will not be an effective motivator and will probably cause more students than usual to score poorly. The two most important results students can obtain in any class are an appreciation of the subject matter and a drive to pursue the subject long after the formal course is over (Harris 1973). These attitudes are not encouraged by the use of threats.

Ridiculing. Some teachers use tests to deride students, as in the following lecture:

> I've graded your papers and the scores are lousy. What did you students do, spend your whole weekend partying and watching TV? If you expect to get a decent grade in this class, you're going to have to study much harder. I don't know, maybe many of you are just too stupid, but in my day with performance like I've seen on this test, I would have been out on the streets long before I got as far as you are now.

Some teachers try to build themselves up by criticizing their students, but putting students down rarely encourages them to study harder or to do better in the future. If such youngsters do study more, it's probably to avoid trouble, not because they're positively motivated toward a goal. While there are cases in which derision has motivated people to achieve success, it almost always begets slowing down or giving up. Why try harder when one's efforts are punished by criticism? As a rule, only encouragement or some other type of reward stimulates students to try harder.

Tracking. As noted previously, grouping students to work on specific common deficiencies can be productive *as long as the groups are temporary and there is continual retesting and re-evaluating.* Group membership should be flexible so that students can move between higher- or lower-level groups as necessary. When students are tracked, or assigned to the same group for most of the year or longer, they may become labeled and progress may be slowed. One successful scientist (who preferred to remain anonymous) summed up his experiences with tracking in an interview with the author:

> Why was I in the lowest reading group in seventh grade when I read everything in sight? I guess because I was a slow reader in the first grade. I was placed into the slowest reading group and just stayed there! At first I didn't know we were grouped according to ability. I thought the Bluebirds and Robins just read out of different books. In third grade I thought the books I was reading seemed awful easy. Besides, my brother told me that books we read in school are dumb anyways—the books at the library were always much better. Being extremely bored with the material we covered in reading, I tended to daydream. Because of that I guess my teacher thought I was slow and I stayed in the same group. My reading skill improved tremendously in the area I enjoyed most— astronomy and space travel—but it only improved slowly in "reading"! When my mother tried to convince my fifth-grade teacher that I was really a good reader (at that time I was reading college-level science books), he said that it would interfere with my progress if I was abruptly put in a group with a much harder book. I felt I already knew everything I needed to know about Dick and Jane—I wanted to know about pulsating quasars. In sixth grade I quit fighting and just accepted school rather passively— my real learning took place in the library at night or during the mini-activities I participated in at school. Thus, school became somewhat peripheral to me—necessary but in the way—something like filing income tax forms—even though I was academically highly motivated.

The primary danger of grouping is that the system can become inflexible and students can get locked into categories without benefit of continuous re-evaluation. To guard against such an occurrence, if there are any indications that a child could succeed or do better in another group, he or she should be transferred, even if more individual attention will be required to ensure assimilation.

Allocating funds. One teacher's experience should illustrate the problem of allocating monies according to test scores:

> During my second year of teaching I was told that my students would be taking a certain standardized test. If our school scored low enough, we would "earn" enough government funds to build a new learning resource center. The principal had a good idea of what was on the test, and because we wanted that learning resource center, we taught only things that were *not* on the test— hoping the students would do poorly enough for us to qualify for additional money. We must have been successful—the next year we had a big, beautiful, new, carpeted learning resource center! (Personal interview with a student in the author's graduate class.)

When funds are allocated according to test scores, there is sometimes a strong temptation to tamper with some of the testing variables. When allocating money, outside agencies should use test scores as only *one* criterion among many others, including the physical state of the school, the income of students' parents, and the needs of the school, justified according to the purposes of the funds.

Summary

Among their many purposes, tests can be used to improve teaching methods, curriculum, teachers themselves, and teaching tools. They can also be used to counsel and help individual children. Of particular importance in any testing situation is the feedback provided to both teachers and students. Teachers must be skilled at obtaining and interpreting feedback in order to be effective. They must also be adept at supplying appropriate feedback to their students. When tests are appropriately constructed and administered, they can be extremely constructive teaching tools that yield useful data for the student, the teacher, the class, the school, the school system, and the community.

Suggested Readings

Gronlund, Norman Edward. *Measurement and Evaluation in Teaching*. 2d rev. ed. New York: Macmillan, 1971. Chapter 1.

Lindvall, C. Mauritz and Anthony J. Nitko. *Measuring Pupil Achievement and Aptitude*. 2d rev. ed. New York: Harcourt Brace Jovanovich, 1975. Chapter 4.

TenBrink, Terry D. *Evaluation: A Practical Guide for Teachers*. New York: McGraw-Hill, 1974. Chapters 7, 8.

3 Giving Feedback: Translating the Need into Reality

The uses of tests in general, and aptitude and achievement tests in particular, have recently been criticized from many quarters. In reaction, the National Education Association (NEA) formed a Task Force on Testing to evaluate the use of tests in the schools. Among their conclusions are:

1. Measurement and evaluation are necessary in the schools. While feedback tools are imperfect and subject to error and misinterpretation, they are indispensable. Thus the question is how we can improve tests, not whether we should abandon them.
2. Some measurement and evaluation tools are highly useful and others are either invalid, unreliable, out of date, unfair, or some combination of these limitations. Clearly there are specific areas that need improvement.
3. Training of many of those using the tools—primarily teachers and administrators—is woefully inadequate and must be corrected.
4. There is much testing done today by people who do not adequately understand the uses of tests and their limitations.

Teachers who understand the use of tests and feedback tools recognize how such materials can improve their teaching and neither accept test results as precise measurements nor reject them as worthless. While many of the NEA's remarks refer to standardized tests, most are also appropriate for teacher-made tests.

After examining standardized I.Q. tests, the NEA concluded that typical intelligence tests are biased against three groups: (1) the economically disadvantaged, (2) the culturally disadvantaged, and (3) the linguistically disadvantaged. The organization also discovered that tests are often used in ways that undermine a student's self-concept. Improper generalization of test results is especially damaging. (For example, a student who does poorly on a test may not have memorized the correct information or may lack test-taking skills. Such results do not necessarily indicate that he or she did not or cannot master the material.) Lastly, the NEA felt the testing industry must update many of their tests and improve (as well as prove) their reliability and validity.

The Role of the Schools

Whether teachers like it or not, the public has placed much of the responsibility for improving society on the shoulders of educators. The schools are often seen as the primary means of solving a broad spectrum of social problems ranging from racial prejudice to poverty. (Gartner et al. 1974) Next to defense, education is the largest economic enterprise in America, and most people would agree that it is probably one of the most important. It serves as the most important force for social change and the primary means of social mobility for many social and economic groups. Our nation is dependent on formally educated people to run its businesses, government, schools, and all other social and cultural institutions.

The educational requirements for most professions have become much more stringent in the last few years. For example, at the turn of the century, a person could become a lawyer without ever going to college, usually by serving as an apprentice and passing a test. Today, to become a lawyer, one must usually spend four years in college, another three or four years in law school, and then pass a state licensing test. Thus, doing well in school (which really means doing well on tests) has become nearly the only way of entering the traditional professions (and to some degree, many occupations).

As education becomes more important, evaluation in the schools likewise becomes more important. Since billions of tax dollars are spent on education, the schools must be accountable to taxpayers. Test results are one important means of communicating the effectiveness of the school's programs to parents and the community.

In addition, tests play an important role in decision making. Usually, the more information available in any decision-making process, the better the decision. Tests and other feedback tools are excellent sources of information, especially in the schools. Since schools are important to our society, the decisions that affect them are important; thus tests are important because they yield information that can influence our instructional system.

Refuting Some of the Arguments Against Tests

Ideally, one should learn because of the intrinsic joy of learning, not merely for the purpose of putting down correct answers on a test. The enjoyment of learning most often has more to do with *what* one is learning and one's attitude toward the subject than with whether or not one is going to be evaluated. Ideally, tests should provide both feedback on learning progress and reward for well-done work. If used properly, tests can increase the enjoyment of learning.

Success in both advanced-level course work and career requires the accomplishment of many intermediate goals. Tests are only one of many means that lead to those goals. An individual test may or may not motivate, but the end goal for which the learning is undertaken should ideally be the primary motivator. Achievement on tests merely represents small steps toward the main goal.

Motivation can increase (as can the enjoyment of learning) if learning is rewarded, and tests can be rewards, especially if a teacher ensures that each student has the knowledge necessary to do well on the test before the student takes the test. It can be rewarding to hit a ball with a bat, but an organized game of baseball is often more rewarding. Batting practice is usually motivated by the goal of performing optimally during an actual baseball game. A baseball game, therefore, is really a test—a chance to publicly demonstrate the skills developed during practice. Academic tests, likewise, are chances to demonstrate previously practiced or learned skills.

A common difficulty in learning is that students lack the ability to assess their own progress and need indicators to assure them that they are on the right track or warn them that they are not and thus need help. Quizzes can provide the necessary feedback. A formal test can then be seen as a final check on a whole unit of activities, each part of which has already entailed many forms of feedback (quizzes, projects, informal evaluations, and the like). Each quiz or test is a step toward the end goal—mastery of a body of knowledge.

Unfortunately, every step in the goal-seeking process is not always rewarding. If the end result is perceived as sufficiently desirable, however, most students will undertake individual steps that they would usually prefer to avoid. For example, pre-medical students rarely enjoy all of their required courses, but they endure them in order to achieve their main goal, which is to become physicians. In such cases, tests can serve as excellent motivators to help students through tough courses like biochemistry. A student may not like to study, even in his or her chosen field, but can usually muster up enough motivation to study *small sections* of material for a test, thus working a "step at a time" toward his or her goal.

True, ideally, students should enjoy all the steps necessary toward their selected goal, but they rarely do and thus need a "push" to help them get by a few of the areas. Schools and colleges which have experimented with eliminating most or all testing have found that most students are not able to work for a college degree without some type of feedback to motivate them to complete a step at a time.

Actually, the discipline provided by tests is an important reason for formal schooling. Anyone, if they wanted to, could learn calculus or German totally on their own. There are hundreds of books available such as *How To Speak German in 10 Days* or *Calculus Made Simple*. One does not need to enroll in a class to study calculus. For that matter, one does not need to go to college to be an engineer. Most anyone, on their own, can learn what is necessary to be an engineer. One of the main reasons we go to college is for the discipline. Most of us could spend five or ten dollars for a do-it-yourself instruction book in German, and with full intentions of learning German, read the first chapter and never pick the book up again. Only a lucky few of us have the discipline to read the book straight through, doing all the exercises and completing the assignments. Further, most books look somewhat overwhelming when we try to read them from cover to cover, but in a college class we often read one chapter at a time; and sufficient motivation to read each chapter is often a weekly quiz. When one chapter is completed, we are assigned another chapter for another quiz. Before we know it, we have completed the whole book. A task which looks overwhelming, when completed a step at a time does not seem difficult when done for a course. Thus we can see that an important function of a school is to provide structure, discipline, guidance, and direction. Tests reward us for completing our work and punish us for not completing the material. Without the discipline of a course, many of us would never read a single textbook from cover to cover.

Tests as Learning Experiences and Teaching Tools

Tests can and should be positive learning experiences. Students can learn from teacher-made tests in the following ways:

1. Studying for tests focuses effort in the appropriate direction and provides a specific, immediate reason for learning.
2. Taking tests allows students to review, generalize, and apply the material they have learned. Much incidental learning can occur if tests are used to encourage students to apply past knowledge to new ideas, applications, and ways of viewing situations.
3. Reviewing test questions and answers provides important feedback. If the correct answers are given and specific reasons why incorrect answers are incorrect are discussed, a test can be an excellent learning situation. Students can also learn a great deal from looking up the correct answers and/or discussing possible alternatives with friends.
4. Taking tests specifically designed to teach can be extremely productive. Take-home, open-book, and performance exams and tests based on case studies can be used to introduce new material at the same time that previous knowledge is measured.

Giving Feedback Outside of the Classroom

To ensure that students receive adequate feedback, some teachers depend on help from older students, parents, college students, or paid tutors. Through individual attention, a tutor can provide a tremendous amount of feedback and ascertain that each step the student completes is correct. The student thus knows that he or she has done well, is on the right track, and can then move ahead with assurance and confidence. In the following example, note that the tutoring session is actually a series of mini-quizzes that guide the student towards answers to simple problems.

TUTOR: I know you've been having problems with math, but see if you can give me the answer to this problem. What is 948 divided by 62?

STUDENT: I'm not very good in division. I don't think I could do that problem.

TUTOR: Well, try. I'm sure that you could get a good start.

STUDENT: (No answer.)

TUTOR: Ok, let's try a different kind of problem. What is 7 times 65?

STUDENT: Well, I can try, but I'm not sure. (Student writes down and works out the problem, arriving at 4,235, an incorrect answer.)

TUTOR: Ok, now we're making some progress. Can you tell me what 7 times 5 is?

STUDENT: 35?

TUTOR: Right, very good! Now you're cooking. *(Note that the tutor tries to determine the highest level at which the student can confidently achieve. The tutor started too high, but rather than discourage the student by telling him his first answer was wrong, the tutor asked progressively simpler questions. In essence, the student failed the first two mini-quizzes and passed only the last one. Now the student can begin to work his way up.)*

STUDENT: I got that one right?

TUTOR: You certainly did. Now, what is 6 times 7?

STUDENT: 42.

TUTOR: Excellent, now what is 7 times 7?

STUDENT: Ah, 48?

TUTOR: Well, that's close. What did you say the answer to 6 times 7 was?

STUDENT: 42.

TUTOR: Now, what would one more 7 added onto 42 be? If 6 times 7 equals 42, then, 7 times 7 would be only one more 7.

STUDENT: It would be 42 plus 7, or 49!

TUTOR: Very good! If you're not sure about a problem, an easy way to work it is to find the answer of one less, then add the additional number.

The sessions would continue similarly, with the tutor *slowly* working the student up to multiplying two-, three-, and four-place numbers. When fluency was achieved there, the tutor could introduce simple division, then more complex division.

Optimizing Positive Results of Feedback

Individualized, concentrated feedback such as a tutor gives is ideal, but every classroom teacher also has many opportunities to provide both oral and written feedback. To ensure that feedback will be optimally productive, the following abuses should be avoided:

Using feedback to punish students. In many cases, a poor grade on a paper or test is adequate feedback; it need not be accompanied by additional oral or written comments, such as "This is a terrible paper. You're going to have to work a lot harder if you want to pass this course." Emphasizing failure is not productive. Rather, a teacher might use small inconspicuous marks to let students know which answers are incorrect, or better yet, place marks or comments *only* next to correct responses. If there are too many incorrect answers, it is often best to ignore the failures and encourage the student with additional remedial attention. It usually does little good to confront a student with an extremely poor paper, and it can often do harm. Failure may cause students to feel defeated, to see themselves as incapable, and put forth less effort in the future.

Occasionally, it *may be useful to return a paper that is poorly done* in order to let the student know that he or she is doing poorly and needs to expend more effort. This method is usually most successful with students who have a *history of success.* In other cases, it tends to discourage rather than motivate.

Using feedback as emotional release. A teacher who has just had a disagreement with the principal may indirectly express some aggression by applying unusually severe grading standards or making harsh comments. Negative feedback can be helpful and is sometimes necessary, but if used excessively, it is likely to be harmful. Of course, very few teachers can completely prevent their feelings from affecting their evaluations, but awareness and control of negative emotions is essential to effective classroom functioning.

Using feedback to show superior wisdom and insight. Teachers sometimes like to show off what they know. Research by Flanders (1969) and others show that teachers tend to dominate the conversations in their classrooms. Most students, however, do *not* learn by listening, but by involving themselves in a learning situation. Functional teaching occurs only when the teacher involves students in the on-going learning process. When a teacher dominates the classroom, the students' needs are subordinated. A teacher's written comments on students' papers may also do more to feed the teacher's ego than to help the learning process. Because they recognize that telling is not teaching, the most effective teachers may briefly present the desired information and then question the class to determine what steps to take next. They are keenly aware of whether or not their students are listening to an explanation and understanding and appreciating it. They are also careful not to give students much more feedback than they can immediately handle. If a sixth grader asks why a comet's tail always points away from the sun, her teacher does not need to explain theories of light and Einsteinian physics. He may simply reply, "The light from the sun forces the tail away like the wind pushes the sail of a ship."

The best and, ideally, the only reason for giving feedback is to help the other person achieve his or her goals more effectively. Experience in working with children, appropriate coursework, reading, and study are all necessary in order to learn how feedback can be most effective. Most important of all, however, is understanding one's motives for giving feedback and tailoring one's feedback to meet students' needs.

Reasons for Inadequate Feedback

Among the possible stumbling blocks a teacher may encounter are the following.

Lack of helpful advice. A teacher cannot always be expected to have a ready solution to every problem. A student, for example, may ask why she always makes a certain kind of mistake. If her teacher does not know why, he should admit it because offering erroneous or misguided feedback can have a harmful effect.

Belief that the student is not ready or is not "in the mood." If the situation has been properly assessed, a student's lack of readiness can be a highly valid reason for a teacher's withholding feedback. For example, one may hesitate to offer feedback at certain times, such as before holidays, when a student is doing poorly in several other areas, or immediately before the class is to take an exam.

Knowledge of human behavior and experience both help in deciding the most appropriate time for feedback. If a youngster fails an important test at a time when he is having severe family problems, his teacher should probably not add to his emotional burden. In such cases, it is preferable to withhold the test results until the child is able to handle the feedback. Another way of responding to this problem would be to present feedback in a very positive way, such as, "I know you've been going through a lot, but, considering your difficulties at home, I think that you're really doing quite well. I want to encourage you to keep up the good work, because I know it's difficult to continue working as hard as you are under your present circumstances." Or, if that would not be appropriate, the teacher might express concern and understanding, offer additional help, and encourage the student not to worry about school for the present time.

Inappropriateness of environment. When others are present, the teacher may feel that negative feedback will put a student on the defensive. If a student is well-liked, the class may turn against the teacher; or, if the student is not well-liked, the feedback may backfire or cause additional problems. If negative feedback is necessary, it is usually best to talk to the student privately, either in the hall or after school.

Belief that feedback will not be helpful. If a student had previously responded negatively to feedback, or has failed to respond at all, his or her teacher may decide that further attempts would be futile. Obviously, a technique that has not been successful in the past is not likely to produce results if it is repeated. Instead the teacher may try another strategy, such as assigning a homework partner.

Belief that feedback is sought for unproductive reasons. Students who know they are doing perfectly well will often ask a teacher how they're doing merely for purposes of ego gratification. Younger children in particular may pester a teacher for constant positive feedback. This can become a serious problem, especially if there are many pupils in the class. The desire for reassurance is a common reason for seeking feedback, but the teacher must ensure that it does not become disruptive.

It should be stressed that giving feedback to reinforce a self-image or to build an ego is not necessarily bad. A teacher should be aware, however, of why a youngster wants feedback and react accordingly. If the child is not looking for honest feedback, but rather is seeking a compliment, a negative response would not be helpful and might be harmful. Obviously, if one cannot answer honestly in a positive way, it may be best not to answer at all.

Obstacles to Offering Feedback

Sometimes teachers find it difficult to give feedback to their students because of our strong cultural norms against the face-to-face expression of personal feelings about someone. A teacher may be able to give a student a grade and point out factual flaws in his or her work but have great difficulty in honestly expressing other important information, such as why a student may have problems getting along with other students.

There are also times when teachers hesitate to offer feedback because they fear negative consequences for themselves. They may believe that if they are honest in their evaluations, their students will be upset; thus, they withhold judgment. Most teachers want their students to like them and some worry that feedback may impede this liking. Fear of losing approval is a common reason not only for withholding feedback, but also for giving higher grades than students deserve. Similarly, feedback may be withheld out of fear of retaliation, perhaps in some schools even in the form of overt physical aggression. Teachers may also fear that students will give them lower evaluations or complain to the principal or other teachers. For nontenured teachers and in school districts that have merit pay systems, this can be a real threat.

Sometimes teachers don't communicate their reactions for fear that their statements will be misunderstood. Because it can be difficult to explain certain things, some teachers may prefer to say nothing. This can be a legitimate reason for withholding feedback. Other times it may be possible to avoid misinterpretation by choosing one's words very carefully, stressing that this is an attempt to *help* the student, and emphasizing that this does not mean that the child is bad, has failed, or cannot make progress, but only that certain shortcomings are presently evident.

Finally, lack of experience may prompt some teachers to avoid offering feedback. In time, many teachers learn how to handle such situations, but the learning process can be difficult. Even after years of teaching, some people never learn how to give constructive feedback, and even fewer develop effective methods for helping students overcome their learning problems. This is one area in which college coursework and in-service seminars could be especially helpful. Familiarity with the kinds of difficulties students face, diagnostic competence, and knowledge of how to help students overcome their problems are the most important skills a teacher can develop. Tests and other feedback tools are useless unless their results are appropriately interpreted, communicated, and used to help students improve.

Students' Reactions to Feedback

Some students simply do not hear the feedback that is offered. Selective reception allows us to ignore some stimuli while focusing on others. Thus, if a youngster is attuned to other stimuli or does not want to hear what is said, the message may never reach the conscious centers of his or her brain.

Another common student response to feedback is to question the teacher's motives. The validity of the comments could even be denied if the youngster concludes that the teacher dislikes him or her, is trying to get even, or is jealous or mean for some reason. Suspicion stemming from differences in social class may cause some students to question not only a teacher's feedback, but also many of the teacher's other actions. Such youngsters may interpret doing poorly on a test, failing an assignment, or any form of negative feedback as an expression of hostility. Under these circumstances, even positive feedback may be disregarded or accepted with reservation.

It is not at all uncommon for students to deny the truth of a teacher's observations. Especially younger children, if they do not want to accept something, cope by denying reality. After doing poorly on a test, for example, a student might conclude that he knew the information, but that the teacher just didn't ask the right questions. While this might be valid to some extent, aside from short essay exams, most tests usually contain a representative sample of the assigned material. Even when the truth of a matter is quite obvious, it can be difficult to convince some students that they are wrong. Most teachers find that in such cases it is best to let the students, in time, discover for themselves that they are incorrect.

Finally, some students may respond to feedback by criticizing or ridiculing the person who is trying to help. Of course, experienced teachers recognize this problem and react calmly by reassuring the student of his or her value as an individual and by emphasizing their interest in improving the youngster's situation.

When planning a feedback session, the teacher should take into account that there are two basic kinds of information:

1. **Objective data** pertain to specifically what happened; they are facts that are universally agreed upon. In reality, since human perceptions are always involved, no data are completely objective, and, in isolation, objective data tend to be somewhat meaningless. Although they enter into decisions, data are not necessarily the most important part of a decision.

2. **Subjective data** reflect feelings, attitudes, values, perceptions, and opinions. Generally, subjective data involve value judgments, or judgments based on criteria that are not readily definable, for instance, "I like math—I don't know why, I just do!" Most evaluations are based on objective data, but they also usually take into consideration subjective and individual factors. For example, a statement such as "Maria is doing quite well in math" may be based on objective test scores, but it also contains a judgment about the student's performance that is open to interpretation. Maria may be "doing quite well" only compared to her own previous performance or compared to other students in her class, or compared to her own ability level.

Timing Feedback

The most appropriate time to offer feedback is immediately after a relevant incident. When an incident is fresh in a student's mind, feedback is more meaningful. For example, if a student tends to have trouble with division, his teacher should first locate the problem, then, when an example of the problem occurs, talk to the child about it. Waiting two or three days before making appropriate remarks is not as effective as dealing with the problem at the moment it occurs.

Another excellent time to give feedback is when a student specifically asks for it. He or she is then probably more receptive and more likely to accept the observations that are offered. If a student wants to know about his or her progress, it is usually appropriate that the teacher give both the information the student wants and some additional information. Robert Havighurst (1970) calls this the **teachable moment**, or teaching when the student is receptive. In such situations, students are more often able to accept negative feedback and are less likely to become defensive.

Before giving feedback, many teachers assess the student's state of mind by asking how things are going, how the child likes the class, and so forth. If it seems to be an opportune time, the teacher then proceeds to offer feedback.

Hints for giving feedback

Certain ways of expressing feedback are more effective than others. A teacher should be tactful, sensitive, aware, concerned, and helpful. It is not always what is said, but how it is said that upsets students. Almost any message can be communicated to anyone if tact is used. Some expressions that are helpful include:

You're doing an excellent job, but I'm concerned about your continued progress, and want to point out that. . . .

I'm really proud of your work. For example, I enjoyed your presentation on. . . . One thing you might find helpful, though, is. . . .

When I have this problem, I sometimes find it helpful to. . . .

One effective method for giving feedback is to follow a sequence that is one-third positive, one-third negative, and one-third positive. That is, start with a positive comment, present any necessary negative feedback, and end with a compliment. Note the following example:

> Willy, I really enjoyed your presentation in class today. It was very lively, informative and well presented. One thing you might be careful about, though, is accuracy. I noted several pieces of information that I don't think are correct. I might be wrong, but you might check. . . . Aside from this, though, most of us found your presentation quite helpful. Keep up the good work!

This approach emphasizes the positive aspects of the student's performance without ignoring weaknesses. The opening comments smooth the way for constructive and tactful criticism. Closing on a positive note helps restore the student's confidence in his performance and encourages optimism about future success.

Summary

The uses of tests have recently been under much criticism. In their evaluation of the use of tests in schools, the NEA finds that the real question is the improvement of tests and testing situations, not their abandonment. The NEA also concludes that typical intelligence tests are biased against certain groups. Evaluation in schools becomes more important with the increasing importance of education. To eliminate testing would be to eliminate motivational feedback which allows students to complete goals a step at a time. The discipline provided by tests is an important reason for formal education. Tests can and should be positive learning experiences. To insure that feedback will be productive, certain common abuses should be avoided. Lack of helpful advice, belief that the student is not ready for feedback, inappropriateness of environment, belief that feedback will not be helpful, belief that feedback is sought for unproductive reasons, fear of negative consequences for the teacher, fear of misunderstanding, and lack of experience are reasons for inadequate feedback from teachers. The teacher should be aware of both subjective and objective data and the timing and sensitivity of the feedback session.

Suggested Readings

Hopkins, Charles D. and Richard L. Antes. *Classroom Measurement and Evaluation*. Itasca, Ill.: F. E. Peacock, 1978. Chapter 1.

Lindvall, C. Mauritz and Anthony J. Nitko. *Measuring Pupil Achievement and Aptitude*. 2d rev. ed. New York: Harcourt Brace Jovanovich, 1975. Chapter 9.

TenBrink, Terry D. *Evaluation: A Practical Guide for Teachers*. New York: McGraw-Hill, 1974. Chapters 7, 8.

Part II
Tests and Testing

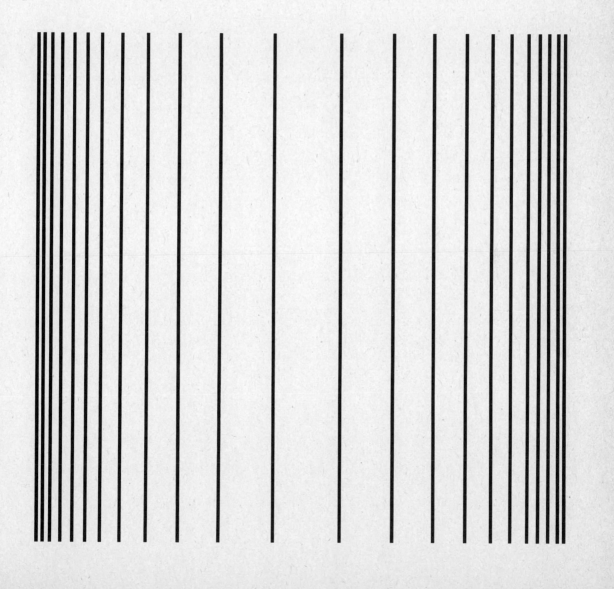

4   Developing a Teacher-Made Test

Two factors basic to the development of effective classroom tests are the ability to use and manipulate the English language (including grammar, spelling, punctuation, sentence structure, composition, and similar language skills) and knowledge of the test's subject matter. Neither of these is discussed in this book. A third essential factor—the understanding of tests and their uses—is, of course, the subject of this book. Unfortunately, there is no simple way of learning how to develop good tests. It is not a skill that can be learned from textbooks, but, rather, one that takes time and practice to develop. A book can present many suggestions, hints, and guidelines, but the key to good test construction is experience.

Many teachers find it productive to write test questions well in advance of the actual exam date and put them aside for several days. Then, a day or two before the exam, they review the questions to see if they are written clearly, are simple to follow, and, in the case of objective tests, have only one answer. This is often the best way to eliminate major problems related to grammar, word order, readability, and clarity.

It can often be very helpful to show test questions to another teacher. Because it is difficult for a person to find flaws in his or her own work, many teachers work out reciprocal agreements to read each other's tests and share comments. Someone viewing a test from a different perspective can often catch problems in wording, content, and grammar that may escape the original writer.

Another method of developing good test items is to present possible questions as a practice test. After the test has been graded in class, each question is discussed. At this time, the teacher is thus able to pinpoint any weaknesses and make appropriate revisions before using the

Time order
Concept order
Cognitive domain
Psychomotor domain
Affective domain
Reliability

Validity
Formative evaluation
Summative evaluation
Behavioral objectives
Behavioral terms
Nonbehavioral terms

questions on the final version of the test. For beginning teachers, this technique can be extremely helpful; and it helps students focus on the information on which they will eventually be tested.

Some teachers find it productive to give students a test exactly as first developed, mentioning that the worst questions will be determined by class vote and that responses to these questions will not be counted. All questions on the test are then thoroughly discussed in preparation for the vote. The teacher can thus gather much useful information that can be used in the revision process all tests continually go through and can eventually develop a collection of effective questions which can be used later.

These "experienced" questions could be typed on 3 x 5 cards and filed according to topic. In time, questions on file for a given fact or concept could be well-varied and easy to draw upon. By selecting questions from the test file, a new test can be developed each term. The new questions need not count until they have proved their value. In this way questions can be developed by trial and error until it is clear that they are effective, and the teacher can continually add to his or her collection of good test questions. The teacher may want to inform the class that there are, say, four or so new questions on the test that will not count as part of their scores—just so the students don't suspect the *whole* test if they should find questions that are ambiguous or otherwise deficient. Professional testing services use this technique to develop new test items.

Organizing Test Material

If possible, in addition to progressing according to level of difficulty, test questions should follow a logical sequence. From the teacher's point of view, a major reason for a logical sequence is so he or she can divide the test questions into groups and score groups separately. The teacher is thus able to evaluate effectiveness in teaching, or testing on, specific units—the Civil War as compared to the reconstruction afterward, for instance. The major reason for ordering the test questions from easiest to hardest is that this way all students tend to be more apt to finish the test. The poorer student will not be discouraged by encountering difficult questions early on in the test. Other students who find it difficult to go on to the next question when they cannot answer a preceding question will not be held up simply because of question order. And the quicker students who reach the more difficult questions at the end will have a chance for enough time for a good crack at answering; others may want to scan the last page of the test to get a feel about how much time they should be spending on the first part. The following sequences are the most useful, and thus the most common.

Time Order Questions are placed on the test according to the dates of the events to which the questions pertain, usually from the earliest to the most recent. Obviously, this system is especially useful for history and social studies exams.

Concept Order Grouping questions according to concept is probably one of the most useful methods of ordering material on a test. The most basic concepts appear at the beginning of the test and there is a logical progression to more complex concepts. For example, on a math test, one might progress from simple division to long division to division with remainders. This method often results in the ordering of questions from easiest to hardest, the ideal sequence.

Learning Domains Grouping according to learning domains is also sometimes useful. The three learning domains are as follows:

Cognitive This is the domain of facts, knowledge, and data. A test in the cognitive domain would concern pure information.

Psychomotor This is the domain of movement, action, and coordination. A test in the psychomotor domain would evaluate ability to perform specific physical activities.

Affective domain This is the domain of attitudes, values, beliefs, interests, likes, and dislikes. A test in this area would tap students' subjective opinions and reactions to events and ideas.

Unfortunately, many teachers have concentrated all too much on the cognitive domain while ignoring the other two. Because reality is made up of all three domains, it seems that all three should be stressed in the schools. If we teach in view of all three areas, our tests should reflect this.

Characteristics of a Good Test

Reliability Reliability refers to the consistency with which a student may be expected to perform on a given test. Assuming that a student does not learn any new information in between administrations of the same test, he or she should earn approximately the same score each time if the test is reliable. For example, let's say that the same I.Q. test is administered four times, and the following results are achieved:

First administration   I.Q. = 80
Second administration   I.Q. = 146
Third administration   I.Q. = 112
Fourth administration   I.Q. = 86

Because the score varies so widely, this I.Q. test is obviously not very reliable. We will discuss this concept in more detail later.

Validity Validity refers to the degree to which a test measures what it is intended to measure. For example, a spelling test that consisted of 45 multiplication problems would be totally lacking in validity because the ability to do multiplication problems usually is not a valid indicator of spelling ability. A history test that was graded according to spelling, penmanship, punctuation, and grammar would also lack validity because the criteria used for scoring do not relate to knowledge of history.

A test may be reliable without being valid, but if it is not reliable, it cannot be valid. Reliability requires consistency, but a measure's consistency may lie in the fact that it is consistently wrong. For example, each time a student takes the previously mentioned history test she may score D, but this does not reflect on her knowledge of history. The test is reliable, but it is not valid.

Ease of Administration Students' performance will suffer if test activities are not kept simple, clear, and straightforward. Test directions should be specific so students will understand *exactly* what they are to do and how they are to do it. If test activities become too complicated, students may be forced to waste valuable time on deciphering instructions and putting them into action.

Fairness The intent of each question should be clear and obvious to most students. "Trick" questions should be avoided. Getting an answer right or wrong should consistently depend on *knowing* the answer, not on "doublethink." Trick questions can destroy testing credibility in the students' eyes. In order to help the students, it is a good idea to underline, capitalize, or italicize all key words, especially such important cues as *not*, *least likely*, and so forth.

Encouraging Positive Attitudes

It is a good idea to announce in advance the type of test that will be given and basically what the test will cover. This helps students to prepare and reassures them of their teacher's intention to be fair. Students should also be given the option of retaking a test on which they do poorly. The knowledge that they may have a second chance helps reduce the anxiety students commonly suffer before a test and enables some to do better than they otherwise might. Although one or two students may occasionally use this as an excuse for not studying, on the whole, it helps to reduce frustration and makes test taking more rewarding and enjoyable.

Summative vs. Formative Evaluation

Summative evaluation refers to the practice of using tests primarily for the purpose of summarizing previous learning and evaluating or judging the students' level of performance. In the past, summative evaluation was the most common type of evaluation in the schools.

Formative evaluation is a radically different approach to testing in which instruction and evaluation are integrated. A test is not merely a measure used at the end of a learning unit; it is an integral part of the entire learning process. Its purpose is to provide guidance that will help the student learn. It is, in essence, a check on how learning is progressing and a guide to future study. With formative evaluation, testing and evaluation take place continually. When using this process, a teacher may start by giving a pretest and developing units of study based on its results. Then throughout each unit, he or she may administer quizzes to determine the effectiveness of each teaching step. There may also be several formal exams to help the student strive toward the unit's final goal.

As you have probably already noticed, this text stresses the effectiveness of formative evaluation. Summative evaluation has its place, but its use should be limited. Formative evaluation uses tests to help students, while summative evaluation uses tests to grade students.

Behavioral Objectives

A test is a tool for determining the degree to which a teacher has *accomplished* his or her classroom goals. Educational goals are often written in the form of **behavioral objectives.**

Behavioral objectives are goals stated in **behavioral terms;** they specifically describe behavior that can be observed, measured, or counted. An example would be: "The student will correctly spell all of the words in list number one." Usually, behavioral goals call for the performance of tasks that can be measured and contain such phrases as: the student will write a paper on . . ., solve, identify, list, and orally describe. The student reaches either the goal or some fraction of it. **Nonbehavioral terms** are words such as appreciate and understand. They refer to abstractions that are difficult to measure. We can measure a student's ability to spell or do math problems, but we cannot measure appreciation very well.

Drawbacks of Behavioral Objectives

Behavioral objectives can help teachers to focus on their goals and can serve as constant reminders that some forms of behavior are easier to measure than others. These are distinct advantages, but there are also some disadvantages to using behavioral objectives. The most commonly voiced criticism is that preparing and writing behavioral objectives can be extremely time consuming. In most cases, if a teacher wants to give a spelling test, he merely writes "Spelling test on Chapter 3" in the class schedule. But if he uses behavioral objectives, he would have to state: "Given 20 minutes, students will spell in written form and with at least 80% accuracy each word found on page 2 of *My Little Purple Spelling Book.* Each word will be repeated orally three times: first in isolation, second in the context of a sentence, and third in isolation again. Each three-phase repetition will be followed by a sixty-second pause during which students are to write the word correctly." Thus we can see that writing all lesson plans as behavioral objectives could become a very cumbersome task and take up a great deal of time that might be better spent with students. In deference to this viewpoint, our discussion will focus on the importance of having *objectives* without requiring that they be *behavioral* objectives. We will also keep in mind the difficulty of measuring activities described in nonbehavioral terms.

Setting the Main Objective

Every book has a main theme; so does every play, song, and painting. The same is true in teaching; every course, regardless of subject mat-

---

*For a complete discussion of behavioral objectives, see the book, *Preparing Instructional Objectives*, by Robert F. Mager, and *Behavioral Objectives and Instruction*, by Robert J. Kibler, Larry Barker, and David Miles.

ter, focuses on a single basic theme. True, these themes may be rather general, but the basic purpose of each and every course from first grade through twelfth grade can be expressed as an individual goal, theme, or **main objective**. Of course, most objectives are dependent upon individual teachers and their likes, dislikes, attitudes, and values, but a few examples of commonly agreed upon main objectives are:

1. Grades 1 through 6: Develop basic communication skills, including reading, writing, arithmetic, talking, listening, and spelling skills.
2. Secondary history: Review the past with the hope of utilizing humanity's prior mistakes and successes as building blocks for a better future.
3. Secondary art: Facilitate individual expression and communication through physical media, including water color, sculpture, ceramics, oils, charcoal, and ink.

Secondary Objectives

Once a teacher has established a main objective, he or she can expand it into a series of 15 to 20 **secondary objectives**. Each secondary objective usually applies to a week or two of work and corresponds to chapters in a book or units in a lesson plan. As a teacher gains experience, he or she will develop a wide variety of secondary objectives that may be easily adapted to differing classroom needs and situations.

Implementing Main and Secondary Goals

A biology teacher's main objective for her students might be the understanding and preservation of life. She may then designate knowledge of the following topics as *secondary* objectives:

1. the cell
2. chemistry of life
3. the digestive system
4. the circulatory system
5. the nervous system
6. the reproductive system
7. the respiratory system
8. the glandular system
9. the muscle system
10. the skeletal system
11. evolution and creation theories
12. ecology

Each secondary objective is then further broken down into a series of specific teaching goals that are used to compile a **table of specifications**. Tests can then be systematically developed from this information. Four steps are usually followed in preparing a table of specifications:

1. Determine the material to be presented.
2. Divide the material into logical blocks of information.
3. Assign a weight or point value to each block, usually according to

the time it takes to cover the information or the pages needed to cover the information in the textbook.

4. Add the weights and divide their total into the number of questions to appear on the test. Then divide that number into the weight for each area to determine the appropriate number of questions.

For example, if I have spent 100 minutes teaching about a certain topic and want to give a 25-question test on the material, I would divide 100 by 25. The result would indicate that I should write one question to cover approximately every 4 minutes of teaching. If my teaching time were broken down into the blocks shown in Table 4.1, I could divide each block of time by 4 to determine the appropriate number of questions per section necessary to construct a balanced test.

Table 4.1 Simple Table of Specifications

Teaching Lesson	Time to Teach	Number of Questions
Nouns	16 min.	4
Verbs	28 min.	7
Pronouns	28 min.	7
Adjectives	28 min.	7
Total	100 min.	25

Why Develop a Table of Specifications? The main purpose of a table of specifications is to help the teacher *balance* a test. A balanced test places emphasis on information in proportions similar to the classroom activities or book being tested from. If 10 percent of class time was spent on a given concept, then 10 percent of the test should be devoted to that concept. Students should be able to judge the importance of a concept by the amount of time their teacher spends on it. If a teacher glosses over a topic, students will interpret this as meaning they may gloss over it too while studying. It would thus be unfair for the teacher to emphasize this material later on an exam.

A table of specifications can help a teacher avoid the tendency to focus tests on material for which it is easy to develop questions. Such unbalanced tests often concentrate on knowledge of isolated facts while ignoring understanding, application, and interpretation. They encourage students to study items which are obviously "testable," such as definitions of words in italics, recall of lists of material, dates, and the like. This produces a situation in which there is a fairly low correlation between success in school and success in the world of work.

A table of specifications forces a teacher to analyze the material introduced during teaching sessions to ensure that at least the basic areas are covered in the test. In correlating the number of test questions with the amount of time spent in class, the teacher can make sure that material is adequately treated in both contexts. Focusing on one topic at a time in order to write appropriate test questions allows the teacher to reassess the nature and amount of material presented and its manner of presentation.

Despite its great usefulness, a table of specifications is *only a guide;* it is *not* meant to be rigidly followed. Some very experienced teachers are able to carry out the same process without written charts, but most teachers find they need to balance their tests on paper, at least at first. While a table of specifications takes time to develop, it saves time in the long run. Teachers who are used to this system find that it is the easiest way to develop good functional tests.

A detailed table of specifications is presented in Table 4.2. We have added to it two elements that are not necessary, but which some teachers find helpful. First, we divided the questions into factual and functional types. Factual questions deal with material that the student has memorized, such as dates, names, definitions, and formulas. Functional questions ask students to *apply* concepts that have been learned to a specific situation.

We have also added columns that allow for adjustments between the ideal number of questions in a given area and the actual number. We may want to develop, for example, four factual questions about the description of neurons, but we may not be able to write four good questions. Therefore, in this case, our actual number of questions would be slightly different from our goal. By keeping track of the actual number of questions, we can readily recognize areas in which adjustments may be made. This will upset our balance slightly, but it should not cause great problems. A table of specifications is only meant to *guide* test development; it can and should be used flexibly.

Summary

There are six main steps in developing a test:

1. Determine the grade level, subject area, and thus the level of difficulty for which the test is to be developed.
2. Identify and keep in mind the single main course objective.
3. List the secondary objectives that pertain to the test.
4. From the secondary objectives, develop a set of specific teaching objectives.

Table 4.2 Detailed Table of Specifications

Teaching Objectives	Time spent (min.)	Ideal Number of Questions		Actual Number of Questions	
		Factual	Functional	Factual	Functional
1. Structure of Neurons					
a. Description (function)	40	4	4	3	4
b. Dendrites	5	1		2	
c. Axons	5	1		2	
d. End brush	5	1		1	1
e. Synapse	10	2		2	
f. Cell body	20	2	2	3	1
g. Myelin Sheath	5	1		2	
h. White-gray matter	10	2		2	
TOTAL	(100)	(20)		(23)	
2. Signal conduction					
a. All or none principle	35	4	3	3	1
b. ATP	15	3		2	
TOTAL	(50)	(10)		(6)	
3. Neurohumors					
a. Acetylcholine	15	2	1	1	1
b. End plates	15	2	1	1	1
TOTAL	(30)	(6)		(4)	
4. Types of Neurons					
a. Sensory neurons	10	1	1	2	1
b. Motor neurons	10	1	1	2	2
c. Interneurons	50	5	5	6	4
TOTAL	(70)	(14)		(17)	
GRAND TOTAL	250	32	18	33	16

5. Develop handouts, presentations, and activities aimed at helping students accomplish the objectives.

6. Develop a table of specifications shown in Table 4.1 and use the data it yields to develop a teacher-made test.

Suggested Readings

Aiken, Lewis R. *Psychological Testing and Assessment*. 3d rev. ed. Boston: Allyn and Bacon, 1979. Chapter 2.

Ahmann, Stanley and Marvin Glock. *Evaluating Pupil Growth: Principles of Tests and Measurements*. 5th rev. ed. Boston: Allyn and Bacon, 1975. Chapter 2.

Hopkins, Charles D. and Richard L. Antes. *Classroom Measurement and Evaluation*. Itasca, Ill.: F. E. Peacock, 1978. Chapter 4.

Mehrens, William A. and Irvin J. Lehmann. *Measurement and Evaluation in Education and Psychology*. New York: Holt, Rinehart and Winston. Chapter 7.

TenBrink, Terry D. *Evaluation: A Practical Guide for Teachers*. New York: McGraw-Hill, 1974. Chapters 12, 13.

5   Helping Students Take Tests

Probably the most serious negative effect of testing is the circular pattern that develops when a student consistently fails tests. Such a youngster, in time, often grows to see himself as a poor student because that is the message his test results communicate. He then begins to behave accordingly, avoiding study in the belief that it won't do any good anyway. Once this negative image is established, he stops trying and directs his efforts to nonacademic areas.

Tests may also cause students to experience such levels of anxiety that effective studying and test performance are impeded. Up to a point, increases in anxiety level can be constructive, but beyond that point, the effect becomes destructive.

To take a test, the anxiety level needs to be high enough for the student to care and to concentrate, but not too high. Likewise, the anxiety level needs to be low enough for the student to relax, but not too low, or the student will not be alert enough to do his or her best. The major problem is that optimal anxiety level varies tremendously from student to student. Only by working closely with each individual can a teacher learn how and when to increase or reduce anxiety levels.

One of the most common criticisms of tests is that they cause too much anxiety and make students uncomfortable, nervous, and upset. Probably the most effective way to reduce some of this anxiety is to give exams more often. If exams are given frequently, each exam has less individual impact on final grades and students can become accustomed to being tested. Repeated exposure to an anxiety-producing situation reduces anxiety if the situation is made as pleasant as possible and the student is rewarded during and after the experience.

Positive and Negative Effects of Tests

Ideally, tests should be a very positive part of the educational process. Even such small rewards as letting students take a break after they have finished will usually cause tests to generate less anxiety. Of course, with poorer students tests should always be used as a guide for learning that can help students pinpoint and work to improve weaknesses. At the same time, it is important that students be aware of and rewarded for their strong points. To properly use tests, it is imperative that each student be retested until he or she reaches the desired level of proficiency. If students do poorly on a test, they must be given appropriate help until their learning gaps are corrected and they can perform successfully. Other tests can then be utilized to determine whether or not their weaknesses have been overcome. Every student should be familiar with how it feels to perform well on a test.

The Correct Answer Mania

By taking the wrong approach to testing, many schools force students into believing that having correct answers is the main goal of education. Class discussion, studying, reading, and lectures tend to be directed toward learning correct answers for tests. Yet in reality, there is often no correct answer but only a better answer or even many good answers.

Extensive research will often cause one to question many if not most assumptions in almost any field of study. There are probably few areas in most fields about which there is not *some* debate. True, there is much less debate in the area of chemistry than in psychology, for example; nonetheless, even in the physical sciences there are lively debates going on in almost every sphere of activity. For instance, concepts accepted by the vast majority of physicists are still being questioned by some physicists with arguments of varying degrees of validity.

Stating that Columbus is the correct answer to the question "Who discovered America?" implies that the answer is a statement of fact that is settled for all time with no disagreement. If professionals in the field can disagree, cannot students likewise disagree? For this reason many teachers prefer to use the following set of directions for true-or-false questions: Put a T by the statement if you believe it is more often true than false and an F by the statement if you believe it is more often false than true. And for multiple choice: Circle the letter next to the answer that is true in most cases.

Problems with the English Language

The literal meaning versus the implied meaning of words presents some problems for us as English speakers. For example, the writer was challenged by a student on the following question: "What street do you live on?" He explained that he did not live "on" any street but lived beside or near a street. "If I lived on a street I would be soon killed," he stated, adding some humor to his point. The word *on* is grammatically correct, but could logically imply several ideas. As anyone who spends some time giving tests knows, similar examples can be multiplied without end—students can tear apart even the most carefully worded question. The problem of language precision probably appears more in the area of testing than anywhere else. Test sentences should be finely tuned and scrutinized carefully so the meaning is unequivocally clear. This is a difficult and, some feel, an impossible goal, but at least this goal should be attempted.

Avoiding the Punishing Effects of Tests

Many students receive low grades primarily, or partially, because they have not learned how to study. They do not know what to look for, how tests are constructed, and how to go about preparing for a test. Failure on a test invariably punishes them for whatever they did do to prepare for the test. If the student continually fails, any behavior that is preparation for a test will likely, in time, be reduced. Teachers can reduce the punishing effects of tests by emphasizing their more positive aspects.

Recapping the Positive Uses of Tests

As previously stated, one of the most valuable uses of a test is that it provides *feedback*—that is, a student may learn both what he or she *does* understand and what he or she *does not* understand. Based on this information, he or she can then more efficiently direct energy to those areas that require the most attention. Tests guide, direct, and help plan a student's future studying and learning sessions. For test feedback to be effective it must occur as soon as possible and be specific. The longer the student waits, the less meaning the feedback will have. Ideally, students will learn the correct answers as soon as they finish an exam.

As noted in Chapter 3, a test also provides an immediate reason to study. Most of us have several books we would someday like to read, but we never do because we have a hard time getting to them. Tests motivate students to reduce procrastination and complete their lessons by a specified deadline.

Another important function of tests, as noted above, is that they can serve as a reward for studying. One who studies hard and does a good job on a test receives the reward of a high grade, or at least the satisfaction of completing the test properly and knowing one has done a good job. Completing a task and knowing one has done one's best is typically highly rewarding.

Structuring the Test to Help the Students

Vocabulary and Phrasing

Every test question should be constructed so that if a student knows the correct answer, he or she will be able to answer correctly, and if a student does not know the correct answer, he or she will not be able to answer correctly. In order to achieve this goal, teachers should make certain that the vocabulary used on tests will be readily understandable by all students. If vocabulary impedes a student's understanding of a question, he or she may answer incorrectly despite knowledge of the correct response. Thus, if a student has trouble with a word, he or she should receive help. Some teachers let students use a dictionary, even for closed book tests, or they circulate about the room answering individual questions as they occur.

If a student doesn't understand an entire question, there are several things a teacher can do to aid him or her. The teacher should begin by rereading the question to the student with emphasis on the key words. Often this alone is sufficient to clarify the situation. If not, the teacher might rephrase the question, using slightly different wording. Or he or she might explain the purpose of the question—for example, "The purpose of this question is to determine if you understand the emotional factors that caused Michelangelo to finish very few of the sculptures he started." Finally, the teacher might give the student a clue that will help him or her place the material the question covers within the context of his or her learning experience. For example, the teacher could prompt: "Do you remember last week when we were discussing maternal deprivation? We talked about an incident in an orphanage where a number of the children were ill and some older children came over to help out. This question relates to our comments during that discussion."

Problems with Helping Individual Students During a Test

The problem with telling one student the meaning of a word is that it may put others in the class at a disadvantage. Only certain students—

usually the more confident, outgoing, gregarious ones—will take the initiative to ask the teacher for help, while shy, quiet students who are reticent to seek aid will be hurt. One way to overcome this bias is to announce the meanings of difficult words to the entire class or to write the meanings on the board after it is discovered that some students are having difficulty. Words the teacher anticipates as problematic could be defined on the test itself. Also, as noted previously, permitting students to use a dictionary during the test can solve the problem.

The definition of difficult terminology can usually be accomplished quickly, but handling individual queries in front of the full class can become very time consuming and should be avoided. The teacher might explain to the entire class any questions that many students seem to be having trouble with and then walk around the room trying to assess how each student is progressing. If it is apparent that several students do not understand certain test items, the teacher can help them individually or briefly present necessary information to the class as a whole. Many teachers, though, do not like to interrupt a class by speaking during a test. In such cases, information can still be conveyed by writing on the board. The best solution to this problem, of course, is to develop questions that are so clear that they don't require additional explanation, a goal that, as we will see, is quite difficult to accomplish.

Reviewing Exams in Class

After an exam is given, scored, and returned, time should be allowed for student discussion, which can be very productive for both the teacher and the class. It may be discovered, for example, that students answered some question incorrectly for perfectly logical and obvious reasons. Sometimes an incorrect answer is obtained for an entirely correct reason. In such cases, if they can adequately defend their answers, they should generally be given credit. This helps students understand that earning a point on a test is not a question of out-guessing the teacher or reading the teacher's mind, but of understanding or knowing the material. On the basis of class discussion, the teacher can then revise ambiguous questions so that they will be less problematic the next time the test is used.

In time, test questions can be refined to a point where discussions of their intent become less common. Some teachers believe that ambiguous questions should purposely be included on tests because the discussions they provoke are often beneficial. Discussions of controversial topics present excellent learning opportunities.

It is also often a good idea to give credit to students who have mis-read a question. If a question is ambiguous and students have inter-preted it to mean something else, they should not be penalized. Note the following example:

The most common error in student-teacher ratings is the

a. generosity error;

b. severity error;

c. central tendency error;

d. logical error.

The above question was intended to determine if the students knew the error that is most commonly made by a supervising teacher when rating a student teacher, but several students understood the question to refer to a student rating his or her teacher, and yet others understood it to refer to teachers rating their students. Thus, the question above could logically be understood in three different ways. Once again, before filing the exam for future use, the teacher should revise such items to ensure their clarity.

It is important that a teacher realize that students often learn a great deal from reviewing their own exams. These benefits of review are often most evident if the students retake an exam. Even if the students exchange their papers in class, the exam still can function as a learning experience.

Compiling a Test

Sequencing test items from easiest to most difficult tends to build stu-dents' self-confidence so that they can do a better job on each question. It also helps them avoid wasting time on questions they cannot answer. Students who progress quickly through a test and then return to the questions they are unsure of tend to do better than those who feel they must complete each question in order. Thus, if a test is not arranged from easy to hard, students whose test-taking style is to work quickly and then return to difficult questions are more likely to be rewarded. These youngsters will do better on the test because of their test-taking style, not because they know more.

Time Limits

A test should be developed so that at least 90 percent of all students will be able to complete it within the time allowed. In addition, as dis-cussed previously, it is a good idea to make special accommodations for the 10 percent who may be unable to finish. Table 5.1 shows the average number of multiple-choice questions students can be expected to answer, depending on their age group.

Table 5.1

Age Group	Number of Questions
College students	50
High school students	40
Junior high students	30
Upper elementary students	20
Lower elementary students	10 to 20 questions per half-hour

Student's Name, Title Page, Page Placement

It is always a good idea to remind students to put their names on their tests. This problem is quite common. Invariably two or three students' papers cannot be identified because the students forgot to include their names. Identification of these is very time consuming and often affects accurate record keeping. On the first half of the front page, in a very conspicuous place, it is a good idea to ask the students for their first and last names.

Generally a title page, a page that is blank except for identifying information, is not necessary except possibly for timed tests. It does give the test a more finished appearance, but in this day of ecology concerns and energy conservation it is not needed. For this reason teachers usually do not use a title page. Timed tests can be passed out face down and turned over at the appropriate time.

Each question should be put completely on one page. A question should not be split up by, for example, having the a and b alternatives on page 9, and the c and d alternatives on page 10. This makes a question very difficult to follow. The typist should be instructed to ensure this does not happen.

Summary

In this chapter, we discussed some of the positive and negative effects of tests. By taking the wrong approach, many schools foster the belief that having the correct answers is the main goal of education. In reality, there is often no one correct answer. Lack of language precision and certain punishing effects of tests are areas of concern. Three main functions of testing are: to provide feedback, to motivate, and to serve as a reward for studying. Tests should be structured to help the student, with questions clear enough to avoid additional explanation. Teachers should realize the value in the review of exams in class. Sequencing test items and allowing proper time limits are two of the areas to be considered in compiling a test.

Suggested Reading

Aiken, Lewis R. *Psychological Testing and Assessment*. 3d rev. ed. Boston: Allyn and Bacon, 1979, Chapter 2.

6   Basic Types of Tests

Before deciding what type of questions to use on a teacher-made test, it is necessary to determine the basic purpose for giving the test. One must consider whether to prepare a mastery or a discriminatory test.

Mastery Tests

Mastery tests are usually used to ensure that students have reached a certain level of mastery of specific material, such as spelling words or multiplication tables. They usually pertain to a small set of specific skills or facts and are therefore comparatively easy for most students to perform well on. Almost all students should be scoring 90 to 100 percent correct on a mastery test. The main purpose is to insure that students have learned a given set of material, thus those students who do not attain mastery level usually repeat the test until the desired percent correct is achieved.

Discriminatory Tests

Discriminatory tests are used to distinguish differences between students. Their purpose is to rank student performance into high, average, and below average categories.

On a discriminatory test, the ideal class average is approximately 50 percent correct, with the lowest score at about 10 percent correct and the highest around 90 percent correct. The average must be around 50 percent in order to have enough spread at each end to discriminate between the better and the best students and the poorer and poorest students. If two students earn perfect scores on a test, we do not know which one knows more of the material. If the test could be made exactly twice as hard, however, one student may still score 100, but the other

Key Concepts   Recognition question   Structured test
                    Recall question   Projective test
                    Specific recall   Product test
                    Free response   Process exam
                    Speed test   External reporting system
                    Power test   Self-reporting system
                    Maximum performance   Nonlearning format
                    Typical performance   Learning exam
                    Performance exam   Convergent question
                    Language test   Divergent question
                    Nonlanguage test

may only score 50 percent. This would indicate that there are differences between the two students that the first test obscured.

Although there are some objections to using tests for this purpose, it must be remembered that in order to help students, one must know in what areas students need help. And the harder the test, the more apt a teacher is to find gaps in students' knowledge. Very difficult tests can be discouraging, but if students understand their purpose and the teacher focuses on the positive by using them as guidelines to direct future learning, there should be few problems. Just as a good physician will try to diagnose and treat a disease before it becomes serious, a good teacher will try to spot and remedy learning difficulties before they become major problems. A "hard" test can help do just that. A rigorous test is like a thorough physical examination—the more thorough the physical, the more likely problems will be detected.

The main objection to developing tests that have means of 50 percent is the belief that with a mean this low, there are too many failing scores. It must be remembered, though, that the percent of correct responses and pass-fail judgments have no direct relationship to each other. A student could pass a test with 30 percent correct answers or miserably fail a test with 80 percent correct if 30 percent is the highest score in the class in the first case and 80 percent is the lowest in the second. While this is not commonly the case, it does illustrate the fallacy of assuming that 90 to 100 means an A, 80 to 89 a B, and so forth.

Another reason for seeking a wide spread of test scores is that in real life a similar spread of knowledge and abilities often exists. If there is much variation in test scores, the test is probably quite representative of reality. It is also safe to assume that factors such as chance and knowing how to take tests were held at a minimum. Finally, when there is a wide spread of scores, it is easier to select a clear grade cut-off point and there are fewer borderline cases. This is illustrated in Table 6.1.

Table 6.1

| | Test No. 1
Range 21-91 | | Test No. 2
Range 62-79 |
Grade	Raw Score	Grade	Raw Score
	21		62
D	34	D	63
	36		64
	58		64
	60		65
	62		67
C	63	C	67
	63		67
	64		69
	68		70
	69		70
	69		71
	74		71
B	75	B	71
	76		72
	76		73
	82		74
	86		75
	89		76
	90		76
	92	A	76
	92		77
	94		78
	96		79

Note that there are very clear-cut differences between the grades on the first test as compared to those on the second test. In the first case, the difference between the highest C and the lowest A is 18 points, but in the second, the difference is only 5 points. The first test is probably a more accurate reflection of the actual classroom situation.

Test Formats

The term **test format** refers to the type of test used, such as multiple choice, open book, or oral. A teacher should use a wide variety of test formats in order to tap students' different skills—memory, creativity, ability to organize information, and the like.

Recognition Versus Recall

Recognition questions require that a choice be made from a given set of responses. Included in this category are true-false, multiple-choice, and matching items. Recognition requires a lower level of mastery than does recall; the student only needs to be familiar with the material so that he or she can recognize the correct answer. The student does not need to have overlearned the material.

Recall questions require students to supply correct answers from memory. The student must know the material well enough that the test question alone will elicit the correct response. Recall questions are usually much harder than recognition questions and require more thorough knowledge of the subject matter. The most common examples of recall tests are fill-in-the-blank and short-answer tests.

Recall questions are sometimes classified as either specific recall or free response. **Specific recall** questions require short responses that are fairly objective. Answers are usually one word or a limited number of words that can be graded by anyone who has a set of answers. **Free response** questions ask students to construct their own rather complex replies; there are no one right answers, but some are better than others. Essay questions are the most commonly used free response items. Usually only the teacher can grade an essay exam because he or she is the only person who knows what has been taught in class and what is expected. One drawback of free response questions is that grading can be very subjective and may depend on personal factors that have little to do with the quality of students' answers. This problem will be discussed in detail in the chapter on essay exams.

Speed Versus Power Tests

On **speed tests** items are simple and quickness is paramount. The best example of a speed test is a typing test. To do well on such a test, one must work quickly and accurately within the specified period of time. Time limits are an important element of speed tests. For example, anyone who knows the alphabet could probably pass a typing test if there were no time limit. Other speed tests included timed tests of athletic prowess and math games (such as flash cards) in which the student with the first answer is awarded a point. In any speed test time is important and the items are easy.

Items vary in difficulty on **power tests**. Usually a quarter of the items are easy, half are of medium difficulty, and a quarter are very difficult.

These are the most commonly used type of test. Theoretically, there is no need for time limits on power tests because additional time would make no difference in a student's score. For example, a student who knows nothing about cube roots would not be able to solve the cube root of 125 without help no matter how much time was allowed. The student either knows the answer or doesn't. Being given additional time will usually not help, or will help only very slightly.

In reality, many tests are a combination of speed and power. A time limit may be given even when the test format does not require one. Often rigidly fixed class periods are more responsible for this situation than are individual teachers. Because of the vast differences among students, however, some thus fare better than others. Most likely to be penalized are youngsters who have a good knowledge of the subject matter but work very conscientiously and carefully and thus take more time. The following suggestions will help teachers meet both the demands of the school and the needs of students.

If a student needs more than the allotted time to complete an exam, he or she might be allowed to come back after school to finish. One difficulty with this approach is that some students might complain that it is unfair for others to have more time to work on the exam. It might therefore be a general rule that who so desires can come after school and continue the exam. Since few students actually want to stay after school, this procedure encourages most to finish on time but allows slower students to finish without penalty.

Schools must accommodate individual differences instead of trying to eliminate them. The reality is that we are all different, and there is no possible way that school can be made "fair" in every way for everyone. Is it fair that the brighter students often have an easier time and earn higher grades with less effort? Is it fair that those from better backgrounds tend to do better in school? Those students who are handicapped in some way, and are thus slower, must be accommodated in ways other than lowering their grade. And being a slow test taker is a handicap just as blindness or mental retardation is a handicap.

The major problem with this approach, though, is that students who return after school to complete the exam have undoubtedly seen many of the questions and may capitalize on the opportunity to look up some of the answers. To prevent this, one might:

1. Identify beforehand those students who are most likely to need more than the allotted time and give them only *part* of the exam. Grade the portion of the exam they have completed, and for the remainder of the exam, which is taken after school, give them a different set of questions that covers the material they have not been tested over. Unfortunately, this procedure can be time consuming

and may create grading problems because the two-part exam may be difficult to compare to the exam taken by the rest of the class. This process actually results in two different exams that must be made of equal difficulty in order to be comparable.

If the teacher simply divides the exam in half, the students who need more time to finish will not see the second part of the exam, but they can still find out about it from their classmates. A similar situation exists where one class takes the exam during, for example, second hour, and another class during third hour. If the same test is used, some students in the later class may find out the questions from someone in a previous class. Because teachers have not felt that the latter situation (where a class who takes the test later can find out answers from an earlier class) is very serious, it would seem that if a few students find out the answers from those who took the whole test, it would also not be a serious problem. One way to minimize this problem is to give all students a complete outline of what will be on the test. Then there is little advantage if students who have not taken the exam find out what is on it.

2. Arrange with other teachers to allow students who usually take longer either to come in early to take the test or to stay after class. This, in many ways, is the most desirable approach, but it requires the cooperation of other teachers. Then there is the problem that a physics teacher, for example, may try to have a student excused from an art class, feeling that "art is not as important or as academic as physics." This can create some problems in that it is not likely that the student is going to need to stay after class to finish an art exam, but it is likely that more students will have to stay after class (or come in early) to finish a physics exam. Care must therefore be taken to ensure in kind cooperation and reciprocity.

3. Grade students on the portion of the test they complete. If a student has completed ten out of twenty questions, and of those ten, eight are correct, the student would have a score of 80 percent. This method can be successful, but there is always the possibility that if students know they will be graded this way, they may not answer questions they are not sure about. Thus, if a student is certain of 30 answers out of 40 and answers all of these, the student will have a score of 100 percent. If another student is sure about only 20 answers out of 40 and answers all of them correctly, his or her score would likewise be 100 percent. Despite obvious differences in performance, students can sometimes manipulate this method to their own advantage, which may negate the benefits it offers slower students. On the other hand, it is a poor procedure to mark problems wrong because a student did not complete them.

Probably the best solution is to help slow workers improve their speed. Sometimes such students are overly cautious and review an answer several times before they are finally satisfied. They would undoubtedly derive many long-term benefits from the acquisition of more effective test-taking skills. This, in many ways, is the best way to deal with the problem of the slow student, but is probably the solution that is least likely to occur. Most of us are very resistant to change, even small changes. Generally, tragic life experiences or a drastic change in the environment are necessary to bring about change.

Maximum Performance Versus Typical Performance

On **maximum performance tests**, students try to obtain the best score possible. Competitive events, such as athletic, music, and art contests, all call for maximum performance. Most classroom tests are also maximum performance tests, but they should really be typical performance tests.

Typical performance tests measure usual performance, or what students normally or typically achieve. A typical performance exam is a more accurate measurement of true achievement than is a maximum performance test. If a teacher is able to measure a student's typical performance, he or she is in a better position to help.

What one can do *under pressure* under favorable circumstances is quite different from what one *normally* does. This situation has caused havoc not only in our evaluation procedures in the schools, but in everyday life. For example, marriage counselors commonly note that a couple's relationship changes after marriage. Before marriage, the individuals usually display maximum performance to each other; that is, they are on their best behavior, are willing to overlook each other's faults and mistakes, and try extremely hard to cover up their own faults and mistakes. According to many marriage counselors, it is amazing how much two people can hide from each other before they are married. After they are married, however, typical performance predominates. This is why many spouses complain: "This is not the person I married. After we were married he (or she) changed tremendously." If couples could assess each other's *typical* performance, the divorce rate would probably plummet. Likewise, schools assess maximum performance and report it in the form of grades, but the everyday world gets typical performance. Partly for this reason many employers have concluded that school grades are not accurate indicators of performance in the work place.

Because most tests developed for use in the schools measure maximum performance, a student can do well on an exam and yet not behave correspondingly in everyday life. In fact, there is a fairly low correlation between job success and grades. Many youngsters can perform well two or three times during a marking period in order to earn a good grade even though their everyday performance is not nearly as high.

The most effective way of evaluating typical performance is to test often—preferably once, twice, or even more per week. Under these conditions, students are likely to spend less time studying for each exam and are more likely to display their normal level of achievement. Furthermore, giving frequent exams tends to keep motivation at a high level during the entire marking period instead of concentrating it into two or three intensive study days.

Objective Versus Subjective

Objective questions have clear-cut answers that are obviously right or wrong. Anyone who has an answer sheet can correct an objective test. True-or-false and multiple-choice are typical kinds of objective questions.

Subjective questions call for answers that are open to interpretation. Only the instructor can grade these examinations, which include such question types as essay or short answer. With the subjective format, evaluation and grading are highly influenced by the grader's personal opinion.

Written Versus Oral Versus Performance

A **written exam** depends highly upon students' reading and writing skills. Unfortunately, some students' true abilities can be obscured this way, if they are either very good or very poor writers. A creative writer can sound impressive even if he or she lacks knowledge of the subject being tested, while a poor writer may have a hard time expressing his or her knowledge on paper. The advantages of this format are its low cost, quickness, and effectiveness in measuring a wide variety of information.

Oral exams were the most common way of testing in the past because paper was expensive and efficient writing implements were lacking. As paper and pencils became more economical, however, oral exams became increasingly rare in spite of the fact that some students actually perform better on oral exams than they do on other formats. By using primarily written exams, teachers inadvertently and consistently favor students who have strong reading and writing skills. Using some oral exams would equalize this situation and enable those who have good oral skills to excel too. Teachers could thus more effectively assess the true abilities of these students.

Another advantage of oral exams is that the teacher can easily ask students to clarify their responses while the test is in progress. On a written exam, a student may lose points if the teacher does not understand a response, but on an oral exam, he or she can be given helpful feedback. The student can then explain an answer more clearly, add additional information, or restate the response in a different way.

An oral exam is a very personal way of testing. In some ways it can be a more effective measure of a student's knowledge than an essay exam because a student is often less able to mask his or her ignorance. With a few well-chosen questions, an instructor can assess whether or not a student knows the material. Some teachers believe that the only way to evaluate a student is through an oral exam because it is the only method that provides sufficient interchange and feedback.

One drawback of oral exams is that they can be very time consuming. For example, the writer decided to give an oral exam to one educational psychology class. Students were scheduled for an hour each, which meant only eight students a day could be tested. The result was that an entire week was used solely for the purpose of giving one oral exam to one class. Then there was difficulty in scheduling every student within the week. If there are 30 students in a class and each is given an individual half-hour exam, 15 hours will be spent on the administration of a single test. Oral exams are thus most feasible in smaller classes or when used only once or twice per grading period.

Another problem with this approach is that a teacher may have difficulty in defending his or her evaluation. Unless the sessions are tape recorded, the teacher has no proof to support his or her judgment. For this reason, oral exams are probably subject to more abuse than are other testing formats. If there is any question, a written exam can easily be regraded, but it is difficult to regrade an oral exam. Furthermore, oral exams can depend upon such nonrelevant factors as personality, self-confidence, fluency, verbosity, and the like. A student may do well on an oral exam not so much because of superlative knowledge as because he or she has a pleasing, outgoing, personality, is verbal, and is able to converse easily with almost anyone. Sometimes the pressure of an oral testing situation can impede a student's performance. Nonetheless, approximately 30 percent of all students *prefer* oral exams to other types. As might be expected, these students are verbal, confident, pleasant, and often outgoing.

An innovative approach to oral exams is to give the students questions and have them record their answers on cassette tapes. If this technique is used, the teacher should ensure that students know how to use a cassette tape recorder, outline their material beforehand, and are quick with the pause button. Most will then do a fairly good job. Even this modification can be very time consuming and difficult to correct accurately, however. A checklist of concepts to be covered can simplify the grading process, provide written evaluation, and standardize procedures. Of course, to grade this way, the questions must ask for specific ideas or bits of information.

Performance exams are highly effective tests. They require students to actively demonstrate specific knowledge or skills. For example, students might be asked to bake a cake or to repair a carburetor. These tests call for the integration of knowledge from a number of areas and measure to what extent students can perform what they have been trained to do. Few students complain about performance exams, for they see them as being useful, relevant, and generally more enjoyable than written or oral exams.

Unfortunately, performance exams can be costly and time consuming. For example, if the final exam in a home economics class is to prepare a well-balanced meal for four people, the amount of time and the cost of ingredients required for each student would be prohibitive. The problem can be reduced if a number of students take the exam at the same time or work in teams, but this tends to lead to somewhat superficial evaluation. Limiting the test group to approximately five students can be more effective, but then there is the problem of what to do with the rest of the class. Many teachers give general assignments during this time to ensure that all students will be busy.

Another drawback is that it is often difficult to obtain the necessary resources to administer a performance exam. In auto shop, for example, a performance exam over the proper method of changing a tire would require the use of several automobiles if the exam were to progress quickly. In spite of these disadvantages though, performance exams are among the best test formats available and should be used as often as possible.

Language Versus Nonlanguage

Most tests are **language tests**—that is, their instructions and questions are presented in words. Language includes reading, talking, listening, and writing.

Nonlanguage tests are used primarily with the deaf, young children, people who do not speak English, and the mentally retarded. As might be expected, such tests are very difficult to administer. The primary means of communication are pantomime, pointing, and signs (all of which could be regarded as language).

The writer once had a student who did not know a single word of English. Consequently, all of her examinations had to be given using pantomime. This was not difficult in math, as she knew enough math to be able to pick up from the book and lectures what she was to do, but in social studies nonlanguage tests were very difficult. Fortunately for us both, she slowly picked up English and in time language exams could be used. A teacher faced with giving a nonlanguage exam is quickly forced to appreciate the utility of language.

Structured Versus Projective

A **structured test** contains very specific and defined items. The student is expected to circle the best answers, fill in the blanks, write short sentences, or compose essays. Almost all commonly used classroom tests are structured tests.

Projective tests present ambiguous stimuli designed to elicit highly individualized responses. Examples of the projective technique include the Rorschach ink blot test, the Thematic Apperception Test (TAT), and the Children's Apperception Test (CAT). Such tests are most commonly used by psychologists in personality testing, but their validity and reliability has recently been seriously questioned.

Many teachers use projective tests in such areas as creative writing, English, social studies, art, and music as a means of stimulating creativity. As such, they more often serve as curriculum tools than as testing tools. They can also be used as interest tests. A commonly used projective technique is to present a set of pictures about which students are asked to write or tell a complete story. The teacher usually directs the students: "Create a story from this picture. Be sure to include a plot and an ending. Let me know at what point in your story this picture describes . . . ."

Product Versus Process

A **product test** emphasizes only the final outcome of the question—that is, the answer, and only the answer. The majority of classroom tests are product tests. In many ways this is very unfortunate. Focusing merely on the answer causes students to direct their attention to a narrow goal that is but one minor aspect of education. They will sometimes try to reach the right answer by *any means,* even by cheating. They may thus find the answer that works, but unless they understand the process (which is the most important outcome of learning), they will have wasted their time. The procedure a student has used to obtain an answer is more important than the answer itself. The reason for working a problem is to learn the correct process.

A **process exam** focuses on how students attack, solve, or work out a problem. On a process exam, each step necessary to arrive at the answer is evaluated. On a product test, a student may obtain the right answer for the wrong reasons. In this case, the student may not get the help needed because if he or she has the "correct" answer, it is assumed he or she knows the correct process. On the other hand, another student may obtain the wrong answer using the correct method and not receive credit. These two incidents would not occur if a process method were used. With this method, a child earns credit for what he or she does correctly, and does not earn credit for what he or she does incorrectly or does not do.

It is also much easier to use a process test for diagnostic purposes. If students know specifically where their weaknesses lie, they can concentrate their efforts in those areas.

External Report Versus Self-Report

When an **external reporting** system is used, an outsider rates the subject. For example, a teacher rates a student, or a principal rates a teacher.

When a **self-reporting system** is used, students grade, evaluate, or report their own behavior. For instance, students might be asked to evaluate their own strengths and weaknesses. This method of evaluation has been sorely neglected in the past. All students need to learn to assess their own behavior, progress, performance, motivations, and interests. Without practice in self-evaluation, students fall into the habit of depending on someone else to give them feedback.

Probably among the most important skills a student can learn are self-discipline, self-evaluation, self-feedback, and self-regulation. These qualities help a person achieve success in adulthood. External report forms of evaluation have been used far too much. Teachers commonly notice that students are unsure about their progress and performance, and, for example, repeatedly come up to ask the teacher how they are doing when it *should* be obvious to the students that their progress is quite satisfactory.

Teachers often do not use self-report tools because they fear that students will grade themselves unrealistically high in every area. Research has not supported this fear (Bergman 1971). In this study, an elementary school initiated a report card system in which students evaluated themselves in each subject area by marking X's in the boxes that represented the grades they felt they deserved. If the teacher agreed with a student's self-evaluation, he or she left the mark alone. If the teacher felt the grade was inaccurate, he or she checked the box that represented the grade that he or she believed the student should have. A detailed study found that teachers marked approximately 15 percent of the grades lower but marked about 28 percent of them higher. Thus students, at least in this situation, tended to underrate themselves. Teachers commonly report that students have unrealistic opinions of themselves and are often more negative than they need to be.

The most common self-report tool is a checklist on which students simply check off the skills they have mastered and rate the skills not yet mastered according to amount of improvement needed. Or they might rate each skill on a four- or five-point scale ranging from excellent to poor. The students then receive help in the areas indicated by the checklist.

Teacher-Made Tests Versus Standardized Tests

A **teacher-made test** is simply a test a teacher makes. The advantage of a teacher-made test is that it is designed for a specific subject, class, school, topic, and teaching style. In short, it is tailored to the teacher's individual needs. The disadvantage of a standardized test is that the teacher does not have national norms available and therefore can compare his or her students only with each other.

Standardized tests are prepared by a test publisher, usually to be used throughout the country and not just in a local area. They are especially useful because national norms are usually developed that allow teachers to compare their classes with other classes throughout the country. Usually, a teacher can make specific comparisons, such as between her fifth-grade inner-city white girls and the national average for fifth-grade inner-city white girls, or between twelfth-grade black students and the national norms for twelfth-grade black students.

Open Book Versus Closed Book

On a **closed book test**, questions must be answered without reference to a book or notes. Closed book essay or short answer exams depend heavily on memory as well as on spelling and writing skills. Although this is the most commonly used form of teacher-made test, it is somewhat unrealistic, because only rarely is one forced to recall information while isolated from reference sources. Furthermore, this type of exam tends to discourage creative thinking (although not necessarily so) and often requires little reasoning.

Open book tests are far less dependent upon memory, writing skills, and spelling because students can rely on their books for spelling, sentence structure, wording, and facts. Likewise, open book exams tend to be more dependent upon understanding, the ability to express one's own ideas, and the ability to evaluate concepts. Open book exams usually ask questions whose answers cannot be easily looked up and copied. For this reason, they generally require a more complex thought process and the evaluation or application of ideas. Open book exams more closely parallel reality in that many work situations require the preparation of reports where access to and use of reference material is encouraged. The quality of the report depends upon the writer's ability to gather the needed material, evaluate and synthesize it, and express it in a logical, coherent manner. Development of these extremely important skills is facilitated by the use of open book exams. The tests are more difficult to grade and require the teacher to have an excellent understanding of the material in order to adequately evaluate student responses, but these "drawbacks" constitute increased demands on the teacher's time rather than a negative aspect of the tests. In many ways, an open book test is a performance exam. Two reasons teachers hesitate to use open book exams are that the grades tend to be higher and that it is more difficult to discriminate better students from average students when trying to assign an objective grade to a subjective performance. Yet, this is an excellent type of an exam, as testing students' grasp of concepts is undeniably important.

Nonlearning Versus Learning Formats

A **nonlearning format test** is primarily designed to determine how much information the student knows rather than to teach *new* skills or information. Generally most tests fall into this category. On the other hand, a **learning exam** requires students to apply previously learned concepts to a new situation, and through the use of logic with information provided on the exam, the student learns something new. The specific, or at least partial, purpose of a learning exam is to teach something. To a limited extent, all tests function as learning exams, but some are designed to be more instructive than others. Open book, process format, and group exams all tend to be learning oriented. We will discuss the subject of learning exams in more detail later.

Convergent Versus Divergent Formats

A **convergent question** purposely leads to one best answer. For example, the question "What is the shape of the average brick?" has one best answer—rectangular. Most teacher-made tests are comprised of convergent questions.

A **divergent question** leads to many possible responses. For example, the different possible answers to the divergent question "What could we do with 10,000 bricks?" could easily fill a page or two. Some examples would be:

1. A woman could carry one in her purse and use it as a weapon.
2. A house could be built out of bricks.
3. A fireplace could be built out of bricks.
4. They could be ground up and used as plant food.
5. They could be covered with felt and used as bookends.
6. They could be stacked up with boards in between and used as a bookcase.

Divergent tests are rarely used because they are extremely difficult to grade, yet they are very useful in developing such skills as creativity, ingenuity, and the ability to synthesize (Torrance 1962). In addition, although they are especially applicable to creative writing, social studies, history, art, and music, they can be used in almost any class. For example, a chemistry teacher could ask students to name as many uses as possible for sodium while a biology teacher could ask students to list as many uses as possible of blood in the body. If these two items had limited numbers of uses, the questions would be convergent, but since there are thousands of uses for sodium and dozens of uses for blood in the body, these questions qualify as divergent.

Scale Measurement Versus Test Measurement

When a **scale** is used, students are rated along a continuum. For example, the *Ayers Handwriting Scale* consists of examples of letters ranging from the poorest penmanship to the best, with small gradations between the two extremes. The teacher determines each student's level of skill by matching the samples with the student's handwriting. The student is then assigned an overall rating in accordance with the scale. Scales are often used in art and physical education as well.

In actual test measurement, each answer is more or less independent and tends to be either right or wrong. Although in some types of tests (such as essay) the answers fall on a continuum, the gradations of the test continuum are less exact than the scale's.

Pretests Versus Posttests

A **pretest** is designed to measure how much a class knows before a lesson while a posttest is intended to determine how much a student knows after a lesson. By using both kinds of tests and comparing the scores, a teacher can evaluate both whole classes and individuals' progress. The same test may be given twice, or two slightly different tests may be developed. Either way, this technique can be very informative because it indicates the teacher's impact on the students. For example, it is not uncommon for the mean score on a pretest to be 65 percent and on a posttest to be 72 or 73 percent. The scores increased, but not greatly. In areas such as mathematics, though, where students are less likely to have been previously exposed to the material, the percentage of gain is often much greater. At any rate, it is helpful for the teacher to know the amount of learning that is taking place and how much students have accomplished.

Pretests can also be used for diagnosis. The teacher can thus determine at what level to begin and which students may need special attention. Results may also be used for the purpose of assigning students to appropriate ability groups. Another purpose of a pretest is to assign students to groups based on ability or knowledge levels, especially if it is obvious that there are gross differences in ability within the class.

Summary

In this chapter we have examined the characteristics of various test formats. Although many teachers tend to prefer and use only one or two formats, it is most beneficial to employ a wide variety. Since some students perform better on some types of tests than on others, the constant use of one format can consistently bias testing in favor of some students and against others. Thus, in order to meet individual needs and help all students achieve maximally, familiarity with and use of many different kinds of tests is desirable.

It should also be noted that there is much overlap among test formats. For example, a process test may also be an open book test. By using various combinations of formats teachers can create numerous different testing situations that can lead to richer understanding of students' strengths and weaknesses.

Suggested Readings

Greene, Harry A., Albert N. Jorgensen and J. Raymond Gerberich. *Measurement and Evaluation in the Elementary School*. 2d rev. ed. New York: Longmans, Green and Company, 1953. Chapters 6, 8.

Mehrens, William A. and Irvin J. Lehmann. *Measurement and Evaluation in Education and Psychology*. New York: Holt, Rinehart and Winston. Chapter 9.

Noll, Victor H., Dale P. Scannell and Robert C. Craig. *Introduction to Educational Measurement*. 4th rev. ed. Boston: Houghton Mifflin, 1979.

Thorndike, Robert L. *Educational Measurement*. Washington, D.C. American Council on Education, 1971. Chapter 9.

7   True-or-False Items

As discussed in Chapter 6, some classroom topics lend themselves better to objective tests while others can be more effectively tested with essay tests. For example, when clear-cut facts are to be tested, the objective format is usually most useful, but when values, concepts, and general ideas are involved, essay exams are more appropriate. In addition, using of several types of questions adds variety to a testing program.

How to Construct Effective True-or-False Items

One of the easiest kinds of objective questions to construct, and one of the easiest to score, is the true-or-false item. It is a statement that is either true or false exactly as written; students must determine which and mark their answer sheets accordingly.

The most common way of developing true-or-false items is to select a true statement and either leave it unchanged in order to elicit a "true" response, or change it slightly by adding the word *not* or changing a key word in order to produce a "false" item. Adding the word *not*, for example, changes the following true statement into a false one:

True statement: Dendrites are extensions of the nerve cell body.
False statement: Dendrites are *not* extensions of the nerve cell body.

This form is common, but unfortunately the word *not* may serve as a hint to students that the statement is false. Those who understand the process of constructing tests will realize that false statements can be easily made by adding the word *not* to true statements and thus conclude that most items stated in the negative are probably false. Such students are then able to select correct answers regardless of their

Enabling skills
Retroactive inhibition
Yes-or-no questions
Fact-or-opinion questions
Cause-or-effect items

knowledge of the subject matter. These kinds of insights into the test-taking process are called **enabling skills**. Students who possess a number of enabling skills are often able to achieve fairly high scores on true-or-false exams without knowing very much about the material. But well-constructed test items can greatly decrease the likelihood that students will be able to obtain correct answers by depending on previously learned enabling skills. Many enabling skills are not directly learned by students but are, to some degree, unconscious. Students learn from experience that certain types of statements are probably false, but most could probably not explain exactly what cues they respond to.

Making a statement false by changing a key word is usually more effective than merely adding the word *not*. For example:

True statement: A *dendrite* is a direct extension of the nerve cell body.

False statement: A *synapse* is a direct extension of the nerve cell body.

Changing the word *dendrite* to *synapse* is more subtle than using the word *not*, but unless the substitute word is chosen carefully, it may give away that the statement is false. The best word to substitute in a false statement is one that is similar to the key word or makes the item almost true. The main problem with this approach is that it is sometimes obvious that a word has been changed, and thus the statement must be false. To avoid this, try to substitute a word that is close, or sounds correct, but clearly is not.

Avoid taking statements directly from the textbook and making only simple word changes. It is a good idea to vary the wording considerably so that if students understand the concept, they will recognize it regardless of the way in which it is stated. The context or the word order should be varied to help students transfer the concept to new situations. Furthermore, since many youngsters study by memorizing from their textbooks, similar wording used on a test may provide clues to the appropriate response. When utilizing formal textbook wording, false statements seem to sound false, even though the student may not know why.

Focus each statement on *only one basic idea*. More complex items can unnecessarily confuse students. Furthermore, many students reason that if there are a number of ideas in a statement, one of them is bound to be wrong, and thus the statement must be false. "In 1492, Columbus, sailing in a ship called the *Nina*, discovered America" actually asks a total of six different questions: (1) *Who* discovered America? (2) What did Columbus *do*? (3) What did Columbus *discover*? (4) *When* did Columbus discover America? (5) What *means of transportation* did Columbus use? (6) What was the *name of the boat* that Columbus was in when he discovered America? Such an item is too complex to be an accurate indicator of what students do or do not know.

A long question does not necessarily test for knowledge, but for reading carefulness, alertness, school concern, and conscientiousness. Careful reading of a question such as the above, often gives the impression it is false, whereas a *superficial* reading gives the impression it is true. In this case the careful students may tend to select "false" as the answer where the faster students may select "true." Ideally, we want to measure the students' level of knowledge, and not their test-taking behavior.

Avoid convoluted wording, such as statements in which one negative term (such as *not*) is negated by another. Such items tend to assess problem-solving ability rather than students' understanding of subject matter. For example, a statement such as "It is *not* true that Washington is *not* the capital of the United States" is unnecessarily confusing. A preferable true-or-false would be "Washington is the capital of the United States."

Use *approximately equal* numbers of true items and false ones. There is sometimes a tendency to include more statements that are true because they are easily adapted from notes or books. In addition, it is difficult to write false items that seem appropriate. We do not usually think in terms of what is not true, but of what is true. For this reason, we may have to expend the effort to develop more false questions. To ensure that a test is balanced in this regard, count the total number of true as opposed to false answers to ascertain that the proportions are approximately equal. With 100 questions, there should be 50 true and 50 false questions. Obviously, if the range is close (48 false and 52 true) there is no problem. But a clear imbalance, such as 28 false questions and 72 true questions, should be corrected. Commonly, in these cases the teacher simply converts several of the true statements into false statements (in the case above, 22 of the true questions are changed into false statements, producing a 50-50 balance). Except for unusual circumstances, a teacher should never develop a test on which all statements are true, or all are false.

A problem with false items is that if students believe them to be true, they may tend to retain the information as factual. To learn what is correct they must then learn new information over old patterns, which can be quite difficult. When questioned, a student may recall both answers and then have to determine which is correct. Such previous learning that interferes with present learning is called **retroactive inhibition**. Some educators see this as a serious argument against the use of true-or-false tests.

Avoid using terms that imply absolutism, such as *always, never, all, none,* and *every,* because they tend to indicate that a statement is false. Rarely is anything always or never true. Likewise, words or phrases such as *generally, some, usually,* and *sometimes* often indicate that a statement is true. In developing true statements, many teachers tend to use these words in an attempt to avoid absolutism. For example, in order for the statement "Neurodermatitis *always* includes exugation of a liquid substance from the skin" to be false, one need find only a single exception. Most students would therefore reason that exugation of liquid must not be true in every case. This feeling is expressed in the cliche "there is an exception to every rule."

Avoid statements that are difficult to read. The longer the statement, the more difficult it is for the student to read. Again, very long statements tend to measure reading ability and comprehension more than understanding of subject matter. Especially sentences involving clauses, many qualifications, or complex ideas are confusing to students. The sentences should be as simple as possible.

Know your subject matter in order to avoid writing seemingly simple, straightforward items that are not as straightforward as they seem. For instance, consider the statement "George Washington was born on February 22, 1732."

Most reference books will say that this information is true, but most history students know that when George Washington was born, the Julian calendar was in use. Thus, according to contemporary records, he would have actually been born on February 11, 1732. This country did not change over to the Gregorian calendar until 1752, which would place his birth on February 22. The same problem is found with many questions relative to Columbus Day, Christmas, the early history of the American colonies, and *any* event that occurred before 1752. The problem illustrated in this example points out the need for the students to at least be given a chance to give a reason for the answer they selected. A knowledgeable student, in this case, could probably teach the teacher a few things.

Make it easy for students to indicate their responses. For example, symbols such as a plus sign for true and a zero for false may create confusion because students must first determine if the item is true or false and then translate their answer into the appropriate code. If students' penmanship is a problem, it is probably most efficient to include the words *true* and *false* by each statement and have students circle their choice. Once again, care must be to focus on the concepts being tested and ensure that students' knowledge will not be obscured by irrelevant factors.

Use statements that are clearly true or clearly false exactly as written. While it is best to ask the student to indicate whether a statement is *most often true* or *most often false,* the answer should still be as clear as possible. A good rule is that a true item should be true in 90 percent of all cases. Many teachers avoid debatable or opinionated statements, while others feel that because such items can stimulate thought, a limited number of debatable answers for which students can earn credit if they can adequately support their point of view are clearly functional and should, at times, be used. Some teachers use statements that are a matter of opinion but preface them with phrases such as *your author stated that . . .* or *your instructor stressed that . . . .* Thus, whether the opinion is right or wrong is beside the point. Other examples would be *Bacon believed that . . ., Einstein's opinion was . . . ,* or *orthodox Freudian psychology teaches that . . . .*

Underline all words that affect meaning (such as *not* and *ideally*) and all key terms, both in the test directions and in individual test items.

Try to write items of uniform length. Often short statements tend to be false and longer ones tend to be true because teachers try to ensure the veracity of true statements by being very specific and including the proper qualifiers. This problem can sometimes be corrected by artificially lengthening false statements. Of course, one must still take care to preserve each item's clarity and limit its content to a single idea.

In summary, true-or-false items can be useful indicators of students' knowledge *if they are used judiciously.* If teachers are aware of both the strengths and weaknesses of true-or-false tests, they can take steps to maximize the beneficial aspects. Hopefully, the above information will not make the reader too pessimistic about using this type of question, but only very cautious.

Variations on the Basic True-or-False Format

It is possible to make some useful modifications on standard true-or-false items. The resulting adaptations provide variety and may be more useful for certain kinds of material than are the standard forms.

Yes-or-No Questions

For younger children and for certain types of information, yes-or-no questions work better than true-or-false items. On the whole, though, there is little difference. For example:

Yes/No   Do you think that $9.00 would be enough money to buy a new automobile tire?

True/False $9.00 is sufficient to buy a new automobile tire.

The yes-or-no question is easier to understand and is thus more useful with younger children. With older students, yes-or-no questions would probably be used mostly for variety.

Mostly-True-or-Rarely-True Items

This format is useful in dealing with generalizations and concepts, especially in such areas as social studies, English, psychology, philosophy, religion, and history. Very few generalizations are strictly true, even in most cases. For example, consider this statement: "The suicide rate is approximately three times higher among males than it is among females." This observation would not always be true, but it would be mostly true. Whether it is true depends upon the age level, ethnic group, specific locality, and other population factors.

Fact-or-Opinion Items

This format is extremely useful to help students discriminate between information that is widely accepted and information that is debatable or depends largely on point of view. Note the following two examples:

F/O   The Chevrolet Citation is a beautiful car.

F/O   Dr. Gus Miller's research found that those who smoke filter cigarettes have a life expectancy of 63 years while nonsmokers have a life expectancy of 76 to 77 years.

The first statement is obviously opinion, whereas the second is fact. In this context, information designated as true may not necessarily be unequivocally true, but it can be verified. Opinions can never be verified. The first item can be changed into a factual statement as follows:

F/O   In a recent survey, 93 percent of 264 people polled agreed with the statement "The Chevrolet Citation is a beautiful car."

The second statement can also be debated, but it would still be classified as fact. It could be changed to an opinion question as follows:

F/O   All other things being equal, the difference in life span between a smoker and a nonsmoker is over ten years; non-smokers live an average of at least ten years longer because they don't smoke.

Notice the statement is now more debatable in that it is difficult to prove that smoking itself *causes* the difference.

Many teachers find that debate over such items can be very productive. Instead of using them as tests, they use them to help students differentiate between various levels of accuracy and the fact-opinion dichotomy. Examples of such questions are:

1. Air conditioning for a car costs an average of $400.00.
2. The *Encyclopaedia Britannica*® is the most useful set of reference books on the market.
3. The cost of a quality pocket calculator is much too high.
4. There is an average of 110 feet of tape in each Scotch tape roll.
5. Children should never be spanked.
6. Blue is the most attractive color.

Answers:
    1. Fact
    2. Opinion
    3. Opinion
    4. Fact
    5. Opinion
    6. Opinion

The important factors in such an activity are the debate that results from disagreement and the process needed to arrive at a solution. Using statements that are clearly fact or clearly opinion and provoke little debate is, in most cases, not as useful.

Cause-or-Effect Items

With these items, students are expected to determine which statements normally are seen as causes of something and which normally are effects. While reviewing a cause-or-effect labeling assignment, students should discover that it is conceivable that anything could be a cause and, likewise, that anything could be an effect, even though we usually think of certain things as causes and others as effects. Again, the debate that results from the ambiguity is highly constructive. Note the following examples:

C/E   The alarm clock did not go off.
C/E   John could not complete his paper because he ran out of typing paper.

The first example is usually thought of as a cause—that is, something that would make someone late for work or school. The second example is more ambiguous—not completing the paper, is an effect of not having enough typing paper, but could it also cause John to fail a course.

Statements That Require Corrections

Statements that require correction are the most useful true-or-false items. The student first marks a statement as either true or false. If it is true, she proceeds on to the next question. If it is false, she must change it in some way that will make it true. This variation converts a standard true-or-false statement into a fill-in-the-blank or short-answer item. In many ways this format is very useful. It reduces guessing and helps the teacher understand specifically why a student answered the way he or she did. It also forces students to reason, analyze, and evaluate both the information presented and their responses. For example, a true-or-false statement requiring correction might read:

T/F   A hebephrenic schizophrenic tends to be either mute and stuporous or dangerously excited and manic.

Students would circle F and either replace the word *hebephrenic* with the word *catatonic* or change the definition to read: "A hebephrenic schizophrenic tends to exhibit silliness, giggling, and childish or foolish behavior."

Summary

The true-or-false question is one of the easiest kinds of objective questions to construct and to score. It is a statement that is either true or false exactly as written. Well-constructed test items can greatly decrease the likelihood that students will be able to obtain correct answers through previously learned enabling skills. This chapter has looked at ways to construct effective true-or-false items, as well as various modifications of the standard true-or-false items. These modifications will provide some variety for the student and may be more useful for cetain kinds of material.

Suggested Readings

Ahmann, Stanley and Marvin Glock. *Evaluating Pupil Growth. Principles of Tests and Measurements.* 5th rev. ed. Boston: Allyn and Bacon, 1975. Chapter 3.

Greene, Harry A., Albert N. Jorgensen and J. Raymond Gerberich. *Measurement and Evaluation in the Elementary School*. 2d rev. ed. New York: Longmans, Green and Company, 1953. Chapter 7.

Lindvall, C. Mauritz and Anthony J. Nitko. *Measuring Pupil Achievement and Aptitude*. 2d rev. ed. New York: Harcourt, Brace, Jovanovich, 1975. Chapter 4.

Mehrens, William A. and Irvin J. Lehmann. *Measurement and Evaluation in Education and Psychology*. New York: Holt, Rinehart and Winston. Chapter 9.

Sax, Gilbert. *Principles of Educational Measurement and Evaluation*. Belmont, Calif.: Wadsworth Publishing Company, 1974. Chapter 4.

Thorndike, Robert L. *Educational Measurement*. Washington, D.C.: American Council on Education, 1971. Chapter 4.

8   Multiple-Choice Questions

The multiple-choice exam is currently the most popular format for both teacher-made and standardized tests. This format can be used to measure a *wide variety* of fairly complex behavior, from memory to evaluation.

Multiple-choice questions consist of a **stem** (the question), three or four **distractors** (also called wrong answers, misleads, or decoys), and the **answer** (also called the correct response). The goal is to select the alternative that corresponds most closely to the stem. Every alternative but one is designed to be clearly incorrect when matched with the stem. For example:

The first mathematical axiom is   **Stem**
         a. reflexive property   **Answer**
Responses   b. symmetric property
         c. transitive property   **Distractors**
         d. distributive property

Basic multiple-choice questions are developed by creating a sentence that is as correct as is reasonably possible; dividing the sentence in some logical place, usually between clauses; and adding three plausible, but clearly incorrect distractors. Multiple-choice test questions take time to develop, but they are quick to correct, especially if machine-scorable answer sheets are used. It takes care and thought to develop four or five tenable responses that seem correct to the naive reader, but which, to the knowledgeable reader, are clearly incorrect. As with all types of test items, the most important skills needed to develop good multiple-choice questions are the ability to use the English language well and in-depth knowledge of one's subject matter.

Stem	Spiral omnibus test
Distractors	Difficulty index
Clang association	Discrimination index
Omnibus method	Item analysis statistics
Cycle omnibus test	

The major problem is to find distractors that sound plausible but are clearly incorrect. A common problem in developing distractors is that the teacher writes some that at first seem incorrect, but upon further consideration, turn out to be correct. Most teachers therefore find it helpful to develop several more items than are actually needed and then select the *best* ones. This process works especially well if the teacher can wait for two to three weeks before rereading the questions and making final selections. It is then more apparent both which questions need reworking and how they can be improved. Or the teacher might consider having a colleague read the questions or using them as part of a pretest.

Hints on Developing Multiple-Choice Test Items

Good multiple-choice items should accurately measure students' knowledge of the subject matter and should not be readily answerable on some other basis. Some factors to keep in mind while writing such items are given here.

To be consistent, the same number of alternatives should be provided for all questions on the test. There is rarely any need for more than five alternatives.

Longer distractors tend to be the correct ones. To ensure that the correct answer is precise, most test writers add several modifiers and qualifiers that make this response longer. Most teachers also reason that there is no need to be precise or specific for incorrect answers. For this reason, the incorrect distractors tend to be shorter in length than the correct responses. Therefore, after having completed a page or so, the teacher should check to see if the answers are noticeably longer than the distractors. If this is the case, one or two distractors in each item should be lengthened.

Alternatives such as "none of the above" and "all of the above" are often used as **fillers** when a test constructor cannot think of a good distractor. Sometimes these fillers are overused, but they can, in fact, be the correct response and do come in handy when an adequate number of logical distractors cannot be devised. For example:

According to the psychology of heightism, all other factors being equal, taller males compared to males of average height
    a.   are more successful in the business world
    b.   are less successful in the business world
    c.   are equally successful in the business world
    d.   all of the above
    e.   none of the above

For this question, it was difficult for the test constructor to think of plausible fourth and fifth distractors. Thus, "all of the above" and "none of the above" were used. In this case they are clearly inappropriate because something cannot be both "more, equal, and less" at the same time, nor can something be anything else aside from "more, equal, or less."

In general, the "none of the above" distractor tends to be incorrect, whereas the "all of the above" distractor is more likely to be correct. This occurs because "none of the above" is often used purely as a distractor, while "all of the above" is a useful response for testing several facts at once. Many teachers find it difficult to write a series of distractors that are all incorrect because they tend to be oriented towards conveying correct information, even on their exams. For the same reason it is common for many teachers to put down a series of responses that are all correct. This type of question is also easy to create from lists presented in the textbook or from lecture notes.

Correct answers should be randomly distributed among the alternatives. There is the tendency for the first answer to be most often correct, the last answer to be next often correct, the third answer to be next commonly correct, and the fourth answer least commonly correct. Thus, if a student purposely selects response *a* most of the time he or she has more than a random chance of guessing the response correctly.

One reason the first answer most often tends to be correct is that when a teacher is making up a question, he or she usually thinks of the question and its answer as a pair and writes the answer down as the first response before it is forgotten. Then, once the question and correct answer are completed, the teacher need only create three or four plausible distractors. If the teacher writes down an incorrect answer first, he or she may forget the answer that was intended when the question was originally conceived. To solve this problem, when writing or typing out questions, the teacher can simply write the question, then enter the correct answer randomly in the *b, c,* or *d* slot, leaving spaces for incorrect answers in the other slots. If a teacher uses dictating equipment, it is more difficult to ensure balance. Usually, in this case, the test must be retyped in order to rearrange the alternatives.

To ensure balance, the teacher should add up the total number of correct answers that correspond to each lettered alternative. The distribution among letters should be as equal as possible. Otherwise, adjustments should be made before the final version of the test is typed. Throughout this process, the teacher should be sure that each alternative remains plausible.

As with true-or-false items, the arrangement of multiple-choice questions should generally be from easiest to hardest. Beginning teachers usually have to estimate the approximate difficulty of their questions, but most experienced teachers can rank questions according to difficulty by using their experience with past tests.

One reason for careful sequencing is that difficult questions placed at the very beginning of a test can increase students' anxiety levels and impede their performance. Another reason the questions should be presented from easiest to hardest is that many students may spend too much time on questions they can't answer and may never reach questions that they could answer easily. Even if they do answer the easier questions, they may be so discouraged that they will not do as well as they otherwise might.

To some extent, to help a teacher find teaching and learning problems, questions should be grouped according to topic. This sometimes interferes with sequencing from easiest to hardest, but many times the two systems can be compatible. For example, on a math test, the questions could be grouped according to both difficulty and topic as follows:

1. addition of single digits $(1 + 4; 3 + 7; 4 + 2)$
2. addition of double digits $(22 + 61; 34 + 18; 14 + 19)$
3. subtraction without borrowing $(9 - 4; 18 - 3; 96 - 4)$
4. subtraction with borrowing $(14 - 7; 19 - 9; 21 - 8)$
5. subtraction with double borrowing $(411 - 41; 100 - 34; 161 - 93)$

Of course, if an entire test is over one to two specific topics, there is usually no problem in grouping according to both subject matter and difficulty. An example of such a situation would be a math test that has only subtraction problems with borrowing. Even when it is difficult to arrange questions both from easiest to hardest and according to topic, it is a good idea to present several very easy questions at the beginning of the test. Usually the first two or three questions should be designed so that most students will be able to answer them correctly.

The Omnibus Method

One approach to the multiple-choice format that tends to be successful because it provides more variety in questions is the **omnibus method**. In this format, both difficulty levels and subject matter are intermixed. For example, an omnibus test might follow a pattern of three math problems, three disarrayed sentence problems, and three practical judgment problems and then repeat three math problems, three disarrayed sentence problems, and so forth. There are two basic types of omnibus tests:

1. On **cycle omnibus tests**, a variety of topics are treated in a patterned sequence and all questions are about equal in difficulty. A cycle is one complete set of questions covering every topic. Difficulty may be represented by a vertical line and variety by a horizontal line.
2. On **spiral omnibus tests**, a variety of topics are also treated in a patterned sequence, but each time a cycle is repeated, the items become more difficult.

More Hints for Developing Multiple-Choice Items

As with true-or-false items, it is a good idea to underline all important words. For variety or special emphasis, all capital letters or italics can be used for some words and phrases.

Every attempt should be made to avoid grammar clues that indicate correct answers. For example, if the stem is plural and only one of the four alternatives is plural, most students will be able to discern the correct answer regardless of their knowledge of the subject.

Verb tenses also serve as inadvertent clues to correct responses. Note the following question, in which only answer *c* fits grammatically:

A survey of most capital cities has found that
    a. the city has grown consistently, especially during the last few years
    b. the city is almost always the largest city in the state
    c. the conditions of these cities are such that crime is often a problem
    d. the population of the city has shrunk in the past ten years

Another grammatical clue results from the use of *a* and *an*. In the following question, the correct answer can be determined because it is the only alternative that fits grammatically.

The most common means of long distance transportation in the 1700s was a
  a. automobile
  b. airplane
  c. horse
  d. animals in general

This problem may be avoided by using *a/an* at the end of the stem or by omitting the article from the stem and including it in its appropriate form in each response.

Avoid the use of clues that may allow students to use their general knowledge to figure out an answer. Note, for example, that there is only one logical response to the following item:

Columbus is the capital of
  a. Christmas
  b. Napoleon
  c. Ohio
  d. Lake Ontario

A better version would, of course, list only states as choices.

Avoid **clang associations**, that is, items for which the answer obviously sounds as if it is or is not correct, such as the following:

The most important seaport in the far eastern part of the U.S.S.R. is
  a. Madrid
  b. Santiago
  c. Vladivostok
  d. Ming Kim
  e. St. Clement

Vladivostok sounds like the name of a Russian city, whereas the other choices do not.

Remember that *above-average knowledge* may actually handicap some students. For instance, consider the distractors for the following item:

Emperor is the name of
  a. a string quartet
  b. a piano concerto
  c. a violin sonata

While this seems to be a straightforward question referring to Beethoven's Emperor Concerto, a youngster who is studying music may also be aware of the Emperor Quartet by Haydn. While this problem is not serious for most tests, it is something that teachers should be aware of.

By discussing test answers and probing why students selected the answers they did, a teacher can discover if this has occurred and modify both the students' scores and the test questions.

Multiple-Choice Tests and Creativity

A common criticism of multiple-choice exams is that they typically do not encourage creativity, independent thought, or other forms of divergent thinking. Multiple-choice questions usually require students to match a stem with a single previously determined correct answer. This activity rarely requires little more than a good memory, and it does not tend to measure the qualities that help scientists, writers, and other creative people see beyond what is tried and true. This does not mean that multiple-choice items cannot be made to tap creativity. Unfortunately, however, such items are difficult both to make up and to grade and, thus, are not commonly used. The best multiple-choice questions force students to find relationships, relate ideas, and form logical conclusions. With practice, most teachers can learn to write such highly effective questions in addition to those that require simple memorization of facts.

Directions

Good directions are important because they set the tone of thinking students will need throughout the examination. To some extent, how students take an exam is based on habit, but directions can, to some degree, affect those habits. Directions should usually ask students to indicate the *best answer* or the *answer that is most often correct* in order to avoid absolutist statements that may be open to debate.

If test directions are given orally, they should be read clearly and with emphasis. It is a good idea for the teacher to type oral instructions, underlining, using commas, etc., so that he or she can properly emphasize needed aspects.

Many criticisms of multiple-choice and true-or-false test items are really criticisms of the English language, especially of its words with multiple meanings, its inconsistent rules of grammar, and its general lack of precision. When wording directions and test questions, the teacher should be especially sensitive to linguistic quirks that may cause students to misinterpret and make unnecessary errors.

When students are asked to indicate the best answer, the test maker should be certain that every response that is considered "best" is also as clearly correct as possible. For example, consider what would be the best answer for the following item:

The total number of different letters in the standard English alphabet is
   a. 3
   b. 20
   c. 30
   d. 50
   e. 102

While *c* is the most nearly correct of the choices given, it is certainly not the best of all possible answers. This kind of item should definitely be avoided. By asking students to indicate the *best* answer rather than the correct answer, the test maker does not escape the obligation to develop the *most correct answer possible*.

Item Cards

After they have taught for several years, most teachers find that they have developed a large set of good questions that they can use over and over. A convenient way of storing such questions is to type them on index cards and file them according to topic. Many teachers also record the *difficulty index,* the *discrimination index,* and the *item analysis statistics* each time the test question is administered. (This useful data will be discussed later.) If the cards are filed so that the topic listing is readily visible, the teacher can quickly choose and rearrange questions to create a new test for each class and yet not spend a great deal of time retyping questions. The questions can be placed inside of a plastic folder and copied on a dry process copy machine. The photocopies then can be used to make spirit duplicator masters. If the teacher wishes to number the questions, she could either have the students number them or number the first photocopy and then make a second copy so that the copy the spirit master is made from is totally a photocopy. This system is quick and easy and saves the teacher a lot of clerical work.

Summary

One of the most popular types of exam is the multiple-choice format. Although multiple-choice items are more work to develop than most question types, they are easy and quick to grade, especially if an answer sheet is used. Multiple-choice questions can be used to measure a student's knowledge of facts as well as concepts and abstract ideas. The first step in developing multiple-choice questions is to create a well-written true statement. Then, the sentence is divided in half and clearly incorrect, but logical, plausible-sounding alternatives are created. To ensure the effectiveness of multiple-choice questions, the alternatives should be all of equal length, and the answers should be randomly distributed among the choices.

The grammar of each stem and set of responses should be carefully checked to ensure that it is correct but that it does not give away the appropriate response. In addition, most teachers find it helpful either to develop the questions, let them sit for several weeks, and reread them later, making corrections from a fresh vantage point, or to give them to another teacher who teaches in a similar area. Most questions should challenge students, but items at the beginning of the test should be easier in order to help the students develop self-confidence.

Suggested Readings

Ahmann, Stanley and Marvin Glock. *Evaluating Pupil Growth: Principles of Tests and Measurements*. 5th rev. ed. Boston: Allyn and Bacon, 1975. Chapter 3.

Greene, Harry A., Albert N. Jorgensen and J. Raymond Gerberich. *Measurement and Evaluation in the Elementary School*. 2d rev. ed. New York: Longmans, Green and Company, 1953. Chapter 7.

Lindvall, C. Mauritz and Anthony J. Nitko. *Measuring Pupil Achievement and Aptitude*. 2d rev. ed. New York: Harcourt Brace Jovanovich, 1975. Chapter 4.

Mehrens, William A. and Irvin J. Lehmann. *Measurement and Evaluation in Education and Psychology*. New York: Holt, Rinehart and Winston, 1978. Chapter 10.

Sax, Gilbert. *Principles of Educational Measurement and Evaluation*. Belmont, Calif.: Wadsworth Publishing Company, 1974. Chapter 4.

9 Improving Tests Through Item Analysis

Multiple-choice items can often be greatly improved through a process called **item analysis**. After a test has been given, item analysis may be used to tabulate the number of students who selected each alternative in a given item and thus determine the effectiveness of each choice in attracting students. Example:

The first year of the "tail fin" on automobiles was

    10 a. 1957
     4 b. 1960
     0 c. 1962
    29 d. 1956

(Ten students selected alternative a, four selected b, etc.)

Once the test has been administered, item analysis may be done by hand or by computer. To calculate item analysis by hand, the teacher simply counts the number of students who selected each alternative and puts a mark in the area for tabulating the responses (see Figure 9.1). If a student selects alternative d for his answer, the teacher would put one mark by d on the sheet used to tabulate the item totals. In Figure 9.1, the teacher found that three students selected a, none selected b, 12 selected c, and 18 selected d.

Figure 9.1   Hand-tabulated Responses for Item Analysis

Stem: The classic handbook of anatomy is called

		Tabulation	Total Selecting
Responses:	a. Roget's Anatomy	III	3
	b. Oxford's Anatomy	0	0
	c. Dorland's Anatomy	JHT JHT II	12
	d. Gray's Anatomy	JHT JHT JHT III	18

The Need for Alternatives to Be Equally Attractive

The first step in improving a test is to determine which alternatives attract the fewest students. Each alternative should be a possible answer. If no one chooses an alternative, it is ineffective and should be altered or replaced. If not a single student selects an alternative, it indicates that alternative weights is obviously wrong and its presence proves nothing.

In Figure 9.1, for example, choice *b* was not selected by a single student. Such a useless alternative increases the students' chances of selecting the correct answer by guessing and reduces the validity of the test. Again, we must stress that a student should not be able to get an item correct if he or she does *not know* the answer, and likewise should not get an item wrong if he or she *does* know the answer. Both situations are undesirable. For a teacher to help a student he or she must be able to assess specifically what the student knows. If a student gets an answer right when he or she really does not know the material, the teacher will assume the youngster knows the material and thus will not offer help.

Determining When to Change an Alternative

Now we shall look at a few sample item analyses to see when and why a question should be changed.

Example 1   The masseteric artery is in what region of the head?
    12   a. parietal
    11   b. frontal
    13   c. temporal
    12   d. occipital

In this example, students had no idea what the correct answer was and thus guessed at random. When answers are evenly distributed, we can usually assume that the class as a whole had no idea of the answer. Quite possibly this material was never covered, or it may simply have been too difficult. In this particular case, since the question depends mainly on memory, it is likely that the material was not covered. A test should contain *very few* truly difficult questions, and they should be placed at the end.

Example 2   The calendar we utilize today is called the

23   a. Gregorian calendar
23   b. Jewish calendar
 1   c. World calendar
 1   d. Russian calendar

In this case, almost the entire class eliminated alternatives *c* and *d*, yet their answers were evenly divided among *a* and *b*. This indicates that the students relied on general knowledge to eliminate *c* and *d*, but still did not know what the right answer was. If a question is effective, most students should select the right answer, even if the question is very hard. Note the following example:

Example 3   The two most well-known attorneys in the Scopes trial were

18   a. Darrow and Bryan
12   b. Clyne and Taylor
 3   c. Dittes and Davis
 9   d. Bear and Kinney

It is obvious that this is a difficult question, yet a clear majority knew that the correct answer was Bryan and Darrow. If the majority *do not* select a response, there is probably something wrong with either the question or the teacher's teaching.

Example 4   The rate of suicide is *most* heavily influenced by

12   a. culture
21   b. individual factors
 4   c. religion
18   d. age

There are obvious problems with this question because most students were unable to select the correct answer, which is *a*. It is likely that the teacher's explanation was unclear or that it conflicted with material studied outside of class.

Example 5   Chlorpromazine is commonly used to treat

 4   a. pain
 4   b. schizophrenia
 7   c. depression
24   d. hypoglycemia

Since the correct answer is *b* and a clear majority selected *d*, it indicates that the students were *not guessing*, but that some incorrect information was presented in class, in the textbook, or elsewhere. If a clear majority select the same wrong answer, the teacher should try to find out why. He or she will probably discover that somewhere along the line some incorrect information was presented. It is unlikely that this many students would select an incorrect answer by chance.

This, then, should give you a general idea of how multiple-choice items can be improved through the process of item analysis. As you can see, it is somewhat of a detective game. Now we will look at other ways of evaluating test questions.

Difficulty Index

A **difficulty index** can be used to determine how hard an individual question is. The index varies from zero, which means that everyone selected the wrong alternative, to 1.00, which indicates that everyone chose the correct response. The formula for calculating a difficulty index is:

$$D = \frac{R}{N}$$

where R = the number of students who selected
the correct answer

N = the number of students who took the
test

To determine a difficulty index for each question, divide the number of students who answered correctly by the total number who took the test. If there are 30 questions, it would take 30 separate division problems to calculate the difficulty levels of all of the questions. For example:

1. If 50 students answered a question correctly, and 50 students took the exam, the difficulty index would be $\frac{50}{50}$ = 1.00. An index of 1.00 means that every student selected the correct answer and that the question was very easy.

2. If, out of a class of 50 students, everyone selected the wrong answer, the index would be $\frac{0}{50}$ = 0. A difficulty index of zero indicates that a question is so difficult that no one answered it correctly.

3. If, out of a class of 50 students, 25 students selected the correct answer, the index would be $\frac{25}{50}$ = .50.

This indicates a medium level of difficulty, or that half the class selected the correct answer and the other half chose a wrong answer.

Generally, the first few items on any test should have an index of .90 or higher (extremely easy). The rest of the items should have indexes ranging from .30 to about .70 or .80. These suggested indexes need not be rigidly observed, but they can serve as guidelines for most, if not all, items. It is a good idea to have a few items that are extremely easy at the beginning of a test and several that are extremely difficult at the end.

For a discriminatory test, the *average* difficulty level for the entire exam should be approximately .50. On a mastery test, the average should be about .90. These figures can be determined by averaging the difficulty levels for *each* individual question. For example, if a test with 10 items had difficulty levels of 1.00, .90, .70, .60, .40, .70, .30, .10 and .20, the *average* would be .50, which indicates the ideal level of difficulty for a discriminatory test.

Generally the spread of a good test should be from .20 to .80. No student should score 100, and, likewise, no student should score 0. Assuming that a class has a normal spread of abilities, most students' scores should be clustered somewhere close to the average, producing a normal curve. Many teacher-made tests produce an average of around 80 percent. This does not adequately differentiate between various levels of achievement. In addition, with a class average this high, several of the more capable students will often reach the ceiling of the test (earn the highest score possible), making it difficult to differentiate between various levels of excellent performance. One of the main advantages of a good spread is that it helps clarify the positions of borderline students. There is usually a clearly distinguishable group of students with top scores who would earn A's, another clear group earning B's, and so forth.

Discrimination Power

In addition to level of difficulty, it is often helpful to know how effectively an item separates students who know the material well from those who do not. This enables the teacher to clearly identify youngsters who need additional help. To determine **discrimination power**:

1. Rank order students' scores from highest to lowest.
2. Select the top third and the bottom third for comparison.
3. Look at an individual test item and count how many students from the top third selected the correct response.

4. Repeat step 3 using students from the bottom third.
5. Subtract the number of students in the bottom group who selected the correct alternative from the number of students in the top group who selected the correct alternative.
6. Divide this difference by the number of students in either of the groups. (As we are using one-third of the highest scores and one-third of the lowest, the number of students in the high group will be the same as the number of students in the low group.)

The formula is as follows:

$$\frac{(\text{Number correct in high group}) - (\text{Number correct in low group})}{\text{Total number in either high or low group}}$$

or

$$\frac{C_H - C_L}{N_{H \text{ or } L}}$$

where C = the number correct
   H = the high group
   L = the low group
   N = the number in either the high group *or* the low group

The discrimination power ranges from + 1.00 when everyone in the top group has the item correct and everyone in the bottom group has the item incorrect, to zero when there is no difference between the two groups, to −1.00 when everyone in the top group has the item incorrect and everyone in the bottom group has the item correct. The following examples illustrate these extremes, which occur in reality only rarely.

1. There are 25 students in the top third of the class. Of these 25, every single student selected the *correct* answer to a question. In the bottom one-third, not a single student selected the correct response. The computation of the discrimination power would be:

$$\frac{25 - 0}{25} = \frac{25}{25} + 1.00$$

This means that the item is a **perfect discriminator**—that is, everyone in the top group selected the correct answer while no one in the bottom group selected it. The item discriminates perfectly between the two groups.

2. Suppose that the previous situation is reversed and that everyone in the bottom group selected the correct answer while everyone in the top group selected the wrong answer. In this case, the computation would be:

$$\frac{0-25}{25} - \frac{-25}{25} = -1.00$$

A discrimination power of −1.00 indicates that the question is a **perfect negative discriminator.** High negative discriminators (more than −.30) are very rare, and, if they occur, they usually mean the answer key is wrong or the question is very poorly worded. The few negative discriminators that do occur are usually only slightly negative (such as −.02 or −.10). A teacher should look carefully at every item that negatively discriminates, and correct or eliminate it. Doing so will usually raise the validity of the test and will often result in a greater spread of scores.

3. Of the 25 highest and 25 lowest scorers, 10 in each group selected the correct response. The discrimination power would thus be:

$$\frac{10-10}{25} = \frac{0}{25} = 0$$

This means that the item does not discriminate *at all* between the bottom and top groups. A discrimination index of zero usually indicates that most students guessed or that there is something wrong with the question. This is not always the case, however, and each question should be judged on its own merit.

Summary

This chapter is devoted to the improvement of multiple-choice tests. One evaluating process is called item analysis. Through this process, the effectiveness of each alternative is determined, enabling a teacher to alter or replace those choices that are ineffective. If a question is effective, most students should select the right answer. A difficulty index is another way of evaluating test questions by determining how hard an individual question is. Using the difficulty index formula, the average difficulty level for an entire discriminatory test should be approximately .50, while on a mastery test the average should be .90. The third evaluation technique is discrimination power. This measures how effectively an item separates those who know the material from those who do not.

Suggested Readings

Aiken, Lewis R. *Psychological Testing and Assessment*. 3d rev. ed. Boston: Allyn and Bacon, 1979. Chapter 2.

Chase, Clinton I. *Measurement for Educational Evaluation*. Reading, Mass.: Addison-Wesley, 1978. Chapter 13.

Noll, Victor H., Dale P. Scannell and Robert C. Craig. *Introduction to Educational Measurement*. 4th rev. ed. Boston: Houghton Mifflin, 1979.

Sax, Gilbert. *Principles of Educational Measurement and Evaluation*. Belmont, Calif.: Wadsworth Publishing Company, 1974. Chapter 7.

10   Other Types of Objective Test Items

Common types of objective test items, in addition to true-or-false and multiple-choice, include matching items, fill-in-the-blank items, odd-man-out items, and various innovative test items. Among the innovative are interlinear tests, tab tests, tests that provide immediate feedback, and in-basket tests. We will look at these one by one.

Matching Items

Matching items are useful when a teacher wants to test students' mastery of a large number of facts, ideas, principles, or definitions. The usual procedure is to list no more than 10 to 12 items in the first column, and the same number plus two extra corresponding items in the second column. The order of items in column A should not directly match the order of the correct responses in column B.

If more than 10 to 12 items are included, it becomes difficult for students to work efficiently, because of the amount of time consumed perusing the choices. Sometimes students must review a list several times before they find the answer they have in mind, and under the pressure of a test, they may fail to find a response they might otherwise easily notice.

There should also be a high degree of homogeneity between the items in a group. For example, all 10 to 12 items should be restricted to names of writers or to names of scientists. When items are mixed, it becomes easier for students to categorically eliminate certain choices and thus, even with limited knowledge, answer many questions correctly. Generally, teachers do not want to measure mere acquaintance with a subject. A matching test should not be a simple guessing game. For example, note the following:

1. Polish anthropologist   a. Werner von Braun
2. Russian physiologist   b. Ivan Pavlov
3. German space scientist   c. Bronislaw Malinowski

In this case, it would be obvious to many students that Pavlov is Russian, Malinowski is Polish, and von Braun is German. Such logical cues should be avoided to ensure that students are tested purely on the subject matter rather than on general knowledge.

To facilitate students' finding answers that they already know, terms in the second column should be arranged in ways that reduce random searching—perhaps alphabetically or chronologically. Guessing can be reduced if responses must be used more than once and if several extra, nonmatching choices are included. If this is the case, the teacher should inform students of these two possibilities in the test directions. The teacher should also check *each* item in column A to make sure that it correctly matches with no more than *one* response in column B.

Fill-in-the-Blank Items

Fill-in-the-blank items are created by removing a key word or words from a sentence and replacing it with a space for writing. The student's task is to complete the sentence by supplying the word that was removed. Fill-in-the-blank items are common in foreign language and social and physical science courses for which students must learn large amounts of factual information. Knowledge of names, places, dates, definitions, and the like can be easily tested in this format. The main problem, however, is that sometimes several different correct answers are possible. For example, in completing the sentence, "George Washington was born in _____," a fifth-grade class produced all the following answers: America, the United States, a hospital, a city, Virginia, a house, Westmoreland County, Fredericksburg, a southern state, the South, one of the older states, a place near a doctor, Wakefield. All of these answers are *technically* correct, but a teacher would need to know a great deal about where Washington was born to assess this fact. In fact, it is not uncommon for a student to supply a correct answer only to have it marked wrong because it wasn't the one the teacher had in mind.

Students cannot be expected to supply a single correct response if the teacher has created ambiguous test items. In view of this, grading a seemingly straightforward question such as "George Washington was born in _____" could be a difficult task. To simplify this situation for both the teacher and the students, the statement could be made more specific: "George Washington was born in the *city* of _____." The answer would then more clearly be Bridges Creek.

Another common problem with fill-in-the-blank items occurs when a single statement contains two blanks. In such cases, one answer may invalidate the other or lead to many unanticipated responses. For example, consider the many correct ways in which one might complete the following sentence:

The American colonies were separate and _____, each having its own government; but at the same time they were _____.
  a. incomplete/complete
  b. independent/interrelated
  c. unified/competitive
  d. organized/growing
  e. distinct/independent

The keyed answer was *e*, according to the person who created the question, yet *d* certainly is not incorrect and *b* is entirely correct. Actually, *a* and *d* are also correct, even though we normally do not think of the American colonies in these terms. This type of question may end up being a guessing game, with the students trying to determine which answers the teacher happens to think are best. Thus, such items are not very accurate indicators of students' actual knowledge.

The Problem of Spelling

Students frequently misspell their answers to fill-in-the-blank items. Therefore, whether or not to insist on proper spelling is an issue that the teacher must confront. If correct spelling is required, the test becomes, at least partly, a spelling test. For example, a student may know both the function and the location of clavicle (the collar bone) without knowing how to spell the term correctly. Should her weakness in one area be held against her in another? Most teachers resolve this dilemma by awarding a certain number of points for knowing the appropriate answer and additional points for spelling it correctly.

Thus, each fill-in-the-blank test would entail two grades—one for knowledge of subject matter and one for spelling.

A related problem occurs when a word is misspelled in a way that makes it difficult to discern if the student knows the right answer. At what point does a misspelled word become an incorrect response? For example, which of the following might be acceptable spellings of the word *clavicle* and which should be marked wrong: klavacle, cviccle, klavical, clavical, klivacal, kalifikel, klivicle, clifikcle? Because misspellings may occur for many different reasons, the teachers must finally rely on personal judgment in allotting credit. Some students may try to obscure their lack of knowledge by poor spelling, while others may actually know the answers very well, but just be bad spellers.

On the other hand, what if the student does have a problem writing—for example, is left-handed, or simply lacks the finger dexterity necessary to write neatly? Giving this student a poor grade would be like consistently failing a blind student because he cannot read aloud from a printed book. Handicaps should be dealt with on an individual basis. It is cruel to punish a child for handicaps he or she has little control over. Obviously, the solution is to evaluate each child individually.

One way to cope with the problem of misspelling is to provide a list of difficult-to-spell words either at the top of the test or on the chalkboard. This also reinforces correct spelling of key terms. One drawback of this method, however, is that fill-in-the-blank questions become matching items. In addition, the level of difficulty of the questions is lowered. Items that would ordinarily require recall only require recognition if the correct response is included in the list of hard-to-spell words.

Odd-Man-Out Items

A variation on the traditional multiple-choice question is the odd-man-out item. In this type of test question, a series of related choices is given and the student selects the response that is *not* appropriate. For example:

Which of the following does not belong?
a. banjo   d. violin
b. ukulele   e. guitar
c. flute

The answer is *c* because flute is the only wind instrument.

This exam format tests for understanding of relationships, classifications, and commonalities and is often used in both I.Q. and abstract reasoning tests. Because such items can be quite enjoyable, they may be used as games rather than as test questions. The same characteristics that can make them into good discussion topics can lead to their being problematic exam questions, as in the following example:

Part of Mrs. Jones' chemistry lesson included a discussion of the differences between a mixture, a compound, and an element. On the test over that material, she gave the students the following question: Which of the following does *not* belong?
a. glass   d. sugar
b. salt   e. water
c. soda

While correcting the students' answers, she found, to her amazement, that an almost *equal* number of students circled *each* answer. No one answer was selected significantly more often than any other. During class discussion of the test, she asked the students to explain their choices. Among the responses were:

LARRY: I selected *a* because glass is the only mixture among the set. All the rest are compounds.

MAVIS: I felt the answer was *b* because it is the only chemical that is classified chemically as a salt. All the others are non-salts.

RYAN: I chose *c* because soda is the only chemical among the group that is medicine. All the others are nonmedicinal chemicals.

KATIE: I thought the answer was *d* because sugar was the only chemical among the group that was an organic compound. All the others were nonorganic compounds.

ROGER: I chose *e* because water is the only chemical among the group that is a liquid at room temperature. At room temperature, all the others are solids.

One student pointed out that water is the only one that will not form crystals, while another said that water is also the only solvent. One student even stated that all belonged because salt, soda, sugar, and water go together to make soft drinks, which are put in bottles that are made out of glass.

The fact that the students were able to provide so many good, logical explanations even though the "correct" answer was supposed to be *a*, or glass, highlights the main problem with the odd-man-out type of question: creative students can often find good reasons for selecting "incorrect" responses. To minimize such occurrences, the teacher should specify objectives and expectations in the test directions and *make sure that there is clearly only one answer that does not belong.* An additional potentially productive solution is to have students write explanations of their choices next to the questions. If their reasons are valid, they can be given credit.

It should be stressed that the problem of multiple defensible answers is *not* typical of well-developed odd-man-out tests. The more factual the material is, the less likely the possibility of ambiguous interpretation. This type of question can lead to enjoyable learning and can be used very effectively if students are encouraged to justify their answers.

Innovative Test Formats

Interlinear Tests

Interlinear tests present expository material with enough space between lines to allow students to write their responses in the body of the text. A typical example would be an English test in which students are required to correct grammar and spelling errors found in a series of paragraphs. Students may also be asked to respond to the ideas and implications presented in a short selection or to add material or modify it in some other way. Interlinear tests are also used in both teaching and testing foreign languages. Students might translate material idiomatically or correct it grammatically and orthographically. This method makes it easy for students to follow the translation and gain a feel for the other language.

Tab Tests

Tab tests offer many exciting pedagogical possibilities. The examinee is given a set of questions in multiple-choice format with each alternative printed on a separate tab. The student indicates his or her choice by peeling off a tab. Under the tab is printed whether or not the student has chosen correctly. If an incorrect answer is selected, the tab explains why the choice was incorrect. Often, even if a correct answer is chosen, *why* it is correct is explained.

The great advantage of tab tests is that students are able to learn immediately whether they have answered correctly, and are able to continue selecting tabs until they locate the appropriate answer. Usually students earn three points if they find the answer by pulling off only one tab, two points if they pull two tabs, or one point if they remove three. A student who pulled off all four tabs before finding the correct response would earn no points. This method gives students credit for various levels of knowledge—that is, the sooner they find the answer, the more points they earn. Underneath the tab, they receive immediate feedback about the correctness of their selection and helpful explanations if they are in error. Tab tests are especially useful in medicine, law, psychology, social studies, and similar areas. For example, note how the following question and its accompanying tab enrich the learning experience:

> A patient complains that he lacks appetite, is nauseous, and sometimes vomits small amounts of mucus and fluid in the morning. He usually feels better later in the day. What is the most likely diagnosis?
>
> a. *Acute Dyspepsia*
>
> Under this response is written: Be careful. In dyspepsia, the urge to vomit appears either in the morning or after meals. Since the cause is too much rich food or too much alcohol, the problem occurs only after meals.
>
> b. *Chronic Gastritis*
>
> Under this response is written: Right, you've diagnosed this correctly. Nausea and the urge to vomit occur in the morning but fade during the day. This differentiates gastritis from, for example, dyspepsia.
>
> c. *Stomach Cancer*
>
> Under this response is written: Wrong! With stomach cancer the symptoms are present all day and do not improve as the day wears on.
>
> d. *Acute Appendicitis*
>
> Under this response is written: With appendicitis, there is specific pain in the middle of the abdomen and vomiting usually occurs only once. Further, with appendicitis, a rise in temperature, tenderness, and a distaste for food are also common.

If a student selected, for example, answer *d*, he would peel the tab away and discover not only that he was wrong, but also specifically *why* he was wrong. And, not only are tab tests among the most effective learning tests developed, but students tend to find them enjoyable, beneficial, and relevant. If such tests are given often enough, students generally look forward to them.

The tabs are designed so that once they are peeled away, they cannot be replaced. Thus, cheating can be avoided, but reuse by other students becomes impossible. Most tab tests are produced commercially, but there are also some a teacher can purchase and print her own questions and answers on. Although this type of test is expensive, its educational benefits may well overshadow its costs.

Answer Sheets That Provide Feedback

Some answer sheets are designed to reveal the correct answers when a student erases the appropriate black mark. If a certain code letter doesn't appear when the student erases the black mark indicating her choice, the response is wrong. She would continue to erase until she finds the appropriate code. The format on the answer sheet is as follows:

$$\begin{array}{l} \text{A B C D} \\ \text{1. T R S M} \\ \text{2. R M T S} \\ \text{3. S R M T} \end{array}$$

Each letter representing an answer is covered with erasable black "ink." If the student selects answer D on the question booklet (regular multiple-choice format) for question 1, after erasing the black, she will find the letter M. If the answer sheet is keyed to M, she knows she is correct. If the answer sheet is keyed to S, and the student selects D, she knows she has selected the wrong answer. Students are told beforehand the letter to which the answer sheet is keyed, and the teacher must prepare the test so that the correct answers will all fall on the appropriate code.

The disadvantage of this method as compared to tab tests is that when the student erases and finds a letter *other* than the key, she knows the answer is wrong but is not told *why*. The fact that she does receive some immediate feedback, however, gives this system an advantage over many others.

In-Basket Test

In-basket tests are commonly used in evaluational processes. A real-life situation is simulated and the test taker is asked to cope with it. For example, a candidate for a vacant principal's job might be given such items as memos from other administrators, notes registering parents' complaints, and outlines of problems that require immediate attention. She would then evaluate according to her reactions and the course of action she devises.

For the classroom, an in-basket test could be utilized especially well in such areas as business, secretarial, and technical studies. A test for a secretarial class, for example, could include a series of reports, letters, and other tasks that students must complete. The variety of activities would parallel those that students would be likely to encounter in the course of an average work day and their performance would be used to evaluate their ability to succeed outside the classroom. This is a realistic situation that helps train the student for future employment.

Summary

Several types of objective test items have been discussed in this chapter. They include matching items, fill-in-the-blank and odd-man-out items. Some innovative test formats were presented. The interlinear test presents expository material with enough space between the lines to allow students to write their reponses in the body of the test. Tab tests offer many educational benefits. Tests are available with answer sheets that reveal the correct answers when a student erases the appropriate black mark. In-basket tests are designed to simulate a real-life situation and the test taker is asked to cope with it.

Suggested Readings

Greene, Harry A., Albert N. Jorgensen and J. Raymond Gerberich. *Measurement and Evaluation in the Elementary School*. 2d rev. ed. New York: Longmans, Green and Company, 1953. Chapters 7, 9.

Lindvall, C. Mauritz and Anthony J. Nitko. *Measuring Pupil Achievement and Aptitude*. 2d rev. ed. New York: Harcourt Brace Jovanovich, 1975. Chapter 4.

Mehrens, William A. and Irvin J. Lehmann. *Measurement and Evaluation in Education and Psychology*. New York: Holt, Rinehart and Winston, 1978. Chapter 9.

Sax, Gilbert. *Principles of Educational Measurement and Evaluation*. Belmont, Calif.: Wadsworth Publishing Company, 1974. Chapter 4.

11   Essay Exams

Aside from oral exams, the essay is the oldest test format still in use today. The usefulness of such written exams, which are simply one step beyond an oral exam, was first stressed by Horace Mann in about 1845. Students are given a clue (the question) that they expand on in writing. A few key words used in developing essay questions are:

discuss	evaluate	describe
explain	compare	translate
outline	contrast	analyze
define		

Although essay tests do not take much time to develop, they are very time consuming to grade. It takes approximately 10 to 30 hours to grade an essay exam for an average high school class (Gronlund 1976). Students' responses may often be hard to read, and even harder to grade. One reason is that essay exams tend to measure such additional skills as penmanship and spelling, grammar and punctuation, and the ability to organize one's thoughts and express oneself clearly, concisely, and correctly in writing.

Grading Essays

The grading of essay exams is highly subjective. In an early study, Ellis (1930) asked a group of teachers to grade the same set of papers twice. The first time the graders did not mark on the essay exam itself and the grade was put on a separate sheet of paper. The same exams were then regraded after an interval of several months. When the two grades were compared, the researchers found only a slight correlation between them. Ellis thus concluded that teachers do not assign grades in a consistent manner. Starch (1912) took a large number of papers in English, geometry, and history and had them graded first by the pupils' own teacher, and then by an independent group of teachers. On the whole, he found a medium correlation between grades, but many papers that were given grades of near perfect by the original grader were given low grades by the second set of graders. Thus, a *single* paper could receive both a high grade and a low one, depending upon who graded it.

More recent research has found that the grading of essay exams can be fairly reliable if teachers follow certain procedures, but grading is often influenced by outside factors, producing, in the case of many teachers, low reliability (Coffman 1971). Other studies have found that in most cases, though, the difference between the grades two teachers would give tends not to be between an A and an E, but between a B and a C, a B and A, and so forth. While the differences between graders' opinions are not usually extreme, they are definitely distinguishable.

Advantages of Essay Exams

One of the greatest advantages of essay exams is that they give students practice in expressing their own ideas. A good essay exam should require students to select relevant information, organize it, and express it clearly. Not only must they know the facts, but they must be able to present them in logical ways to support their arguments. Essay exams should force students to think about the material covered in class—ideally, in new ways.

Another advantage of essay exams is that they generally require a more useful and rewarding method of study. Students tend to learn ideas, concepts, and the general flow of events rather than a mass of isolated facts. Better than any other test format, essay exams reward the abilities to think, organize, and apply knowledge. Meyer (1934) found that the kind of studying done for essay exams produced greater achievement than did study techniques for other types of exams, no matter what type of exam was actually given.

Although essay exams were commonly used up to the 1960s, they temporarily lost some of their popularity, partly as a result of the student demands on schools in the 1960s (Coffman 1971). Recently, as a result of the Back to Basics movement and the belief that students' writing abilities are declining, some educators have begun to encourage increased utilization of essay exams. Others argue, however, that objective exams can be equally reliable gauges of many skills that essay exams are supposedly unique in measuring. They believe that well-constructed multiple-choice questions can measure the same levels of understanding as essay exams and that they can do it without some of the disadvantages, such as lack of precision in grading. But, in spite of the criticism of essay exams for subjectivity, the time needed to correct them, and the like, many teachers still favor them as useful learning and teaching tools. Thus essays can be very useful, but they do have clear limitations. If a teacher recognized these limitations, and endeavored to improve his/her ability to develop and utilize essay exams, essay exams could be quite useful, especially as a learning tool.

Steps in Developing Good Essay Questions

The key to developing good essay exams is to write questions that are clear, specific, and to the point. One of the most common problems with essay questions is that they are too vague and general. They may thus confuse students or lead to too wide a variety of answers. For example:

Too general: Discuss the causes of the Civil War.
More specific: Discuss the role of slavery as a cause of the Civil War.
Too vague: Why do nations go to war?
More specific: Either support or refute the theory that humans are innately aggressive.

To ensure that the questions are clear, specific, and to the point, it is a good idea to have someone else read the entire exam. Ideally, another teacher could both proofread the questions and attempt to answer them. Since actually responding can be very time consuming, however, a thoughtful review will often suffice. This process can also help teachers familiarize themselves with each other's work and lead to the exchange of ideas in addition to ensuring better, clearer exams.

Once a set of questions has been developed, it is usually helpful to set them aside for a few weeks. Then, when they are reread at a later date, it will be possible to spot problems that were not apparent when the questions were originally constructed. It is also a good idea for the teacher to write out what he or she believes to be the best answers, outline them, and compare the outlines with the questions. If the questions don't specifically ask for most of the material in the outlines, they may have to be expanded. This step will also simplify the grading process, for the teacher can then utilize the outline in assigning points for specific information that should be included in the students' answers.

Optimizing the Teaching Potential of Essay Exams

Teachers can help the student take essay exams in the following ways:

1. Tell students as much as possible about the exam in advance, including number of questions, length, material covered, and the like. This helps students direct their studying and general preparation and reduces their fear and tension while taking the exam. In addition, studying tends to be more rewarding because it is more directed.
2. On the exam, indicate the preferred length of answer for each question, either in number of paragraphs or in number of pages.
3. Specify the information or issues on which students should focus their attention. When questions are too vague and open-ended, too wide a variety of responses is possible. This makes it extremely difficult for the teacher to compare and grade the papers. To prevent this problem, it is best either to ask for a series of short answers or to break one question down into several. For example:

Discuss the implications of the concept *maternal deprivation*. Be sure to include:
   a. a definition of maternal deprivation (5 points)
   b. a discussion of two well-known studies and their findings (5 points each)
   c. a discussion of the influences of feminism and changing sex roles in relation to children and maternal deprivation (10 points)
   d. the implications of the concept of maternal deprivation for the future care of children (10 points)
   e. apply the results of the research on maternal deprivation to the concept of *paternal deprivation* (5 points)

Note that the general question (discuss the implications of maternal deprivation) is broken down into a series of short questions and that a point value is given for each part. This helps students allocate their effort, gauge the length of their answers, and concentrate on the important areas. It also simplifies grading, for there is one basic answer for each part of the question.

Hints on Grading Essay Exams

Because the grading of essay exams is so subjective, a teacher must be able to adequately defend the grade given each student. This requires specific statements about why a certain grade was given and exactly what could have been done to earn a higher grade. If the student asks the teacher, "What should I have done to earn an A on this question," the teacher should be able to tell the student specifically what was omitted or what was incorrect. This is much easier to do when the teacher has developed questions that ask for short answers on specific subjects and has prepared an outline of his or her ideal answers to the questions. He or she can then check each paper for specific factors that are either present and correct, or not present, or not correct.

Outlining a good answer also helps the teacher develop a realistic set of grading standards. Teachers sometimes expect better answers from students than they themselves can produce. Preparing their own answers may help them reassess the level of their expectations. A teacher-prepared ideal answer and corresponding outline can thus be used simultaneously to improve test questions, the grading process, and grading standards.

It is usually helpful to assign points to each part of each essay question. This makes a paper fairly easy to grade, for the grade is not based on a global impression of a long answer, but on part-by-part scrutiny, with points awarded for each aspect that is correct.

In order to grade an essay exam as fairly as possible, it is generally best to give separate grades for spelling, grammar, writing style, clarity of expression, and ideas presented. The first four factors are important language skills. The last is often the main purpose of the essay test, however, and this grade is the one that should be used to determine the grade for the course. Penmanship and spelling problems similar to those discussed in the chapter on fill-in-the-blank items may also come into play, and the same considerations that apply to fill-ins may also be applied to essays.

A real problem with essay exams is that if a student does not know the answer, he or she may write carelessly in the hope that the teacher will not bother to struggle through the sloppy penmanship and will just give the paper a C. The student hopes that the teacher can "find" in a carelessly written essay an answer that is in fact not there. Or, the teacher may pick out key words and assume that the student has the answer when in fact he or she does not. Further, if a student is weak in spelling and grammar, or is unsure of important facts, he or she will often write carelessly to cover these weaknesses. In response, some teachers provide cassette tape recorders, typewriters, or even dictaphones to help those students with serious handwriting problems, especially if the problems seem to be physiological or even psychological.

Other Grading Suggestions

It is usually best to grade the same question on every paper before proceeding to the next question—that is, grade question 1 on each paper first, then grade question 2 on each paper, and so forth. This allows the teacher to develop an accurate set of expectations for *each* question. When the teacher knows the quality of work students can be expected to produce, he or she will find it much easier to grade their answers. Usually, for the first few papers, a teacher expects a great deal and grades according to very high standards. Then, as the grading proceeds, he relaxes his standards and awards higher grades. To reduce this problem, many teachers *regrade* both the first and the last five papers.

Grading essay tests one question at a time also minimizes the **halo effect**. Sometimes, when a teacher likes a student's first test answer, the favorable impression will influence his perception of the student's other answers and he will grade them equally high. On the other hand, if the teacher does *not* like the first answer, he may grade the rest of the answers *lower* than he otherwise might. This halo effect may be largely subconscious, but it will often influence a grade even if the teacher tries to be objective.

Multiple grading is another way of minimizing subjectivity. When multiple grading is done, the same teacher grades each paper twice, but on separate occasions, or two different teachers each grade the same papers. Some teachers read all the papers first without grading them; then, a week later, reread and grade them. Other teachers read all the papers once and assign them grades on a separate sheet of paper. At a later date, they reread each paper and give each a second grade. When they compare the two grades, if they are identical, the paper is given that grade. If there is a difference (for example, a B for the first time and an A for the second), they either read the paper a third time or average the two grades. When two different teachers grade the same set of papers, they usually use the average of the two grades or both grades—A/B, C/D.

The Problem of Empty Answers

A common problem with essay exams is that students may be tempted to use many words to say nothing. Some students can construct a superficially impressive essay that is in actuality so vague that it could answer almost any question. Such answers are frequently very well constructed, contain highly appropriate vocabulary, and, in many ways, sound knowledgeable. Some students even develop a set of pat answers that they can use to answer partially, or at least to fill up space, on almost any essay exam. A teacher must be aware of this possibility. The previously mentioned suggestions, such as asking very specific questions, help to avoid this problem.

Should We Use Essay Exams?

If the basic ideas set forth in this chapter are taken into consideration, essays can be rewarding, useful examinations. If the teacher is flexible about grading and stresses her willingness to discuss and reevaluate grades, most students will feel that essay exams are rewarding. If the teacher is open about the difficulties of grading essay exams, students will better understand her position and be more willing to work with her in arriving at equitable grades. And if essay exams are used to help students learn more by thinking about classroom material in new ways, their pedagogical benefits become unquestionable.

Summary

One of the oldest test formats still in use today is the essay. Although essay tests do not take much time to develop, they are very time consuming to grade. The grading of essay exams is highly subjective, but grading can be fairly reliable if teachers follow certain procedures which are outlined in this chapter. The key to developing good essay exams is to write questions that are clear, specific, and to the point. Essay exams can be very useful learning tools, but they do have their own limitations.

Suggested Readings

Ahmann, Stanley and Marvin Glock. *Evaluating Pupil Growth: Principles of Tests and Measurements*. 5th rev. ed. Boston: Allyn and Bacon, 1975. Chapter 5.

Gerberich, J. Raymond, Harry A. Greene and Albert N. Jorgensen. *Measurement and Evaluation in the Modern School*. New York: David McKay, 1962.

Greene, Harry A., Albert N. Jorgensen and J. Raymond Gerberich. *Measurement and Evaluation in the Elementary School*. 2d rev. ed. New York: Longmans, Green and Company, 1953. Chapter 9.

Karmel, Louis J. and Marylin O. Karmel. *Measurement and Evaluation in the Schools*. 2d rev. ed. New York: Macmillan, 1978. Chapter 15.

Lindvall, C. Mauritz and Anthony J. Nitko. *Measuring Pupil Achievement and Aptitude*. 2d rev. ed. New York: Harcourt Brace Jovanovich, 1975. Chapter 4.

Mehrens, William A. and Irvin J. Lehmann. *Measurement and Evaluation in Education and Psychology*. New York: Holt, Rinehart and Winston. Chapter 8.

Sax, Gilbert. *Principles of Educational Measurement and Evaluation*. Belmont, Calif.: Wadsworth Publishing Company, 1974. Chapter 5.

Thorndike, Robert L. *Educational Measurement*. Washington, D. C.: American Council on Education, 1971. Chapter 10.

12   Scoring Exams

Once a test is administered, it must, of course, be scored. This, in many ways, is the most tedious aspect of testing, and thus it is this point at which error is most likely to occur. It is therefore important for each teacher to experiment with various ways of scoring exams in order to find the ones that are most appropriate to his or her needs.

Probably, the easiest way to score exams is to have the students themselves do the correcting. This method is quick and makes results immediately available. In addition, as the exams are being corrected, the students can discuss the pros and cons of the correct answer and/or the answers they selected. This is an excellent way to provide feedback.

Problems in having the students correct their own papers include haphazardness and cheating. These difficulties can be dealt with in a number of ways. If students correct their own papers, the teacher can have them mark their original responses in black and then correct them in red. To reduce cheating while papers are being corrected, no black pens or pencils would be allowed on top of desks.

Another common way of reducing the amount of cheating is to have students trade papers and then correct each other's work. If they trade papers with whomever they choose, they may be tempted to "help each other out" by not properly correcting all of the responses. This possibility can be reduced if papers are exchanged in a more systematic way. Among the most common systems are:

1. Ask each student to pass her paper to the student behind her. The last student in each row would then bring her paper up to the first student in her row.
2. Ask the student in the first seat of each row to exchange papers with the student in the second seat. The student in the third seat would

then exchange papers with the student in the fourth seat, and so forth. If there is an uneven number of desks, the students in the last row can exchange papers with the student on their right or left.

3. Have each student exchange papers with the student diagonally across from him or her.
4. Have each student pass his paper to the person on his left. Those in the far left row would bring their papers to students in the far right row.

Most teachers alternate among several of these methods or develop systems of their own. It is usually a good idea to have students put their names at the bottom of the paper they correct. The teacher can spot-check to ensure that the papers are properly corrected. If a teacher discovers that certain students consistently do a poor job of correcting papers, he or she can give them special help to improve their skills. Even when they exchange papers, students should use one color pen or pencil (usually black or blue) while taking a test and another color (usually red or orange) while correcting it. As discussed above, the teacher should ensure that only the proper color of pen or pencil is used each time, for this tends to reduce the possibility of cheating.

It is important, though, that a teacher not communicate suspicion or treat the students as if they were dishonest. If the teacher projects the belief that the students are dishonest, the students may pick it up. Then, through the Pygmalion effect, this projection may adversely affect their honesty.

Answer Sheets

The easiest way to correct objective tests is with a machine-based system. Optical scoring systems such as the IBM answer sheets described here are the most common. Hand scoring is more time consuming, but may be preferable under certain circumstances or when a machine is not readily accessible. Hand scoring, however, is far less accurate than machine scoring. In one study of 51 third- and fourth-grade teachers, errors were found in 28 percent of the standardized tests they had scored (Bergman 1970). In other words, 28 out of 100 papers they scored had at least one or more errors in scoring.

When IBM answer sheets are used, students indicate their answers by filling in the space between two parallel lines below the letter of the answer they prefer (see Figure 12.1). The sheets can then be quickly corrected by a computer. Or, to score the sheets by hand, it is possible to purchase an IBM answer-sheet punch that enables a teacher to punch holes anywhere on an $8\frac{1}{2} \times 11$ sheet of paper. To make a master answer key, the teacher first marks the correct answers on a regular IBM answer sheet, then punches a hole through each correct answer. By laying a student's answer sheet under the answer key, the teacher can align the student's marks with the holes in order to quickly check the work. If there is a mark visible through the hole, the student has marked the correct response. If there is no mark, the teacher places a red X on the student's answer sheet to show which answer is correct. Finally, the teacher removes the answer key and counts the red X's to find the number of wrong responses. While doing this, the teacher should check to ensure that the student has selected only one answer for each question. If the student selected two or more answers for a question, and one was correct, the teacher would not know that an incorrect answer was also marked because it would be covered by the answer key. Thus, the teacher must review each answer sheet twice. This review may be avoided if a clear sheet of plastic is used in place of an opaque answer key.

To punch out the plastic, place it over the answer sheet, then punch out the holes as usual. A hole would be punched through both the opaque sheet and the plastic. Then the opaque sheet would be removed, and the plastic used to grade the answer sheets would be used by itself. The teacher then could see whether or not the students marked two answers without having to go over the answer sheets twice. A notch could be cut out at the top of the answer sheet so that the teacher could write the student's score directly on his or her answer sheet with a minimum of paper shuffle. The only problem with this technique is that the $8\frac{1}{2} \times 11$ scoring sheet could be accidentally reversed or flipped over. To prevent this, one corner should be notched, preferably the same corner that is notched on all IBM sheets.

Tests may also be scored quickly using a spirit duplicating machine. Simply place a spirit duplicator or mimeograph stencil *underneath* a prepared answer sheet and draw a dark circle around each correct answer. The correct answers can be overprinted on each student's answer sheet by running sheets through a mimeograph or a spirit duplicator just as if they were blank paper. The problem of alignment can be solved by running several blank answer sheets through the machine to ensure that the circles are being printed in the correct places. Alignment marks can also be placed on the stencil and compared to the overprinted answer sheets to ascertain that circles are printed directly upon the correct answer.

The teacher must be careful that the mimeograph machine does not tear any of the answer sheets. Once the master is lined up and working properly, this should not be a problem. When circles are printed on the correct answers, all the teacher has to do is count up the circles that do

Figure 12.1 The Grid of an IBM Answer Sheet

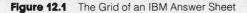

not have a student-made mark in them and subtract this number from the total possible score. This procedure, which gives the number correct, is quick and easy.

Strip Answer Key

If students have not used an answer sheet, or if the test has been written in matching or fill-in-the-blank format, the correct answers can be put on a narrow slip of paper that can be placed alongside the student's answers for easy comparison. This method of placing the answer key as close as possible to student answers eliminates some of the errors that can occur in hand grading.

Correction Formula for True-or-False and Multiple-Choice Tests

The correction formula is utilized to try to reduce the effect of guessing. To illustrate the effect of guessing, note the following example.

If a student knows 20 true or false questions out of 100 and guesses on the rest, he or she will likely earn a score of about 60 correct. We know this is true because we know that by blindly guessing a set of true and false questions, the student can get up to 50 percent correct. If the student knows 20 questions out of 100, he or she will get 50 percent right of the remaining 80, which means he or she will likely get 40 questions correct. If the 40 correct guesses are added onto the 20 known answers the student will end up with a score of 60, or about a D score according to common grading standards. This grade, of course, is not a clear reflection of what the student has learned.

The probability that a student guessed on a total of twice as many as he or she got wrong is the reasoning behind the following formula: The number right minus the number wrong equals the "true score" for T-F questions, or "T.S. = R − W."

With true and false questions, guessing actually becomes an important factor because chances are very high that a score can be improved purely by chance. And, the fewer questions a student gets right, the more important guessing becomes. If, out of 100 questions, a student only misses 10, he or she probably guessed on 20 questions and therefore knew the answers to 80 questions (100 − 20 = 80). Thus, guessing in this case would not significantly alter his or her score. Of course, if the teacher was grading 90 percent A, 80 percent B, the student's grade would go down from a low A to a low B; so even at this level, guessing could be important. But, if a student missed 40 questions out of 100, he or she probably guessed on 80 questions, or knew only 20 questions. Guessing added about 40 points to the score, giving that student a score of 60 or a D for knowing about 20 percent of the material.

With multiple choice questions, guessing exerts less influence on the final score. With three choices the student will end up with about one question correct by chance. With four choices the student will also end up with about one question correct by chance.

Using this reasoning, the following formula is obtained: the true score, corrected for guessing, equals the number correct minus the number wrong, divided by one minus the number of alternatives, or

$$\text{T.S.} = R - \frac{W}{A + 1}.$$

For example, if there are two alternatives as in true and false, we have the following formula:

T.S. = Score corrected for guessing

$$\text{T.S.} = R - \frac{W}{A + 1} = R - \frac{W}{2 + 1} R - \frac{W}{1} = R - W.$$

R = Right answers
W = Wrong answers
A = Number of alternatives

With four responses (the common multiple choice question) we have the following formula:

$$\text{T.S.} = R - \frac{W}{A+1} = R - \frac{W}{4+1} R - \frac{W}{3}.$$

Sample Problems:

If Mindy receives a score of 70 correct out of 100 questions (has 30 wrong) and each question has a total of four alternatives, what would her true score be? Answer:

$$70 - \frac{30}{3} = 70 - 10 = 60.$$

On the other hand, if Mindy guesses on 24 questions, she will probably end up with how many correct by chance? Answer:

$$24 \times \frac{1}{4} = \frac{24}{1} \times \frac{1}{4} = \frac{24}{4} = 6 \text{ or } \frac{24}{4} = 6.$$

If Mindy earns a score of 82 out of 100, her true score is probably what? Answer:

$$82 - \frac{18}{4-1} = 82 - \frac{18}{3} = 82 - 6 = 76.$$

Problems with Using the Correction Formula

The advantage of a correction formula is that it tells a teacher specifically how many of the questions it is likely that the student knew the answer to minus guessing. This in itself can be a valid measurement tool for the teacher. As far as grading is concerned, however, there is no real need to use the correction formula, because if all students answer all items, the rank order before and after the correction formula is identical. The lowest students are still lowest, and the highest students are still the highest. Grades are generally based on ranking, not on absolute score.

Furthermore, using the formula with students could create several problems. First of all, students may resist this formula because they literally lose points from their score. Even if a teacher explains that the formula will not affect their grade because the rank order stays the same, students still may tend to object. Use of the formula may also discourage students from guessing and, by and large, guessing on a test is often not totally blind. In fact it is rare that a student clearly knows many answers and unequivocally knows incorrect choices are incorrect. To some degree, we can say that students guess on each and every question.

Finally, guessing is clearly not the only manner in which students answer test questions incorrectly. The correction formula simply does not take this into account. For this reason, most teachers decide to use the correction formula only for their own purposes and not openly with the class. As long as the teacher understands the part guessing plays, the formula can be very useful.

Summary

Probably one of the most potentially boring aspects of teaching is scoring exams, especially objective exams. Thus, the teacher should endeavor to find a quick, effective scoring method. One of the most common quick and accurate methods is the use of an answer sheet having a "key" with the answers punched out. When the student circles the answer directly on the test booklets, a method used especially in the lower grades, the most effective method is a strip answer key. The correction formula for determining guessing can be a valid scoring tool for a teacher, as long as its limitations are recognized.

Suggested Readings

Aiken, Lewis R. *Psychological Testing and Assessment*. 3d rev. ed. Boston: Allyn and Bacon, 1979. Chapter 2.

Gronlund, Norman E. *Measurement and Evaluation in Teaching*. 2d rev. ed. New York: Macmillan, 1971. Chapter 11.

Mehrens, William A. and Irvin J. Lehmann. *Measurement and Evaluation in Education and Psychology*. New York: Holt Rinehart Winston, 1978. Chapter 11.

Noll, Victor H., Dale P. Scannell and Robert C. Craig. *Introduction to Educational Measurement*. 4th rev. ed. Boston: Houghton Mifflin, 1979.

Thorndike, Robert L. *Educational Measurement*. Washington, D. C.: American Council on Education, 1971. Chapter 8.

13   Evaluating and Using Tests

Now that we've examined the basic types of test questions, let's look at how they can be used and improved in order to help students.

The teacher should endeavor to improve every test by utilizing feedback from students. To do this the test's contents must be divided into subgroups of specific learning units. For example, a test on the nervous system could be divided into sections on the brain, the spinal chord, neurons, synapses, neural transmitters, and so forth. Usually, the divisions follow the table of specifications (see p. 59). By computing a score for each subgroup, the teacher can evaluate the effectiveness of each specific unit of instruction. In order to respond appropriately to learning units on which the entire class did poorly, the teacher should examine the following possibilities:

1. It may be that the material was poorly explained in class. This is probably the most common reason for poor student performance. A teacher may simply lack experience in presenting the material, or sometimes a teacher, after teaching for years and explaining the same material to class after class, inadvertently falls into making careless presentations. Since he knows the information well, he tends to assume that students already know more than they actually do.

    To diagnose the problems, a teacher might discuss a test on which the entire class performed poorly and specifically ask the students what *they* feel the problem is. If they do not understand the material, quite likely a poor or incomplete explanation is at fault. Sometimes presenting the material in a different context or providing more basic background material leads to improvement.

2. The concepts or material covered may be too difficult for most students in the class. To rectify this, the teacher may need to explain

Inventory test	Criterion referenced exam
Survey test	Age norm
Aptitude test	Grade norm
Readiness test	Score band
Placement test	Obtained score
Sequential test	Content validity
Multilevel format	Criterion validity
Survey test battery	Concurrent validity
Raw score	Predictive validity
Norm referenced exam	Construct validity
Standard	Ideal discriminate validity
Reference group	Reliability

the material more thoroughly, and/or use more examples, illustrations, quizzes, or individualization. It is also possible (but less likely) that the material is inappropriate to the age level or the specific class, which may occur if the class is immature or lacks the social or academic background to master the material.

3. The students may see the information as unimportant. Most curricula include several subjects whose importance is difficult for students to perceive. In these cases, the teacher may have to develop ways to help the student recognize the material's relevance. Merely telling students that someday they will understand why a subject is important usually does not suffice. The teacher must actively help students understand its significance through examples and demonstrations, such as putting them into situations where it is obvious the material is needed.

Finding an average class score for each subtest and analyzing each part of the total teaching process in light of that information is probably the most fruitful, useful, practical, and economical way of improving instruction and diagnosing learning problems.

Using Teacher-Made Tests for Multi-Diagnostic Purposes

An important function of all teacher-made tests should be to identify gaps in students' learning. To do this, a test should be subdivided according to skill dimensions, which requires that each question be evaluated independently to determine if it tests the criteria the teacher is concerned with. For example, reading tests can sometimes be used to assess word recognition, reading comprehension, vocabulary, rate of reading, story comprehension, identification of sounds, and syllabi-cation simultaneously, with each paragraph focusing on one or more skills. To evaluate the student's mastery of each aspect, the test is scored seven times, each time with a separate key. To save time, the keys can sometimes be combined so that several factors may be assessed at the same time. In addition, highly individualized learning programs can be developed to assess each student's specific strengths and weaknesses.

Inventory Tests

Inventory tests are used prior to instruction to assess students' back-ground learning. Results of these tests can be used to place students in appropriate instructional groups and also plan teaching sequences. For example, the writer's first year of teaching was spent in an open class-room "house" situation. About 350 students and six teachers worked together in one large octagonal room. During the first week of classes, a series of general inventory tests were used to place the students in six groups, one for each subject taught. There were then six levels for math, six for social studies, and so forth. Placement in each level was based on the knowledge demonstrated on the test. The students' actual grade levels were from third to sixth, but the math groups, for exam-ple, ranged from a group that was equivalent to first grade to one that was starting at the high school level. Although it is difficult to accom-modate such a wide range of aptitudes in one class, it is commonly found. Inventory tests can help the teacher recognize and adapt to the situation.

Survey tests are used to evaluate students' general abilities in one area. A survey test covers a wide range of abilities and usually yields one score. Examples would include final examinations and grade placement tests.

Aptitude tests are used to measure potential or to assess possible suc-cess in restricted fields. They are standardized tests with emphasis placed on predictive validity, or how well the *future* performance of the student may be predicted. An example of an aptitude test would be a clerical assessment survey that predicts likelihood of success in a cleri-cal area. Aptitude tests are used to place students in various courses of study, especially trade school programs. They also are used to place potential employees in various positions in industry. In addition, apti-tude tests are used to measure students' ability to profit from certain fields of study and their probable success in specific lines of work. Note the following:

Wally is an eleventh-grade high-school student who is unsure of his career goals. His interests seem to lie in the areas of electronics and foreign languages. Because he enjoyed his Spanish class, he also began taking German and is doing quite well. He has always felt that he would like to get involved in some area of electronics, although he has no experience in this area aside from that gained in the home electronics shop he assembled as a hobby. Because he felt a need to begin planning for college. Wally requested help from his guidance counselor, who gave him a series of aptitude tests. According to the tests, Wally has clear ability in foreign languages, but lacks aptitude for electronics. His manual dexterity is not high, and he has other problems that would make working with technical instruments difficult. The counselor was careful to advise him that tests are *not infallible* and that these were only *part of* the many factors that should be considered in making a decision. Wally was very satisfied with the results of the test and decided that he would definitely prefer to study languages at the university. He felt that his interest in electronics was one of many hobbies he had but that when it came to a career he would be happier in something related to languages. He also felt he was more competent in that area.

An aptitude test can be quite useful if its predictive validity is high. Such tests could be applied broadly to help millions of people facing decisions about their life's work, avoid frustrations, disappointments, and loss of time and money.

Readiness tests are designed to assess whether or not a youngster has developed the skills necessary to succeed in a specified area. For example, reading readiness tests determine if a child has the skills needed to begin learning to read by examining his or her knowledge of the alphabet and word sounds, eye-hand coordination, and other skills related to the reading process. Algebra readiness tests may assess a student's ability to add, subtract, divide, multiply, and work with fractions and decimals. Since these skills are thought to be necessary to success in algebra, it is assumed that a student who has mastered them is ready to study algebra.

It is generally best to avoid trying to teach a skill before a student is ready. If a student is required to begin learning something before he or she has acquired necessary background skills, he or she may develop a mental block that will make it more difficult to learn the subject later when he or she *is* ready. The use of readiness tests can thus help simplify the learning process and help both the teacher and the student avoid frustration. In addition to their more specific functions, readiness tests may assess a variety of other factors, such as the student's general maturation and even quality of eye movement. Although readiness tests are available commercially, most teachers who use these tests develop their own, especially in such areas as math, physics, chemistry, and foreign languages.

Placement tests are used to place a student at an appropriate learning level. For example, students entering a college foreign language program usually take placement tests to assess the level at which they should begin their studies. The scores they achieve are important factors in determining where they are placed; the higher the score, the higher the level at which a student begins.

Diagnostic Test Formats

Sequential tests are constructed so that the difficulty of each item is determined by the student's response to the item that preceded it. A student is asked one question at a time. If she answers correctly, she is given a harder question; if she answers incorrectly, she is given an easier one. Usually, if she passes one item and fails the next, the difficulty level of the third question will be in between that of the first two. This format is often presented on a computer or printed on cards with each difficulty level clearly marked. When cards are used, the student selects questions according to self-scored results; or a teacher works individually with the student.

When **multilevel format** is used, one standardized test is designed so it can be utilized for several grade levels usually from first to sixth or from fifth to twelfth grades. For example, for first grade, there may be both an easy and a difficult format, or even an easy, a medium, and a difficult format. This enables a teacher to choose the test that is most appropriate to his or her class's abilities. Often, a teacher uses several multilevel standardized tests, matching each with a specific group of students.

A **survey test battery** is usually a standardized test designed to assess a student's very *general* level of ability. Usually a survey test battery is extremely short but covers a wide range of material. For example, the Wide Range Achievement Test (WRAT) begins at preschool and ends at college level, yet is only three pages long. The first questions about math, for example, are extremely easy (counting), while the last ones are extremely difficult (college-level calculus).

All of these tests can be very helpful guides for a teacher to use in planning a course of instruction. It is important to stress, however, that the types of tests discussed above and their definitions refer more to the use of a test than to its content. There is actually little difference, for example, between an aptitude test and an achievement test except for the ways in which the results are applied.

Using Test Scores to Help Students

After a student takes a test, the teacher usually corrects it and counts the total number of points earned. The result is commonly known as a **raw score**. By itself, a single raw score does not have much meaning; it must be compared with something else, usually the scores of the rest of the class. For example, if we are told merely that Nicole earned a 28 on her last exam, we have no idea what that score means. If, on the other hand, we know that six other students took the exam and that their scores were 12, 26, 18, 29, 9, and 14, we would have some notion of how Nicole compares to her classmates. When a student is compared to the rest of the class or some other population, he or she is being evaluated according to what is known as **norm reference** criteria.

Norm Referenced Exams

On **norm referenced** exams an individual score is interpreted by comparing it with the distribution of some **standard**, or norm. The norm, or comparison group, could be fifth-graders, twelfth-graders, eighth-grade rural females, six-year-old blacks living in the inner city, or some other designation. A comparison is made between one individual and a **reference group** that is similar in some way. Sometimes we compare students with national norms (the performances of a large sample of students throughout the country) for the same grade level or age. More commonly, we compare one student with the rest of his or her class.

Criterion Referenced Exams

There are several problems in comparing a student's performance with that of other class members. Since the individuals in a given class differ in so many ways, it is sometimes difficult or meaningless to compare one with another. For example, if Dave is the only deaf student in the class, his performance should be compared with that of other deaf students as well as with that of his nondeaf classmates.

For this reason, **criterion referenced exams** can be extremely useful. On such tests, comparisons are made with a preestablished set of mastery goals. The term *criterion referenced* means that the standard of comparison is something other than statistical norms. For example, a teacher might determine that a certain level of performance is desirable for a certain student and then try to help him reach that level. The desired level would be based on the student's individual abilities, goals, background, and other factors rather than on what is average for his grade, age, or sex.

This method allows for more individualization than do norm-referenced exams. There is a wide range of abilities and aptitudes among fifth graders, for example, and a teacher should thus have different expectations for each student. The goals for a bright, capable student who has performed well in the past should differ from those for a less gifted student. The criteria used to judge a student's performance should reflect his of her individual goals, needs, and abilities.

Another common basis of comparison for criterion referenced exams is the student's own past performance. With this approach, a student is expected to perform at a specified level above his or her past achievements. A student is thus expected to improve only in reference to his or her past performance and is *not* compared with others in the class or with national norms. This evaluational procedure can be especially productive, with students who are doing poorly. A student who falls far below class or national norms may find it extremely discouraging to be constantly compared against standards that seem unattainable. But being compared only to him- or herself may be a very powerful motivator. On the other hand, students who perform considerably above the norm may suffer from reduced motivation for opposite reasons. They may feel that because they are already far above average, they don't need to work as hard. Thus, for both these groups of students, criteria referenced exams can be very useful.

Percentile Rankings

As noted previously, to give a measurement meaning we need a reference population. An exam score of 128 means nothing in isolation from other scores. The most common statistic used to help a teacher understand what a score means is a percentile (discussed in more detail in Chapter 20). A percentile is a comparison between an individual student's score and another *group* of scores. The reference population could be the whole world, an entire country, all males within a certain country, all females in a certain country attending a certain type of school (such as Catholic schools), or all Spanish-speaking fifth-graders in large cities. These types of comparisons are called **norm reference scores**.

The population to which a student is compared strongly affects the meaning of his or her score. A sixteen-year-old boy who is 79 inches tall is considered quite tall compared to other sixteen-year-old American boys, but would be quite average compared to sixteen-year-old Watusi boys. Thus, all comparisons require judgments about the *most appropriate* reference group. A teacher should always know what comparisons are being made and the source of the data used for the comparisons. Is the source a standardized test and the comparison group a randomly selected sample of all twelve-year-olds? Or is the source a test the teacher made up and the comparison group the other students in the class?

These populations are important for another reason. If Ray receives scores of 74% on an algebra exam and 83% on a French exam, it is possible that the algebra score is actually a better score in relation to the performances of other students. If the class average for the French test is 85% and the average for the algebra test is 70%, Ray's score is above average in algebra and below average in French. Thus, before a comparison is made, we need to know more about the reference population. A score is meaningless without some type of a reference population.

Common Reference Populations

The most common standards of comparison used in education are **age norms** (comparisons with students of the same age) and **grade norms** (comparisons with students in the same grade). On standardized tests, both of these norms are usually recorded in terms of years and months. For *age norms* scores usually begin with 4-0, which means the child is four years and zero months, and increase in units of one month, which in this case would be 4-1, 4-2, 4-3, to 4-11 (because there are twelve months in a year). If age norms are used, a child who is four years and seven months old would be compared with other children who are four years and seven months old.

Grade norm annotations are similar to age norms, except that the first number indicates grade level rather than age. Thus, a student in the first month of fourth grade would have a grade norm of 4-1, and a student in the second month of the fourth grade would have a grade norm of 4-2. As there is generally no school during the summer months, grade norm would then jump from 4-10 to 5-1.

Other commonly used norm comparisons include sex, race, and educational level. Sometimes comparisons are also made by geographical region and urban versus rural residence.

Score Bands

On standardized tests, each score is actually only an *estimate*. Therefore, one must consider **score bands** rather than a single score. An **obtained score** of 75, for example, is probably close to the true score, which, on the basis of the obtained score, could be expected to fall between 73 and 77. It is unlikely that the true score would be as low as 60 or as high as 90. Score bands show the range within which there is a high probability that a given true score will fall. When test results are

Figure 13.1   Score Bands for I.Q. Scores

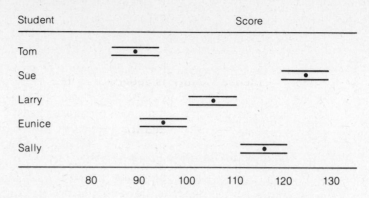

Center Point = Obtained Score
Lines = Range of True Score

reported using score bands, the center point is the student's obtained score (see Figure 13.1), and the student's true score most likely lies somewhere within the band. When students' test results are jointly diagramed, if two score bands overlap, it means that no significant difference exists between the two students' performances, and when bands do *not* overlap, one can assume that there is a significant difference. Based on Figure 13.1, for example, we could conclude that Tom and Eunice performed similarly on this test, while Sue clearly outperformed both of them.

Validity

A test's **validity** is a reflection of how well it measures what it was designed to measure. A test designed to measure spelling ability that contains nothing but math problems would obviously lack validity. Other cases, though, are more subtle. A history exam that is graded to reflect strong emphasis on spelling, penmanship, and grammar rather than knowledge and understanding of historical events is also lacking in validity. Another example that is much less obvious forms the basis of the controversy over I.Q. tests. Can a series of vocabulary items be a valid measure of what we commonly think of as intelligence? Since many group I.Q. tests are heavily weighted with vocabulary items, this is an important validity question. It is these types of questions that validity studies explore.

Types of Validity

Content validity pertains to how well the content of a test measures what is intended to be measured. The previous example of a series of math problems being used as a spelling test typifies lack of content validity. This is both the most common and the simplest kind of validity to check. Comparisons between the material on the test and that which we want to measure is usually all that is needed to quickly determine content validity, although more complex methods are available.

Criterion validity is reflected in the relationship between the test results and some predetermined measure, or criterion. The criteria could include a previous test, prior classroom performance, or peer ratings. A test is checked for criterion validity by correlating its results with the other measure. Students who do well on one should do well on the other, those who earn average scores on one should have average scores on the other, and so forth. The higher the correspondence between the two, the higher the criterion validity.

There are two types of criterion validity that differ only in terms of the amount of time that lapses between the first and second measures. The first type, **concurrent validity**, is of concern when the second measurement is made as soon as possible after the first. **Predictive validity** cannot be measured until criterion data are gathered several months or years later.

When the results of one test are compared with those of another for which the validity is already known or accepted, it is a check on concurrent validity. For example, if we develop a new I.Q. test, the way to ensure that it is valid is to correlate its scores with those from a standard I.Q. test for the same group. A problem with this method is that one must assume that the other test is itself valid, which may not be the case.

Predictive validity is similar to concurrent validity except that the second measure is obtained much later and is usually a performance measure. To check predictive validity, one might administer a job aptitude test to a group of people and then, six months later, measure their performance on the job for which they were tested. Those who score well on the job aptitude test should perform well on the job, those who exhibit average performance on the aptitude test should perform similarly on the job, and so forth.

When these conditions occur, there is a high correlation between the test and the criterion. The greater the deviation from the ideal, the lower the correlation and the predictive validity. Predictive validity itself has high validity because the test is checked against the actual performance that it is designed to predict. The purpose of most tests is either to evaluate past performance or to predict future performance.

Predictive validity is an issue for those tests that are used to predict future performance.

Some critics of aptitude tests are concerned that there may be a relationship between predictive validity and self-fulfilling prophecy. What they do not take into consideration, however, is the fact that if a test cannot predict future performance with some degree of accuracy, there is simply no reason to give the test. If a large number of students who failed the test were to succeed later, it would be a waste of time to give *anyone* the test. It is important to use tests that have high predictive validity because the results can be used to advise and help students. If it is possible to predict that someone is likely to fail, appropriate remedial steps can be taken. The test has thus served a very useful purpose. If a student would have failed without teacher intervention, and if the test helped determine the need for intervention, the test can still be seen as valid.

Construct validity relies on the use of reason to determine how well a test conforms to its underlying theory. Our theory, for example, may be that certain skills are characteristic of good football players. We would first analyze the skills needed. If fast reaction time, muscular strength, and knowledge of the rules were found to be important in successfully playing football, then we would try to develop a test to measure these skills. Presumably, if a student scored highly in these three areas, he or she would be able to play football well. Likewise, if a student's scores were uniformly poor, he or she would not be likely to play football well. Construct validity is probably the most difficult type of validity to determine, and is the most debatable. Determining construct validity tends to be an ongoing process because a test must be evaluated a number of times to obtain an accurate indicator of this measure.

In contrast to construct validity, **ideal discriminate validity** is probably one of the easiest types of validity to determine, and, in some ways, it is the most important for the average classroom teacher. Ideal validity, in essence, measures how well a test discriminates between students who know the subject matter well and those who do not. When a test has high ideal validity, a student who knows nothing about the subject should do *very* poorly, a student who knows a fair amount about the subject should receive an average score, and one who knows the subject well should do well.

Reliability

Reliability, as discussed previously, refers to *consistency*. If a student takes a test several times and has not grown in the area the test measures, he or she should earn a similar score each time.

The most common way of determining a test's reliability is to administer it to the entire class and rank the students. Then, the entire procedure is repeated. If the test is reliable, all scores will improve on the second administration, but student rankings will remain very similar. To obtain accurate results, it is important that retesting be done fairly soon after the original testing. If one were to wait, for example, for two years, differences would occur because the students would have matured and changed at different rates. Thus, the rankings would be different because of *real* differences in the subjects and not necessarily because the test is unreliable.

Reliability Coefficients

A reliability coefficient is determined by calculating the correlation between obtained and estimated true scores on a given test. If the reliability coefficient equals .00, the test reflects total unreliability. If the coefficient equals 1.00, there is no error in measurement whatsoever; that is, every individual in the class would have obtained the same ranking on both administrations of the test. If the reliability is less than 1.00, there will have been a change in the rankings of one or more persons between testings. The lower the coefficient, the more changes in rankings there have been and the lower the test's reliability. It is important to remember that a reliability coefficient is only a measure of the amount or magnitude of inconsistency; it does not tell us *why* inconsistency exists.

Methods of Determining Reliability

The most common method of determining an exam's reliability is the **test-retest method**. As explained previously, the same test is given to the same group on two separate occasions, usually only a few days apart. The correlation between the two tests becomes the coefficient of reliability. Since rankings rather than raw scores are used to compute the correlation, the fact that most students usually do slightly better on the second test will not greatly affect final results. The real problem with this method stems from students looking up answers after the first test. Some students may not look up any answers, while others may look up as many as they can remember. This would reflect intervening learning and would likely cause their scores to rise disproportionately. The same problem may occur when students talk about the test among themselves. We could expect that those who. discuss the test will improve their scores, whereas those who do not discuss it will not improve or will improve only slightly.

Another way to determine reliability is **split-half correlation**. Each student's test is divided in half, usually with odd-numbered items making up one-half and even-numbered items making up the other. This, in essence, produces two tests for each student that are then correlated with each other.

A third method is to correlate some students' scores on *equivalent forms*, or two tests that cover the same material although the specific questions are different. For example, the first test might contain the math problem 47 × 93, while the second contains 93 × 47. It is impossible to develop two tests with different questions that are *exactly* equal in difficulty, but we can make them fairly close. These two tests are then administered within a fairly short time period, and, as before, the results are correlated. The problem with this method is that it costs time and money, and it is hard to ensure that the two tests are equal but different.

How the Teacher Can Increase Reliability

The various methods of determining reliability can never yield precise measures of a test's unreliability. Correlation coefficients are only *estimates* or, more precisely, *averages*. For a teacher, the *most important concern is how to increase reliability*. The following causes of unreliability should be avoided:

1. The sample of test items is skewed—that is, some material only briefly mentioned in class is made an important part of the test, while other material extensively covered in class is only briefly touched on. If a test is not well balanced and does not test material in proportion to the emphasis it was given in class or in the text, reliability will be lowered. To remedy this situation, a table of specifications should be used to balance the test.
2. Wording of instructions and questions is ambiguous. This common problem may cause students to misinterpret the intent of a question or a portion of the test. Ambiguity may be reduced by revising test questions in accordance with feedback from other teachers or based on the results of previous use, either in a practice test or with other classes. For example, the following question is so ambiguous that all four answers could be correct:

Maternal deprivation is generally an important concept for
a. teachers   c. nurses
b. parents   d. teenagers

In order to be a good test item, the question must be much more specific about the one aspect of maternal deprivation the test maker has in mind. A better version would be:

Direct application of the implications of maternal deprivation is likely to be most important to:

a. teachers   c. nurses
b. parents   d. teenagers

The correct answer is now more clearly choice b.

3. Too many difficult items can lead students to do a great deal of guessing. Chance then plays an important role in final scores. The more difficult a test is, the more its final scores are affected by chance. To solve this problem, the test should be made easier. The average difficulty level for a nonmastery test should be about .50, as discussed in Chapter 6.

4. A short test usually has lower reliability. Probably the easiest way to increase a test's reliability is by lengthening it. An average test that contains only 10 questions often has very little reliability, whereas a test of 70 questions of equal quality is likely to have a greater reliability. The larger the sample, all other things being equal, the more accurate the assessments of students' levels of achievement usually are.

Although longer tests have more reliability, there is a point of diminishing returns. The problem of timing and the fact that an extremely long test can fatigue students sometimes counteract the advantages gained from a long test. It is usually desirable to develop items that can be answered quickly so that as much information as possible can be obtained within the allotted time. In terms of reliability, it is generally better to have 70 easy-to-answer questions than 30 longer, more complex, involved ones. Depending on subject matter and grade level, of course, there are times when it would be preferable to have fewer and longer questions.

5. Restrictive time limits can force hasty reading and responding, which affect students' final scores. Students should generally be given plenty of time to finish a test. This ensures that they answer thoughtfully and minimizes quick guesses.

Outside Factors That Affect Reliability

Fatigue, illness, emotions, motivational level, attitudes, and values all affect reliability. Although these are common elements, they are difficult to control. Sometimes the effects of fatigue and illness can be controlled if the teacher allows students to take the exam later if they do not feel well. This may, of course, cause some students to malinger in order to gain more time to study or find out from other students what is on the test. Although illness can affect an obtained score, the results are usually not great. Motivation is probably a more important factor, especially the motivation to study *before* taking the test.

A student's personality characteristics may affect his or her test scores. Students with certain personality patterns tend to be better test takers than others. Sociable persons who enjoy communicating are apt to perform better on many types of tests. People who are able to express themselves fluently, are confident, and enjoy writing will also often score higher than people who lack such characteristics.

Students' past experience with tests will influence their performance on subsequent tests. Youngsters who have taken a great many tests and have received good feedback to help them learn *how* to take tests will usually do better on almost any exam. This produces consistency, which, in turn, increases reliability. If students vary their test-taking strategies, reliability will probably be reduced. For example, some students work fairly rapidly to complete a test and then return to those questions they are unsure about. Other students carefully answer each question and do not continue until they are confident they have put down the best answer. The first method is much more productive and will likely result in a higher score.

Also important is the *quality* of students' past experiences with tests. If they have often achieved success, their attitudes and skills are likely to be ones that will help them to be consistently successful. On the other hand, students who have had several negative or disappointing experiences with tests may have a much more difficult time because of factors totally unrelated to knowledge of subject matter.

Such additional factors as students' I.Q., memory, fluency, and the like also enter into the reliability of a test. The higher these factors, the more reliable the test. Other more transient factors, including lapses in attention, boredom, distractions, poor ventilation, and the like may serve to reduce a test's reliability to some extent.

In most cases, a teacher can increase reliability simply by ensuring that all students clearly understand test directions, are marking answer sheets correctly, and are not interrupted during the testing process. Elimination of distractions and maximization of students' comfort through good lighting, ventilation, and heating can also contribute to higher reliability.

Summary

Teachers should endeavor to improve every test by utilizing feedback from students. An important function of all teacher-made tests should be to identify a student's learning gaps. A survey of tests that are available to aid the teacher in placement of students and planning of course instruction has been presented in this chapter. This chapter has also provided information for using test scores to help students. A student's raw score does not have much meaning, but must be compared with something else. A test's validity and reliability are two areas to explore. A test's validity is a reflection of how well it measures what it was designed to measure. There are several types of validity to examine. A test's reliability refers to its consistency. Both of these factors are important in evaluating a test.

Suggested Readings

Ahmann, Stanley and Marvin Glock. *Evaluating Pupil Growth: Principles of Tests and Measurements*. Boston: Allyn and Bacon, 1975. Chapter 8.

Gerberich, J. Raymond, Harry A. Greene and Albert N. Jorgensen. *Measurement and Evaluation in the Modern School*. New York: David McKay, 1962.

Greene, Harry A., Albert N. Jorgensen and J. Raymond Gerberich. *Measurement and Evaluation in the Elementary School*. 2d rev. ed. New York: Longmans, Green and Company, 1953. Chapters 3, 4, 7, 13.

Hills, John R. *Exercises in Classroom Measurement*. Columbus, Ohio: Charles E. Merrill Publishing Company, 1976. Chapters 23, 24, 25, 26, 27.

Hopkins, Charles D. and Richard L. Antes. *Classroom Measurement and Evaluation*. Itasca, Ill.: F. E. Peacock Publishers, 1978. Chapter 8.

Lindvall, C. Mauritz and Dale P. Nitko. *Measuring Pupil Achievement and Aptitude*. 2d rev. ed. New York: Harcourt Brace Jovanovich, 1975. Chapter 5.

Thomas, Murray R. *Judging Student Progress*. 2d rev. ed. New York: David McKay Company, 1960. Chapter 10.

Thorndike, Robert L. and Elizabeth Hagen. *Measurement and Evaluation in Psychology and Education*. 4th rev. ed. New York: John Wiley and Sons, 1977. Chapters 3, 4.

14   Tests as Curriculum

Teachers tend to view tests as nonlearning tasks tacked onto the ends of learning units. They are necessary, teachers feel, in order to satisfy administrative demands to grade students. This approach is called **summative evaluation**. When tests are used as an *important part of the curriculum*, the process is known as **formative evaluation**, which is the focus of this text.

Tests that are specifically designed to help students learn are appropriately called **learning tests**. In reality, as discussed previously, most students will learn from almost any test. The process of repeating information while taking a test serves as review. Each time the student reviews a given set of material, progress from mere familiarity to mastery learning is made.

Types of Learning Exams

To function as a learning tool, tests are often used to guide *future* studying. A student retakes the exam until he achieves a high level of proficiency, usually at the 90 to 100% level. When tests are an integral part of the curriculum used to guide learning towards a specified level, as noted above, they are called **mastery learning tests**. In mastery learning, tests or other types of feedback are an indispensable part of the curriculum.

Short answer, essay, and, to some extent, fill-in-the-blank exams can all serve as learning tests. These testing formats can be designed to help students think about new relationships, look at ideas in new ways, reevaluate previously learned material, and apply their own thinking to ideas introduced in class discussions, lectures, and readings. This requires teachers to create interesting or even provocative test questions. Essay exams in particular can be made to force the students to *integrate* what they have learned as well as review old material in a new context. While essay exams are commonly used, many rely largely on recall skills rather than divergent thinking and thus have little potential as learning tools. Properly designed, though, essays can be one of the best formats to use as learning tests.

ABC Tests

On ABC tests, A refers to material learned in class discussions and readings, while B is a paragraph or so of *new material* that is presented *on the exam itself*. Students must then combine the two to produce C, a synthesized answer. Even students who do not know or cannot recall the material presented in class lectures or readings will at least be exposed to (and often learn) the new material presented on such an exam. In order to answer the question correctly, a student must know and understand the material presented in lectures or readings (A) and integrate it with the new information (B) by synthesizing, comparing, and contrasting. The process of creating an original response (C) often results in new learning. For example, basic principles of economics may be presented in class; then, on the exam, a *specific* situation may be provided for students to analyze. Students apply previously learned economic principles to the specific case and their analyses are evaluated by the teacher. In the process, students must think divergently to match appropriate principles to a situation similar to real life.

Some specific examples of ABC test questions and their uses are:

1. In Phase A of an experiment, a white male rat was trained to run through a maze and was rewarded by food placed at the end. This procedure was repeated until the rat was fluent in running through the maze. During Phase B of the experiment, food was no longer placed at the end of the maze. On the first trial, the rat found its way through the maze quickly but did not find food at the end. The rat

continued to run, but he took longer to complete each trial. Eventually, when placed in the maze, he no longer made any effort to find his way to the end.

Based on this information and our class discussion, the most probable reason for the rat's not running to the end of the maze during the later trials would be

  a. The rat was too tired.
*b. The rat was no longer being reinforced.
  c. The rat didn't remember the way.
  d. The rat was no longer hungry.

This question is useful for testing students' understanding of the reinforcement process. If several examples are given and discussed in class, the students should be able to discern very quickly that the rat no longer works his way through the maze because he has no reason to do so—that is, he is no longer being reinforced. In this case, the concept of reinforcement was taught in class (A), new material was presented on the exam (B), and a question was asked whose response (C) requires awareness of both A and B.

2. Inflation in 1984 will be higher than originally predicted. Which of the following assumptions is most likely to serve as the basis of this statement?

  a. Inflation increases progressively from year to year.
*b. Predictors are optimistic and always predict a lower inflation rate than will actually occur.
  c. Inflation in 1984 will be higher because of price increases in all manufactured goods and a freeze on salaries.
  d. The Council of Economic Advisors does not have plans to stop inflation from rising, thus an increase will occur in 1984.

This kind of question might be used in economics, logic, political science, and history classes. After students have learned what inflation is, how predictions are made, and what cannot be assumed from any prediction, this question tests their ability to apply that information. Although it does not ask for specific factual information, it does require previous knowledge to answer correctly. The information called for is very basic and would require familiarity rather than memorization.

3. Eloise's mother told her many times not to play in the street. One day her mother wanted to bake a cake. So she asked Eloise to go to the supermarket with her sisters to buy some eggs. Instead of going with her sisters, Eloise slipped away to play ball in the street. Soon a speeding car raced by. Although Eloise wasn't hurt, her new jacket was torn. Poor Eloise! Her mother sent her to bed without any cake.

This story is much like one of the stories we just read in class. Which of the following stories is most like the story of Eloise?

    a. Jack and the Beanstalk
*b. Peter Rabbit
    c. Snow White and the Seven Dwarfs
    d. Little Red Riding Hood

Variations on this type of question can be used in classes ranging from elementary reading to graduate-level literature. They are more subtle than those that ask for mere factual information, such as Peter Rabbit's mother's name or the names of the seven dwarfs. Instead, this kind of question probes whether students have grasped the meaning of the story they've read and can generalize it to their situations.

Other Types of Learning Exams

While reading test questions, students generally show high levels of concentration. However, as noted previously, concentration may be impeded if anxiety level is too high. Although anxiety can be lowered by allowing students to repeat an alternate form of the exam if they do poorly, a more effective method is to give exams more often. Further-more, *if learning exams are used and it is stressed that their function is actually for learning, the students tend to fear exams less and, at the same time, learn a great deal from them.* There are many kinds of learning exams in addition to the ABC format, so it is possible to test often and still avoid monotony.

Performance Exams

On performance exams, as discussed previously, students demonstrate their knowledge by performing a specified activity. They are then graded according to the skills they display. Because performance exams provide additional practice, and because usually the more practice students have, the more skilled they will become, performance exams are almost always learning exams. A teacher can also increase learning on a performance exam by introducing a new variation on a familiar procedure.

Group Solution Exams

On most exams, each student independently completes his or her own work without consulting other students or resources. On a **group solution exam**, however, several students work together to produce an answer or set of answers. In many ways group solution exams better reflect reality than do individual solution exams because many or most decisions in both the business and academic worlds are made in group situations. These exams provide students with valuable experience in developing solutions in collaboration with others.

There are several ways in which group solution exams can be used. Each is a learning situation, but how much a student learns depends on individual differences. The writer's experience with this type of exam is that poor students learn proportionately *more* than better students. Thus, the group solution exam is one of the few teaching techniques that *tends to equalize original differences*. A student who already knows most of the answers will probably not learn much from this experience, but one who is not as well prepared is likely to benefit a great deal. Group solution exams can be used in any of the following ways:

1. Students are assigned a joint project and individual responsibility for a specific section of it. The entire project is given one grade, and each student receives that grade. This encourages better students to work with poorer ones and ensures that the entire project will be of high quality. Usually the groups are balanced by assigning an equal number of high-, average-, and low-ability students to work together. Or, groups can be divided so that better, average, and below-average students work separately. This forces the better students to challenge each other and gives the slower students a chance to excel among their peers. The main problem with this situation is that the more talented groups often do much better and almost always earn A's while the slower groups almost always earn poorer grades. When this arrangement is used, the teacher may decide not to grade the students or to grade on another basis, such as effort.

2. The class is divided into four- or five-member groups and given an objective test (multiple choice or true or false). Using only *one* answer sheet for all four or five members, each group must unanimously agree on one correct answer for each question. Once agreement is marked on the answer sheet, only then can the group proceed to the next question. Since only one answer sheet is used, each member of the group receives the same grade. This forces students who disagree to discuss their objections with the rest of the group, which should lead to additional learning in addition to agreement on the correct answer. When this technique is used, the group almost always selects the correct answer and enjoys a great deal of discussion and learning in the process.

3. In a variation of the previous method, each student is given a *separate* answer sheet on which to record his or her own answer. The

students can discuss the questions with each other, but if one remains adamant about his own answer, he can use it on his answer sheet and take his own chances on earning or losing a point. There is usually not a great deal of difference between this method and the previous ones.

Group solution exams encourage students to *learn from each other*. In addition, the participants develop the skills needed to solve problems in group situations. Teachers can present new material in this way or use a modified form of an ABC test. New material can be presented in class; then, from additional material given in the group solution exam, the group can work together to find an answer. The answer requires students to use the material learned in class, the material presented in the exam question, and the material from group discussion to produce an answer. Obviously, with this type of exam, most grades tend to be very high and do not reflect individual differences. For this reason, teachers usually don't use group solution exams more than three or four times per marking period. Grades resulting from such activities may also be counted as a regular grade rather than as test grades. One problem with this process, though, is that unless students are highly motivated to complete the assignment, they tend to digress into discussions of nonacademic subjects. If the grade is made an important part of each student's final class grade, digressions may be minimized.

Process Exams

Process exams focus on how students *attack, solve, evaluate, or go about arriving at solutions to problems*. With the process exams, one looks at the total process from beginning to end and, in essence, each step used to find the answer is evaluated. This type of exam produces a great deal of learning because students are able to see specifically where they erred and are rewarded for exactly what is completed properly.

Open Book Exams

Open book exams are probably the most commonly used learning exams. They encourage learning by allowing students to apply their own thoughts and ideas in conjunction with material found in books. As already noted, open book exams tend to be more dependent upon innate understanding, self-expression skills, and ability to reason and evaluate and less dependent upon skills such as writing, spelling, and memory for details. The latter can easily be looked up in reference books or the textbook.

Open book exams, by their very nature, are almost always learning exams. Students are confronted with problems whose solutions they are encouraged to seek in outside sources. Finding the answers results in learning, or at least in increased familiarity with the correct responses. Often, too, in searching for an answer, a student will come across much other information that is of interest, or at least he or she will be exposed to new material.

Take-Home Exams

Homework projects are frequently assigned but not often considered as tests, although they could well be graded like exams. Assignments such as interviewing a local newsmaker or learning to play a musical selection make excellent take-home performance exams. The format works well as long as the learning task is obvious and easily measured and the assignment is very specific.

Divergent Tests

The most commonly used test formats are convergent—that is, each question has a single best answer. Divergent tests, whose questions lead to many possible solutions, are usually used only to measure creativity. These can clearly be learning exams, however. Since students are encouraged to devise many interesting solutions or answers, a great deal of learning can take place. If students are asked the same question again, they can usually answer much quicker and can often increase their number of responses. Repeated exposure to this type of question not only helps students learn, but also improves their fluency, confidence, and familiarity with divergent thought processes (Torrance 1962). There is some evidence that practice with divergent questions leads to increased creativity. In group solution situations, especially if groups are small, this kind of test can be highly productive. If it weren't so difficult to grade, it would probably be used more often.

Essay Exams

Probably the most common learning exam is the essay exam. As stressed in Chapter 11, such tests should *not* merely ask students to repeat what was learned in class, but should have them *apply* previous knowledge in new contexts. For example, in American history, students may study the relationships between America and England from 1620 to the late 1700s and then, on an exam, be asked a question such as: "In what way was America of the 1700s like an apple on a tree? Hint: When a certain stage of ripeness occurs the apple falls off." This question helps students to find a pattern in the various facts they have learned and draw conclusions about certain historical realities. Since students arrive at these conclusions independently, they are more likely to be remembered than information gleaned straight from a text-book or a lecture. Furthermore, in seeking examples to support their conclusions, they are forced into thinking divergently.

Summary

In the process of formative evaluation, the use of learning tests, which are specifically designed to either present new material to students or to require the synthesis of material previously presented in the class-room, becomes an integral part of a curriculum. Some types of learning tests are ABC tests, where new material is presented on a test itself, performance exams, in which learners actually perform a specific activity, group solution exams, in which several students work together for answers, and a whole list of tests with self-evident labels: process, open book, take-home, divergent, essay. Tests as curriculum point away from tests as exclusively measurement tools and toward tests as sources of discovery in the classroom.

Suggested Readings

Aiken, Lewis R. *Psychological Testing and Assessment*. 3d rev. ed. Boston: Allyn and Bacon, 1979. Chapter 11.

Hills, John R. *Exercises in Classroom Measurement*. Columbus, Ohio: Charles E. Merrill, 1976. Chapters 23, 24, 25, 26, 27.

15   Standardized Tests

In Chapter 1 we discussed the history of testing, much of which is actually the history of standardized tests. In this section, we will discuss the specific types of standardized tests and the increasing amount of criticism that is being aimed at them.

Standardized tests are usually defined as tests that are designed by professionals whose sole or primary job responsibility is to develop, evaluate, and refine test questions; produced commercially and sold to school systems, psychologists, and other consumers in the educational marketplace. Most commercially produced tests would be classified as standardized tests. The other type of test, which is the main focus of most tests/measurement and evaluation courses, is the teacher-made test. Such instruments are designed by the classroom teacher to test specific material he or she has taught and take into consideration the needs, abilities, and limitations of a limited group of students. Teacher-made tests are highly individualized, whereas standardized tests are intended to be administered to large numbers throughout the nation and the world.

Standardized tests allow for the comparison of an individual student, group of students, whole class, entire grade, or even an entire school or school district to an even larger group. For example, a teacher may want to know how his or her students' knowledge of English grammar compares with that of *all* other American students. A standardized test would enable the teacher to compare his or her class's scores with a set of norms based upon hundreds or even thousands of students. A teacher may also compare the scores of her fifth graders with the national norms for just fifth graders, or she might measure her fifth grade males' results against the national norms for fifth grade males. Similarly, she might want to check how her students compare with youngsters from parochial or private schools or with children from different geographic regions. Thus, an important purpose of

Key Concepts
Interest inventory
Forced-choice format
Comparable forms
Test battery
Reading readiness test
Diagnostic test
Aptitude test

standardized tests is the making of comparisons that can lead to the location and correction of academic weaknesses.

Standardized tests are also valuable research tools. As time passes, certain tests, such as the *Minnesota Multi-phasic Personality Inventory* (MMPI), generate much useful information. These data help us to understand many things about the different groups that have taken the test. If the MMPI is used for new research, the researcher is better able to interpret his or her findings because of the body of data that already exists from prior studies. For example, researchers may have found that individuals who score in certain ways on the MMPI have predictable personality characteristics. If we then did some new studies, we could rely on past research and assume that those individuals who score in similar ways in our research do so because they also have the personality characteristics the previous research found. We could then conclude that the current research results were produced partly *because* the characteristics found in previous studies are also present in the current subjects. In time, this process helps researchers become very familiar with certain tests. They learn their limitations, usefulness, and expected results in various forms of research.

Evaluating Standardized Tests

One of the best sources of information about tests is the *Eighth Mental Measurement Yearbook* edited by Oscar Buros. The first volume appeared in 1933 and updated editions are published periodically. Different tests are reviewed in each volume, although there is some overlap, and the newer tests, of course, are examined in the more recent editions. Since many of today's tests have been in use for quite some time, their reviews are likely to be found in the earlier volumes.

The reviews in the *Mental Measurement Yearbook* are grouped according to test type, such as achievement tests, vocational tests, interest tests, character tests, projective tests, nonprojective tests, and the like.

And, since the reviews can be quite critical, they can be good indicators of a test's value and limitations. In addition to reviews, each volume includes detailed list of references on each test reviewed.

The Development of Standardized Tests

Standardized tests are developed in a number of ways. The development of an academic standardized test often begins with a survey of the material frequently taught about a given subject. The leading textbooks in that field are analyzed and questions on their content are prepared. For example, for a standardized biology test, professional test writers may study the ten most commonly used biology textbooks. If most of them include a discussion of mitosis and meiosis, then several questions on this topic will appear on the test. If most of the books underscore ecology, the number of ecology-oriented test questions will probably be in proportion to the amount of emphasis the subject received in the majority of books.

This brings us to a major problem with standardized tests—they do not take many possible individual differences into consideration. For example, because textbooks tend to be several years behind current research and thinking, some teachers prefer to use handouts of articles from newspapers, magazines, or paperbacks. In addition, what is stressed in some classes, may not be emphasized in others. Mr. Gomez may feel that biological survival and clinical biology are very important, and thus spend much time discussing them. As a result, if his students take a standardized biology test, they may not compare well to national norms even though they may actually have strong knowledge of several aspects of biology. If the material that the teacher presents does not correspond to the material on the test, the students will probably not do particularly well. A teacher should clearly keep this in mind when using a standardized test.

Today standardized tests are available in almost every school subject—math, art, music, biology, chemistry, history, government, modern and classical languages, and even shorthand and bookkeeping, to name a few.

The Case Against Standardized Tests

Over the past few years, some standardized tests have been severely criticized. For example, an article in *Time* magazine (25 February 1980,

p. 44) discussed criticisms of the Bar Exam, which individuals must pass in order to practice law in most states. Although requirements vary from state to state, the examination is usually made up of approximately 200 multiple-choice items and a set of essay questions. Some people believe that such tests are not relevant measures of competency in the actual tasks required by the profession. As the article stated, "A basic question is whether Bar Exams are good measures of who is qualified to be a lawyer. The major criticism is that while they do test memory, they do not probe ability to do legal research, conduct interviews and argue in court." According to *Time*, California officials have considered conducting an experiment in which Bar applicants would be evaluated on the basis of various innovative tests, including a quiz on a videotaped "mock arbitration proceeding." The argument that the ability to answer multiple-choice and essay questions is not necessarily an indication of the qualities needed to function well in the real world is true of *all* standardized tests—especially those that purport to screen entrants into professions (teaching, medicine, accounting, and the like).

Others feel that such tests may be manipulated to artificially raise requirements and thus keep the number of new professionals low. Since there is a limit to the amount of business available, practicing professionals (and those who administer exams usually fall in this category) may be anxious to reduce the number of new practitioners. This can be easily accomplished by raising the minimum passing score. While some may argue that this is one way in which the professions may raise their standards, as has already been noted, there is little cause to believe that higher test scores reflect higher competence in performing practical tasks. One can thus see why some might argue that these tests for the professions, and even in the public schools, serve the purpose of reducing competition primarily by reducing numbers.

Standardized Tests and Bias

The most common objection to standardized tests is that they are biased against various groups, especially the poor and minorities. Study after study has shown that black students consistently score lower on standardized tests than do white students. For example, in North Carolina 18 percent more blacks failed a standardized math test at the junior-high level than did comparable whites. Middle-class black students failed more often than middle-class white students—and even the sons and daughters of black college graduates failed more often than their white counterparts.

A common reaction to this state of affairs is to attack the tests—their validity, reliability, relevance, and, especially cultural bias. Those who find the tests culturally biased contend that because blacks are raised in a different cultural milieu than whites, they should be tested *on their knowledge of their own culture* rather than on their familiarity with the white culture. In an article in *Newsweek* (22 October 1979, p. 27) Jordan, an opponent of this viewpoint, argued that such criticism is not well-founded. He states:

> The bottom line is this: if we try to defend our right to be incompetent, we lose. . . . None of the excuses we use for failure, no matter how valid the excuses seem to be, change a thing. When blacks fail, blacks suffer. We must become the masters of our own destinies. We must accept full responsibility for our failures and stop blaming "the system." Only then can we begin accepting full credit for our successes. Instead of opposing the competency tests, let's conquer them. Let's make sure our children pass them. If they write them in Greek, let's teach black kids Greek. . . . Whatever we have to do, let's do it to make sure our children pass these competency tests. Black people simply can't afford to enter the 21st century rated "incompetent."

The seemingly endless debate about standardized tests will probably continue for some time. Hundreds of articles on this topic have appeared in newspapers, magazines, professional journals, and other publications, and the reader is encouraged to consult the *Education Index* and *Readers' Guide to Periodic Literature* to familiarize further information about both sides of the argument.

Interest Inventories

Among the more successful standardized tests are interest inventories, used mainly in vocational and educational guidance. They help people determine their general interests and preferences and guide them in considering alternatives.

Because students have so much freedom of choice among occupations today, many need assistance in determining those that suit their abilities, talents, and interests. A number of occupational interest surveys have been developed to meet this need. A typical question in such a survey might ask a student if he or she would prefer, for example, to study and do research on plants, to own a plant store and sell plants, or to write stories about plants for an ecology magazine. The student must indicate both the most favored and least favored activities. This is called a **forced-choice format**: the student must respond in a definite and specific way to a restricted set of items. Note that by selecting both the most and least preferred items from among three choices *rank ordering* automatically occurs.

Many interest inventories are developed by writing vast numbers of questions and posing them to people who are happy or successful in their work—salespeople, teachers, electricians, cosmeticians, writers, dentists, and so forth. From this, a set of norms are developed—that is, it is found that successful teachers tend to answer in certain ways while successful electricians tend to answer in others. When an individual takes the inventory, his or her responses are compared with the norms for various professions. If the test taker's profile is very similar to that of successful bankers, it is assumed that he or she has the characteristics that could make him or her successful in that line of work. If a subject's profile is totally different from that of successful salespeople, it is assumed that he or she does not have the characteristics that would lead to success in that area. For example, most salespeople who like their jobs would probably rather own a flower shop and sell flowers, while most scientists who like their jobs would most likely prefer to do research on flowers. Such logic, though, does not hold for all questions.

An individual may select the answers that are most similar to those of a successful nuclear physicist without having the necessary intelligence, ability or opportunity to become one. These interest inventories *do not predict* that a person will be successful in certain occupations; they only indicate that such fields should be explored. Once an occupational preference scale indicates that a student, for example, would make a good mechanic, he or she can investigate the possibilities by interviewing mechanics, reading appropriate books and magazines, and talking with teachers, counselors, friends, and family about this possible career goal. These tests can be useful guides, but they should not be allowed to dictate behavior. There are many cases in which they are clearly wrong—although most of the time they tend to be quite helpful.

The Kuder Preference Test

One of the better-known interest surveys is the Kuder Preference Test. There are a number of forms, such as the General Interest Survey, which is used primarily in high schools, and the Kuder Record-Vocational, which has higher-level vocabulary and is more often used for high school graduates, college students, and college graduates. All of the forms are very similar in their use of such forced-choice questions as:

Select the activity in which you would most like to involve yourself, and then select the activity in which you would least involve yourself:

a. Do surgery.
b. Film surgical operations.
c. Write books on surgery.

An advantage of the Kuder is that many forms are accompanied by a self-scoring answer booklet. The student records his or her responses to each question by putting two pinholes on the answer sheet—one under the most preferred category, and one under the least preferred category. When the answer sheet is removed and the booklet is opened, the student can follow a series of lines and circles printed on the back of the sheet to arrive at his or her total score for each area. The Kuder usually profiles each of the following general areas of interest: (1) outdoor, (2) mechanical, (3) computational, (4) scientific, (5) persuasive, (6) artistic, (7) literary, (8) musical, (9) social service, and (10) clerical. Despite the usual accuracy of the scales, to avoid unnecessary errors, Kuder now suggests that scores should be interpreted according to the basic categories rather than matched to specific occupations.

Strong's Vocational Interest Blank (SVIB)

In the same category as the Kuder Preference Tests are Strong's Vocational Interest Blank, the Minnesota Vocational Interest Inventory, and the Ohio Vocational Interest Inventory. The earliest and probably the best, is Strong's. Cronbach (1970, p. 460) states the Strong's "has been a landmark in testing history, as renowned in its way as the Stanford-Binet." The research for Strong's was begun in the 1920s, and although researchers have revised the original format, the changes have been minimal.

Dr. Strong based his original test on the theory that those who were successful in a particular occupation probably shared similar traits and had similar interests and personalities. From these interests, a profile can be developed. For example, it may be that successful engineers tend to enjoy doing puzzles in their spare time but do not enjoy playing football. High school seniors who have a similar profile may, likewise, be good engineers.

The main concern about all vocational interest inventories is the stability of what they purport to measure. Do an individual's interests change so drastically that at age 37 they are totally different from what they were at age 17? Campbell (1969) found that "test-retest correlations over 30 days averaged slightly over .90, dropping to about .75 over 20 years for adults and .55 over 35 years for men first tested at age 16." Thus there is a good deal of stability, but over a long period of time interests do change. Although, for example, a high percentage of college students change their major field of study, this may or may not be reflected in changed scores on the Kuder. Many researchers have concluded that many basic personality traits become fixed at an early age.

These traits include aggressiveness, gregariousness, bookishness, and other broad styles; others argue that a student's failure to develop new interests in college could indicate an unstimulating *college program* and would not clearly prove that interests do indeed remain stable. Finally, it is important to stress again that a person's *interests* in an area, even if very stable, do not necessarily indicate appropriate ability, although it would seem that areas one is interested in do provide the impetus for doing well in related occupations.

Interpreting Interest Surveys While classroom teachers are occasionally called upon to discuss the results of interest surveys with students, this is primarily the task of counselors, psychologists, and others involved in vocational counseling. For the most part, students tend to be less threatened by interest questionnaires than they are by psychological or ability tests. Thus, to some degree, these tests may serve as starting points for discussions about interests and abilities. For those who lack extensive training in their interpretation, these tools are of limited usefulness, but every teacher should have a general understanding of their use, possible abuses, and limitations.

Standardized Achievement Tests

Because the number of standardized achievement tests has increased tremendously, we will discuss only a few of the more common ones. Most have similar formats and are based on the same theory, so familiarity with a few will allow one to understand and use most of them. Among the best known and most popularly used standardized achievement tests are the California Achievement Test, the Iowa Test of Basic Skills, and the Stanford Achievement Tests.

The first step in the development of a standardized achievement test is the delineation of topics to be covered and the grouping of this material into sections. For example, an elementary school mathematics test should obviously cover addition, subtraction, multiplication, division, fractions, decimals, mixed numbers, simple story problems, money, and counting. The next step is to develop questions and attempt to rank them in the approximate order of difficulty. The proposed questions should then be field tested on a sample group of students from different geographic regions, school sizes, abilities, and economic levels and the results utilized to revise the test. During the revision process, it is important that each question be thoroughly discussed. Gronlund (1976, p. 285) suggests that the following procedure be used in evaluating test items:

1. The difficulty of each test item should be determined.
2. The discriminating power of each test item should be calculated.
3. The effectiveness of each distractor for each test item should be determined.
4. The equivalence of the items in the various forms of the test should be estimated.
5. The adequacy of the directions, the time limits, and the test format should be evaluated.

Items that are judged too easy or too difficult and items that do not discriminate between high and low achievers are often removed from the test. Although there are no strict cut-off points, questions that are correctly answered approximately 98 percent of the time and those that are incorrectly answered just as frequently are often omitted. Usually, though, test developers leave one or two extremely easy items at the beginning of the test and one or two extremely difficult ones at the end. Some tests go through one or two revisions before they are finally produced commercially, while others must go through several. Ideally, all tests should be continually revised.

Before a test is marketed, its final form is administered to a representative group of students to establish norms, reliability, validity, and other measures. One of the main advantages of standardized tests is the availability of national norms—thus the pretesting process is important to the development of an effective, useful final product. As previously discussed, it is very difficult to develop good questions. Except in some basic areas, such as mathematics, it is extremely difficult to construct a good standardized test. The development of good social studies, history, science, and English tests requires a tremendous amount of expertise and experimentation.

Comparable Forms

Many standardized tests offer **comparable forms**—that is, one series of tests (all of which are similar except for degree of difficulty) that can cover all levels from grades one through twelve. One form may be used for grades one to three, another form for grades four to six, another for grades seven to nine, and a final one for grades ten to twelve. A school system often adopts one brand of test and uses the same forms year after year so the results can be compared. For example, one may want to know how a first-grader's performance compares to that of others at the same level, how her performance in third grade compares with that of other third graders, and also how well she is doing in grade three compared to her performance in grade one. Even though she may still be below the national norms, she may have improved tremendously since grade one. In addition, if comparable forms are used, it is fairly easy to determine the specific areas in which a student has or has not improved.

Test Batteries

Standardized achievement tests that cover a large number of academic skills are called **test batteries**. This format makes it possible to evaluate a student's strengths and weaknesses in specific areas. For example, one student may be clearly above average in math, but below average in spelling. In addition, each major subject area often has a subtest: the reading part of a test battery may include both vocabulary and comprehension.

Most schools use test batteries to evaluate their learning program as a whole. No one lives in isolation; everyone must eventually compete to some degree with others in the outside world. It is therefore useful to evaluate individuals in comparison to most people (or certain people) throughout the country. Test batteries help educators to do this. A school's program may lag behind, for example, in spelling or computational skills while concentrating on other areas—and its administrators may not realize that this is happening. Standardized achievement tests help schools to continually evaluate their effectiveness and the amount of progress (or lack of progress) being made. Thus we can see that the interpretation of standardized achievement tests is an important skill for teachers and administrators to acquire.

Achievement Tests in Specific Areas

In addition to evaluating students' skills in such basic areas as language arts, math, and social studies, many teachers want to assess progress in a specific area, such as reading ability, or explore students' aptitudes. We shall now discuss some of these kinds of tests.

Reading Tests Reading tests are probably the most commonly used standardized achievement tests because reading is recognized as the most important skill needed to do well in school. A good reader who has a high level of comprehension is likely to do fairly well in most courses. Although standardized tests are usually used to evaluate the effectiveness of an entire reading program, they are also commonly used to identify pupils who need remedial work in individual areas of weakness. Because reading is such a crucial skill, most school systems try to provide extra help in this area. Such well-known standardized tests as the Gates-MacGinitie Reading Tests, the Nelson Reading Test, the Davis Reading Test, and the Iowa Silent Reading Test help them to identify both areas of their reading curriculum and individual students that require special attention.

There are also a number of **reading readiness tests** that indicate whether or not a student has developed sufficiently to begin to learn how to read. One well-known reading readiness test, the Boehm Test of Basic Concepts, evaluates a student's grasp of such basic concepts as biggest (Which of these dogs is the biggest?) and nearest (Which boat in the picture is nearest to the dock?). These exams test a student's grasp of the ideas and concepts believed necessary to begin learning to read. They are most concerned with a youngster's maturity—his or her understanding of verbal communication; recognition of letters, words, and numbers; recognition of words in simple sentences; and ability to copy symbols, letters, and numbers. To some degree, reading readiness tests are actually achievement tests in that they tell whether or not a student has achieved what are considered to be the prerequisites of learning how to read.

Diagnostic Tests

Diagnostic tests, another kind of standardized test, attempt to determine specifically *why* a student has difficulty in some areas, such as reading. They indicate the level at which the student is performing and whether or not he is having problems in given areas. To some degree, such tests are also achievement tests, but they tend to have more test items that measure specific reading functions, and the questions can be isolated by type to provide scores for each function covered. In addition, the test items are often based on a detailed analysis of specific skills related to successful performance. These test items are usually developed by studying pupils' most common errors—for example, missing the meaning of a sentence because punctuation was ignored. Although diagnostic tests are available for many subjects, they are most commonly used in reading and arithmetic. Among the most widely used diagnostic reading rests are the Gates-McKillop Reading Diagnostic Tests, the Stanford Diagnostic Reading Test, and the Doren Diagnostic Reading Test.

As we have noted, diagnostic tests are similar to achievement tests—but they are designed for pupils of below-average performance and intended to identify learning weaknesses. For this reason, they do not indicate the level of proficiency of above-average students. A high score on a subtest means only that this is not an area of weakness for the pupil—not that she is highly proficient. Furthermore, although a diagnostic test may indicate both the frequency and kinds of errors a student tends to make, they do not directly explain the cause of the errors. It is not usually difficult to identify errors, but determining and remedying their causes can be quite a challenge. For example, if a student consistently ignores punctuation, it would seem that he should be trained to be more accurate in obeying punctuation signs. This, though, may not be the solution to the problem. It could be that the student rushes his reading or reads phrases and not words, which causes him to miss punctuation signs (as happens to most of us, even the best readers). On the other hand, it may be that the student does not fully understand the concept of punctuation and needs to be taught the rules or given practice in applying the rules.

Aptitude Tests

In theory, aptitude tests are designed to predict *future* performance while achievement tests are intended to assess *present* performance. Actually, however, there is not a great deal of difference between the two. It is difficult to measure aptitude without measuring achievement. For example, it is difficult to accurately measure the math aptitude of a person who has never been exposed to mathematical concepts; exposure tends to greatly affect the indicators of aptitude.

Nonetheless, aptitude tests evaluate how well an individual can perform in one area and this information is used to indicate potential achievement in the same or a related area. As Gronlund (1976, p. 316) states:

> A common distinction is that achievement tests measure what a pupil has learned, and aptitude tests measure his *ability* to learn new tasks. Although this appears to be a clear distinction, it oversimplifies the problem and covers up some important similarities and differences. Actually, *both* types measure what a pupil has learned, and both are useful for predicting his success in learning new tasks.
>
> The major differences lie in:
>
> 1. the types of learning measured by each test, and
> 2. the types of predictions for which each is most useful [or successful].

Kinds of tests can be classified on a continuum that ranges from tests on specific content (for instance, something that a student learned in a class) to tests of general skills and abilities that are not based on traditional learning (such as working with mazes or reproducing designs with colored blocks). Although to some degree, one may learn how to solve mazes or reproduce designs, most schools do not have specific programs to teach students these skills. Therefore, they tend to be somewhat more dependent upon innate abilities or early home environment than on formal education. Practice may make perfect in some cases, but for the most part, even though it can improve performance, practice usually cannot increase abilities a tremendous amount in a short period of time. A child who consistently scores around 60 on I.Q. tests will probably never become a cardiovascular surgeon or a Supreme Court justice—no matter how hard he or she studies or practices.

What are now called aptitude tests have traditionally been known as intelligence tests. The change in terminology occurred because many people began to associate the concept of intelligence with such inherited traits as eye and hair color and because there is much debate over the definition of intelligence. To avoid controversy, the term *test of scholastic aptitude* was adopted because it more accurately describes what is actually being measured. We will thus use the more recent terminology throughout this book even though in most cases one could substitute the term *intelligence test* without distorting meaning.

As already noted, scholastic aptitude tests measure performance based on learned abilities rather than strictly innate capacities. Of course, it is accepted that such performance is dependent on both innate intelligence and previous experience. By necessity, any conclusions we draw concerning capacity for learning must be inferred from the results of these tests.

Although some scholastic aptitude tests yield only a single score, most provide a series of separate scores for each basic area. The advantage of single-score tests is that they are quick and easy to administer—often taking only a half-hour or so. The Otis-Lennon Mental Ability Test and the Henmon-Nelson Test of Mental Ability are good examples of this type of exam.

Many group tests are designed to yield both verbal and nonverbal scores. The California Short-Form Test of Mental Maturity is a good example of this variety. It contains four separately timed subjects—vocabulary, analogies, sequences, and memory. To obtain a verbal score the vocabulary and memory subtests are combined, and to obtain a nonverbal score the analogies and sequences subtests are combined. It is important to differentiate between verbal and nonverbal scores because academic success tends to require verbal abilities, whereas the success in many occupations requires nonverbal skills. A child could be quite bright and clearly have excellent nonverbal skills, but if she is deficient in verbal skills, she will probably do poorly in school, or at least have a more difficult time. A verbal score provides the best prediction for academic success. Nonetheless, some handicap or problem could cause a bright student to be deficient in this area, a situation that may be indicated if a high nonverbal score occurs in conjunction with a low verbal one. This is why Gronlund (1976, p. 323) concludes that both nonverbal and verbal scores provide a more satisfactory estimate of a pupil's underdeveloped learning potential than does a single score.

Most standardized aptitude tests yield both verbal and nonverbal scores and provide several other measures as well. For example, the Academic Promise Test has four parts—verbal, or the ability to understand word meanings; numerical, or the ability to use math skills; abstract reasoning, or the ability to reason and manipulate concepts; and language usage, or the ability to use or recognize correct grammar, punctuation, spelling, and word usage.

The Wechsler Individual I.Q. Test

David Wechsler was for many years a clinical psychologist at the Bellevue Hospital in New York City. As part of his clinical work, he was required to help people with many kinds of mental and emotional problems. Wechsler believed that a person's intellect was an important factor to consider in making decisions about psychological disposition. Furthermore, he was convinced that intellectual performance was a complex product of both biological development, genetics, and experience. Because most of the available I.Q. tests gave only a single score, Wechsler decided to develop a new test, which he completed in 1939 and called the Wechsler-Bellevue Scale. Although at first designed for children, it was later revised for use with adults. The original Wechsler-Bellevue had almost a dozen subtests for each age level, with each subtest devoted to a single basic task. This form became the standard instrument in military clinical testing, especially for cases in which there was brain damage or emotional disturbance from World War II.

The Wechsler series in use today consists of three basic tests—the Wechsler Preschool and Primary Scale of Intelligence, for children from ages four to six and a half; the Wechsler Intelligence Scale for Children (WISC-R)—Revised Version, for ages seven to sixteen; and the Wechsler Adult Intelligence Scale (WAIS). These three scales follow the same basic format and include many similar kinds of tests that are adjusted to appropriate levels of difficulty. Scores are reported as norms for grade and age levels. Used primarily in special placement cases, the

Wechsler tests are individual I.Q. tests that, in most states, must be administered by a licensed psychologist or other highly trained person. Teachers, though, should be familiar with these tests and their uses.

Summary

Standardized tests are usually defined as tests that are designed by professionals whose primary job responsibility is to develop, evaluate, and refine test questions; they are produced commercially and sold to school systems, psychologists, and other consumers in education. Standardized tests allow for comparison of individual students or groups of students to an even larger group. They are valuable research tools. References and reviews for standardized tests are available to the teacher. One of the more successful standardized tests is the interest inventory that is used mainly in vocational and educational guidance. Standardized achievement tests help schools to evaluate the amount of progress being made, and their interpretation is an important skill for teachers and administrators. Diagnostic tests, which attempt to determine *why* a student has difficulty in some area, and aptitude tests, (intelligence tests) which in theory are designed to predict future performance, are discussed in this chapter. In the past few years, there has been much criticism of standardized tests, including their bias against certain groups. The reader is encouraged to familiarize further information about both sides of the argument by consulting *Education Index* and *Readers' Guide to Periodical Literature*.

Suggested Readings

Aiken, Lewis R. *Psychological Testing and Assessment*. 3d rev. ed. Boston: Allyn and Bacon, 1979. Chapters 5, 6, 7, 8, 9, 10.

Gronlund, Norman E. *Measurement and Evaluation in Teaching*. 2d rev. ed. New York: Macmillan, 1971. Chapters 12, 13, 14, 15.

Noll, Victor H., Dale P. Scannell and Robert C. Craig. *Introduction to Educational Measurement*. 4th rev. ed. Boston: Houghton Mifflin, 1979.

Sax, Gilbert. *Principles of Educational and Psychological Measurement and Evaluation*. Belmont, Calif.: Wadsworth, 1974. Chapters 11, 12, 13, 14, 15, 16.

Thorndike, Robert L. and Elizabeth Hagen. *Measurement and Evaluation in Psychology and Education*. 4th rev. ed. New York: John Wiley and Sons, 1977. Chapters 8, 9.

Part III
Grading, Rating, and Social Measurement

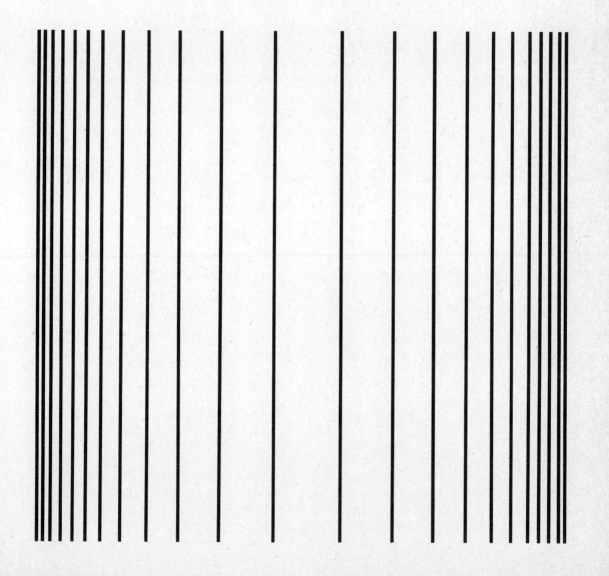

16   Grading

Grading is an important aspect of the entire educational process. To parents, and often to students, a grade represents a sacrosanct evaluation of a youngster's overall level of performance, ability, and achievement in a course of study. It is often said that students work primarily for grades, and that grades are the main means of communicating to parents how well their child is doing. Thus, in our education and achievement-oriented society, rightly or wrongly, grades are important.

Assigning grades is frequently a difficult task. Grades are actually quite imprecise measures based on subjective judgment. Can a teacher really know whether a student has more artistic ability than practical ability or whether he or she is just unmotivated? Even in areas such as mathematics and science, where objective tests are used, subjectivity remains, especially in borderline cases. In addition, grading represents a tremendous amount of tedious, repetitive work for teachers. Grading 200 math papers or 200 essay exams, most of which may well say about the same thing, is probably one of the most unrewarding aspects of teaching. Nonetheless, students and parents generally *want* grades, and teachers find that grades are one way to affect students' behavior.

Grading Systems

Letter Grades

A **letter grade** is an evaluation that is condensed into a single symbol. The most common grading system is ABCDE (or F). Sometimes numerical equivalents are assigned, with an A equal to 4, a B equal to 3, and so on. Other systems are also used, such as an A equal to $\sqrt{++}$, A B equal to $\sqrt{+}$, a C equal to $\sqrt{}$, a D equal to $\sqrt{-}$, and an F equal to 0.

Letter grades are a quick, easy, convenient, and familiar method of summarizing a student's progress. They seem to be useful as motivators for many students and are also good predictors of future grades. Unfortunately, their meanings often vary within schools and among teachers and they may encourage competitiveness that can lead to cheating and unnecessary anxiety, reflect bias, force academic conformity and stifle creativity, and do not have a correlation with future occupational success.

Pass-Fail

The **pass-fail system** is actually a capsulized form of letter grades. Because only two grades are possible—pass or no pass (fail)—it is probably the easiest and most convenient grading technique and removes the pressure of competing for letter grades. Some educators believe that this system encourages creativity because students may explore areas they find interesting or pertinent to their needs without concern about earning low grades. Since only gross assessments are made, the pressure on both the students and teachers is reduced. On the other hand, some believe that the pass-fail system encourages only the minimal levels of performance needed to earn a passing grade. The grades cannot be used to predict future academic success and make it difficult for employers and others to differentiate varying degrees of academic achievement. Furthermore, when only two grades are available, drawing the line between acceptable and unacceptable levels of performance becomes especially difficult, and more substandard students are likely to be passed.

Checklists

A common criticism of letter grades and pass-fail systems is that they do not help a student direct his or her energies in directions that will facilitate improvement. Therefore, many educators feel that in addition to, or instead of, the familiar letter grades, detailed feedback that identifies strengths and weaknesses should be utilized. Many school systems have developed detailed *checklists* that examine performance in specific areas. For example, a mathematics checklist for elementary grades may evaluate skills in basic addition, addition of three or more numbers, addition with carrying, basic subtraction, double-digit subtraction, subtraction with borrowing, and so forth. Mastery within each of these categories is indicated as high adequate, inadequate, or nonexistent. Even such an elaborate system can fail, however, if parents, students, teachers, and administrators do not take the time to utilize it. In fact, many teachers protest the tremendous amount of work the lists entail. The fact remains, though, as Feldmesser has stated:

> To a student in a biology course, for example, it is not enough to know that his lab work was weak while his grasp of abstract concepts was strong, and that he was high on understanding of cell structure but low on understanding of ecological relationships and middling on understanding of reproductive systems. He will also want to know what it all adds up to: whether, all things considered, he did well or poorly or something in between. The grade thus satisfies a natural curiosity, but, while that seems like a virtue in itself, the grade does more. It helps a student decide whether, taking one thing with another, biology is a field in which further inputs of his resources are likely to be productive for him, or whether he should switch to another field. (1972, p. 67)

Furthermore, Feldmesser found that when grading was dropped, instructors spent much less time on evaluation and either directly or indirectly conveyed to their classes that they did not care about students or helping them with their work.

Letters to parents may be used instead of checklists. They are usually extremely individualized and discuss each student's strengths and weaknesses without some of the extraneous material checklists might include. They allow the teacher to emphasize desired topics and to phrase suggestions in ways that will not discourage parents or students. Specific individual problems, such as difficulty in concentration, or consistent failure to bring needed supplies to class, can also be mentioned. Unfortunately, personal letters can become quite time-consuming, and if a teacher is not well acquainted with each student, he or she may be forced to overgeneralize, giving feedback that is not really useful. In addition, some teachers are not skilled at tactfully conveying students' weaknesses to parents. Because this system is quite subjective, it makes it difficult to compare students and to reach decisions that will justify failing a student or putting the student in a slower class.

Parent-teacher conferences may also be used to supplement or replace other grading systems. They open lines of communication, allowing teachers to comment on students' performance and parents to ask questions and raise specific issues. Teachers can thus learn more about each student's home environment while parents gain important familiarity with and understanding of the school situation. Unfortunately, time restrictions can make such meetings difficult to schedule with every parent. In addition, many teachers and parents find such encounters uncomfortable and lack the communication skills that are needed for optimal benefit. Finally, if parent-teacher conferences are used in place of other grading systems, there are usually no written records for parents to take home and they are left with only general impressions.

In theory, some combination of all the grading techniques we've examined would probably be most effective. Since each method has its strengths and weaknesses, utilization of all of them, at least once during the school year, should yield the best assessment. In practice, many other alternatives to the traditional A-B-C-D-E gradings system have been tried, but in almost all cases, schools eventually return to this traditional system. Despite its limitations and drawbacks, in the United States this system is consistently chosen over others.

For example, one school system attempted to do away with the letter grades and substituted an experimental program in which more meaningful evaluational comments "works well (adequately, poorly) by him or herself" were used. After two years the parents and students overwhelmingly voted to reinstate the traditional letter-grade system. The only ones who wanted to keep the new system were the teachers! The students themselves simply changed the evaluations the school used into letter grades. For example, they thought of the comment "works well by him- or herself" as an A. To utilize the best of *both* systems, many schools have decided to compromise, giving both letter grades and some other more meaningful evaluational mark. Thus, established patterns and certain advantages of the letter-grade system seem to require its continued usage.

Systems for Judging Student Performance

There are probably as many systems of assigning grades as there are teachers. Nonetheless, most usually use some combination of the following basic methods.

Grading by Absolute Value

Under this approach, 90 to 100 equals an A, 80 to 89, a B, 70 to 79, a C, 60 to 69, a D, and 59 and below, E. The problem with this system is that it is difficult to use in creative courses, such as art, or when students are expected to achieve mastery, as in foreign language and mathematics. Even though D may be a passing grade, a student who has received a D in Spanish is unlikely to possess the basic skills needed to progress to a higher level of complexity.

Grading by a Curve or Distribution of Scores

A teacher who used this system might give the top three students A's, the next six students B's, the middle twelve students C's, the next six students D's, and the bottom three students E's. This system is not difficult to use if the class curve is normal (which is not likely for teacher-made tests; see Chapter 23 for a discussion of the normal curve). In the past, the majority of students received C's based on the concept of the normal curve, but presently as a result of grade inflation, the most common grade is a B. Thus, a teacher may elect to give the top 25 percent of the class A's, the next 40 percent B's, the next 25 percent C's, and the last 10 percent D's and E's. When using a curve in everyday classroom contexts, there are no rigid rules to follow. But it is usually a good idea for teachers to look at the distribution of grades and the level of test difficulty in other similar classes to ensure that their grading standards coincide with those of other teachers and of the school system in general. While a teacher may prefer not to pattern his or her teaching after that of colleagues, comparisons are nonetheless necessary in order for him or her to develop what the students perceive as reasonable standards. Many teachers also use their own grade distributions from previous years for purposes of comparison.

Criterion-Referenced Grading

Grading by absolute values and according to a curve are norm-referenced systems; that is, a class norm is used to evaluate each student and assign a grade. Criterion-referenced grading, on the other hand, is based on individual goals, standards, and needs. For example, Sam may take biology as an elective and seek to learn only the basic concepts, while Janine may intend to become a biology major and hope to lay a firm foundation for further study. The grading standards for these two students would differ according to their goals—simple familiarity with versus in-depth understanding of the subject matter. Their grades would depend on the degree to which each reached his or her goals. Obviously, Janine would be required to learn a great deal more about biology in order to succeed. On the other hand, if Sam wants to be an English teacher, while Janine only seeks a basic knowledge of English in order to facilitate communication, their roles and tasks would be reversed in English class. Sam would be required to perform at a higher level than Janine in order to earn the same grade. To accommodate differing student goals, some schools offer chemistry for future science majors, for example, and chemistry for future home economics majors, as well as chemistry for youngsters in non-college preparatory programs. Such a system combines both criterion-referenced and norm-referenced grading; that is, students in each class meet certain basic criteria, and from these a set of norms is developed. However, even within special-interest groupings students' goals will differ, and this factor should not be overlooked.

Another form of a criterion-referenced grading is based on each student's past performance. If a student has always done very poorly in spelling, for example, but shows some improvement, he or she may merit an A, regardless of the fact that the improved performance remains substandard in comparison to the spelling skills of others in the class. This form of grading is somewhat difficult to use, however, in that it is easier for students at lower levels of performance to improve and thus earn higher grades. Furthermore, since it is often assumed that if a student has earned an A, he or she excels in that area, grading according to degree of improvement rather than relative performance can be very misleading. In arguing for criterion-referenced grading, Lindeman et al. (1979, p. 200) observed: "There seems to be a tendency among teachers to regard a mark as a kind of composite reward (or punishment) for good (or bad) behavior, for trying hard (or not so hard), and for accomplishment (or lack of it) of instructional goals. As such, a grade is almost entirely without utility." They believe that a grade should be a reflection of specific course goals and not a measure of how well a student comprehends or follows directions or gets along with others. In actuality, however, these factors and other equally subjective criteria probably play extremely important roles in the grading process.

One of the most important functions of a grade is to motivate, but as Feldmesser notes (1972, p. 11), "If a grade is to motivate, then a high grade must be a never guaranteed but ever possible outcome; a low grade, therefore, must be an avoidable but also ever possible outcome." In other words the possibility of a low grade should produce levels of anxiety in students that can be reduced by studying. Feldmesser's evidence indicates that this function of grades is effective only when the anxiety level is moderate, and when the student is confident that he or she is able to do well, has a history of doing well, and has the skills and abilities to achieve.

Grades, of course, are far from infallible. There is much evidence to show that it is difficult to predict performance in the workplace or future academic progress on the basis of past grades. Those who are forced to make such evaluations should be familiar with the possible pitfalls. Grades are no more than estimates, and, as Feldmesser states (1972, p. 71), "A grade is not a judgment of [a student's] moral worth, but merely an informational statement, and a tentative and fallible one at that. . . . In the end, it is their lack of validity that emerges as the most legitimate criticism of grades. Whatever valuable functions they could perform in the abstract will not be performed if grades are not valid measures of learning; and all too often, they are not."

Components of a Grade

Generally a course grade is a summary of performance on homework, class projects, tests, quizzes, and the like. In the past, teachers often relied heavily on objective examinations that were given two to three times per marking period and a final exam that was intended to provide some measure of a student's retention of material learned early in the course, as well as his or her ability to integrate information presented throughout the entire course. Nowadays, teachers tend to test more frequently and include other criteria in evaluating performance, but most underutilize the wide variety of exams discussed earlier, such as performance, group, oral, and take-home. In most cases, the larger the number of measures and the greater the variety of examinations, the more accurate the final grade will be in assessing a student's ability in a certain academic area.

Organizing Information into a Grade

The easiest way to determine a grade for a course or semester is to establish the weight of the various elements of performance and average accordingly. Teachers usually try to work out a system that is simple and efficient. For example, exam scores may comprise mathematically 50 percent of the total grade and all other scores the other 50 percent. Two averages are then calculated: one for exams and one for all other coursework. The average of these two scores then becomes the final grade. If exams are worth 75 percent of the final grade, separate average scores for exams and for all other coursework are similarly calculated, but they are combined differently. The exam score average is given three times as much weight as the other average. For example, if a student has a B average on exams (B = 3 points) and an A average on other coursework (A = 4 points), her grade would be determined thusly:

$3 + 3 + 3 + 4 = 13$; $13 \div 4 = 3.25$.

Components of a final grade usually count half, a third, a fourth, or some equally simple fraction in order to make the calculations easy.

Problems of Validity and Reliability of Grades

Grades are of more concern to students than any other aspect of school. Yet all too often the usefulness of grades and tests as predictors of performance are called into question by such occurrences as:

London—Twenty-four of twenty-five students in a high-level psychology program at West Ham College of Technology graduated with honors recently. They had all previously been rejected as college material because of low test scores. (*Parade,* 24 April 1966)

The federal Upward Bound program selected 20,000 high school students whose grades failed to match their ability and sent them to 220 college campuses for summertime remedial work. Eighty percent later entered college and only 23 percent failed to finish their first year, which is roughly similar to the average freshmen dropout rate. (*Time,* 3 October 1965)

This demonstrates that students who did poorly in high school, based on their grades, could succeed in college when given appropriate remedial work. Their high school grades were not accurate predictors of their college performance.

Studies of grades often find that they have little or no predictive value or, even worse, that they have a negative correlation with other criteria. Hoyt (1965), after analyzing over 45 studies, concluded that college grades bear little or no relationship to any measure of adult accomplishment.

Dr. Eli Ginzberg studied a group of Columbia University graduate students who had won fellowships between 1944 and 1950. The study attempted to determine how successful the 342 students had become 14 years after the completion of their degrees. The findings found that "students who graduated from college with honors, who had won scholastic medals, or had been elected Phi Beta Kappa, were more likely to be in the lower professional performance levels than students who had not distinguished themselves in college." Those who are successful at earning grades are evidently not as successful at earning their way in the world of work. In reference to this situation, Harold Fitzgerald (*Look,* 23 January 1968, p. 52) said: "Always be kind to your A and B students. Someday, one of them will return to your campus as a good professor. And also be kind to your C+ students. Someday, one of them will build you a two-million-dollar science laboratory."

Another survey, conducted by a research team headed by Dr. Philip B. Price, found that there is almost no relationship between the grades a medical student receives and his later performance. Dr. Price stated, "It is a shocking finding to a medical educator like myself who has spent his professional life selecting applicants for admission to medical school" (personal interview). He added that his research has caused him to question the adequacy of grades, both in selecting candidates for medical school and in measuring students' progress.

While grades in general may not be good predictors of career performance, most studies conclude that, in general, high school grades *are* good indicators of success in undergraduate school. In one study of 383 students who ranked in the lower portions of their high school classes and went to college, 64 percent later withdrew because of scholastic difficulties and 73 percent had unsatisfactory grades. Only two students out of the 383 earned grade averages of B or better. The primary reason that high school grades quite reliably predict success in college is that *college grades measure essentially the same qualities that high school grades measure.* Both reflect students' performance in those areas that contribute to earning good grades, such as memory, communication skills, and willingness to conform. And it is likely that the standards of performance are very similar at both educational levels.

The fact that high school grades are good predictors of college grades but that neither relates to professional success should be of serious concern. First of all, it calls into question the *validity of grades* and the criteria teachers use in assigning grades. Secondly, it should cause educators to consider the effects that grades can have. Some form of evaluation is necessary and desirable, and thus tests are clearly necessary and desirable. Yet, it is equally clear that most commonly used evaluational procedures have serious shortcomings. Those most likely to suffer are the recipients of poor grades, for they are, in effect, labeled as failures.

Common Biases in Grading

Virtually every teacher can readily identify and justify the objective criteria he or she uses in assigning final grades—test scores, class participation, and the like. But few would be equally aware of the more subtle factors that influence their grading decisions. These include race, socioeconomic status, and sex. One study at Michigan State University, compared the grades of 225 black students with those of 511 randomly selected white students and found that cumulative grade point average for blacks was 2.27 as compared to 2.72 for whites (Kallingal 1971). Using a series of standardized verbal and mathematics tests, it was found that the blacks' grade point averages were actually *higher* than might have been expected. That is, if the scores from the standardized tests were controlled, blacks would be expected to receive lower grades than whites (Kallingal 1971). Why this occurs is difficult to say. Some contend that teachers are under pressure to give blacks higher grades or at least not to fail black students. Others believe that education is a more important route to socioeconomic advancement for blacks than it is for whites and that as the blacks are thus apt to invest more effort than whites into academic achievement. A number of studies have shown that minority-group membership can lead to attempts at compensation that produce such effects (Wineburg 1973).

The problem of cultural fairness also arises when various racial groups are compared. Darlington (1971) notes that construing a test table fair carries "various connotations which generally conflict with each other, so that no single test (except perhaps one with perfect validity) can meet all the specifications likely to be made for a culturally fair test." First of all, it should be stressed, as Thorndike states (1971) that it is the use of a test, not the test itself that is fair or unfair. If a test is used to help a student, fairness or unfairness should not be major considerations. If a test points out that a student has certain deficiencies and is a good measure of skills important to the student or to society as a whole, then the test has served its purpose well. Certain minority groups may very well exhibit deficiencies due to lack of exposure to the majority culture, and a test that reflects on this lack may in some sense, be biased. But, if the test results are used by the instructional staff for remedial purposes, the test is not biased. For example, on a test on Chinese culture, we would expect native Chinese to do quite well but Americans to do quite poorly. The test would actually indicate that the native Chinese know a great deal about their culture while Americans do not. If the only purpose of the test is to measure cultural understanding, it is not biased. On the other hand, if this test served as the basis for admission into college, its cultural fairness could be questionable.

Biases based on sex can also play subtle but important roles. Generally, in the past, males have done better on performance and objective tests, and females have done better on essay and oral exams. In addition, on standardized tests, males tend to score higher in nonverbal portions while females tend to do better in the verbal portions. (Cronbach 1978) Whether this is caused by biological differences between males and females or by sex-role training has been debated considerably in recent years. Regardless of their basis, it is clear that the differences are not great and that they can probably be overcome by training (Wimby 1978).

Because tests may reflect differences between races, cultures, and sexes, some teachers develop separate sets of grading norms—one for non-native speakers of English, for example and one for native speakers. The top ten percent in each group may then be given A's. Thus, a non-native speaker of English could earn an A even though a native speaker of English would be given a B for the same score. Most teachers probably compromise between using one and several sets of scores for all students by taking into consideration each student's performance relative to the entire class and relative to his or her subgroup.

The Effects of Grades

Gordon Keller, Educational Director for the Work Education Program at Camp Oakland in Oxford, Michigan, who works with wards of the Oakland County Probate Court, has stated, "It is becoming increasingly apparent that our schools are conditioning from 20 to 40 percent of our children to accept failure" (Sidney Harris, *Detroit Free Press*). He stressed that many of the children he worked with found nothing in school but failure, defeat, rejection, and indifference. In fact, many students are actually punished for their academic efforts and may eventually develop defense mechanisms that distort their normal needs for achievement.

The Results of Constant Failure

Teachers often remark that some students don't seem to care that they receive low grades. What such teachers fail to recognize is that youngsters who have received constant signals that they are academic failures, are bound to stop caring about academic achievement. They turn elsewhere for rewards, usually to peers who are in similar situations. They may even brag about their poor grades, failure, and inability to achieve academic goals. Poor grades influence their value systems so that they learn to prize other achievements and negate the importance of academic performance. Eventually such youngsters *learn* not to care about school and school-related values.

Understanding Low-Achieving Students

Many educators take the position that a child *cannot* fail, *only a teacher can fail*. To prevent this failure, a teacher must first of all become a diagnostician who seeks the *reasons* for learning problems. He or she then must be able to help students overcome the problems that are discovered. But academic diagnosing is only a small part of understanding the problems of students who do poorly in school. A teacher must deal with the whole human being. Children who fail are especially likely to have family, cultural, and emotional difficulties in addition to their academic problems. Some may also have been born with intellectual, physiological, or neurological weaknesses that interfere in the educational process. It is up to the schools to find methods of meeting these youngsters' greater and different needs. If the schools cannot correct children's social or emotional problems, they should at least offer an environment where every child is encouraged to realize his or her full potential. It does not help these students to be given low grades.

Grades as Motivators

Grades can be a powerful motivator for many students, especially the better ones and those who know that good grades are within their reach if they work hard. For example, a county correctional worker left his job to work on a master's degree in social work. As part of his academic program, he was assigned to do field work in the same job he had just left. He found, however, that he worked much harder and was more conscientious when working for a grade than he had been when working for a paycheck. The reason, he said, was that while working for money he knew that he would automatically be paid the same amount as long as he met minimal requirements. In the master's program, however, better performance would be rewarded with a better grade.

Given the problems of fairness, labeling, and misinterpretation, some people have questioned why students must be graded at all. The most obvious answer is that many students want a concise assessment of their progress beyond simply being told they are doing fairly well or could be doing better. Parents and the community also seek specific indicators that summarize academic performance and allow for comparisons among individuals. Furthermore, as students progress through the educational system, teachers and administrators at each level depend on reports of past academic performance in order to ensure academic continuity and plan for students' futures. Our present system of grading may require improvement. But a formal educational system without the historical and motivational structure that grades provide would result in ambiguity that students, parents, the community, and the system itself would find difficult to tolerate. A society as progress-oriented as our own of necessity seeks and values constant measures of that progress. Our school systems cannot hope to escape such strong societal pressures.

Used correctly, grades can help students gauge their progress towards their goals. If their performance does not meet required standards, they know that they should review the material before continuing. Such evaluations do not penalize, but merely indicate levels of progress. Emphasis is not so much on finishing a certain amount of material in a certain length of time as it is on reaching a desired level of competency before moving on. Grades can then be assigned to indicate levels of performance within an acceptable range. Grades should have a value that can be recognized by parents, other schools, and prospective employer, and they should serve students as both feedback and motivation for improvement.

The ABCI System

The most equitable solution to grading problems is to adopt a system that stresses *uniform criteria* and *standardized system of testing*. One system that does this a system that assigns grades of A, B, C, or I (or incomplete). The I grade would replace the usual grades of D and E (or F) and remain on the record until the student achieves a satisfactory level of performance. A student who is given an I has *not failed,* nor can he or she ever fail. A student receives credit only when he or she has achieved the *minimum level of acceptable performance,* both on standardized tests and according to the instructor's own uniform standards. This is similar to a credit-no credit system, except that it is possible to reward various levels of acceptable performance.

The ABCI grading scale provides a set of ratings for *acceptable performance,* (A, B, and C), as well as one other symbol that indicates that a student has not, as yet, reached the *minimum* standards. An I indicates performance only *at the time of examination.* If the student *later* reaches a higher level of performance, a different grade may be given. In addition, if a student wants to try to improve his or her performance later, he or she can earn an improved grade. The policy of giving a student an E and refusing to change it at a later date is both stifling and misleading. To continue to penalize a student for something he or she didn't know before but *does* know now is nonproductive.

A student's present knowledge and performance are more relevant than past knowledge and performance. A youngster who does poorly and then improves demonstrates a perseverance that will be of lifelong usefulness. Many studies indicate the most important quality for success is *motivation* (Roe 1962). Under the ABCI system, students are motivated to improve their performance because they may always be reevaluated and awarded a higher grade, whether their initial grade was an I or a B.

Other Advantages of the ABCI System

The ABCI system also counters a student's tendency to perceive the *goal* of education as a *grade.* He or she is encouraged to *work for the accomplishment that is reflected in the grade, and not for the grade itself.* A student works until he or she achieves the necessary or chosen level and then is rewarded with a grade. Tests guide growth until a level of performance that satisfies both the teacher and the student is reached.

We have stressed that an important aspect of any learning situation is feedback, which requires some form of evaluation. Such evaluation is often limited to the assignment of grades. The result is that in many classes, especially at the high school and college levels, evaluation is rarely used in ways that facilitate learning. The ABCI system, on the other hand, encourages constant assessment of strengths and weaknesses so that students' energies can be effectively channeled.

Central to the ABCI system is the requirement that a certain minimum level of performance be reached before the student is assigned an actual grade. This level should, ideally, be set by the school system, or even relevant state agencies. This would ensure that grades had uniform meaning and that an A in one school would be more or less equivalent to an A in another school. This uniformity would greatly facilitate such matters as transfer of credits and grade-level placement for students who move to new school districts, and, in addition, would help employers judge the scholastic performance of job applicants.

School systems often must communicate more about a student than simply that he or she received credit for taking a certain class. If schools do not provide more detailed evaluations of students, outsiders are forced to do their own evaluations. Colleges, industry, and other institutions must make selections from among many candidates. If they cannot base their selections upon grade point average and other information provided by the schools, they are forced to establish their own evaluation systems. To do this, they have produced tests designed solely for the purpose of reducing the pool of candidates.

If faced with 350 people applying for five job openings, an employer must adhere to rigid selection procedures. If many of the candidates come from schools whose policy is to give all students high grades or who use pass-fail systems, the employer's task is complicated by the fact that she lacks basic information that could help her make distinctions. Schools do not benefit students by giving blanket A's, but can benefit them by providing fair evaluations that help discriminate true ability levels. If schools provided useful and reliable evaluations, colleges and industry would see less need for entrance and employability examinations and could instead base their judgments on the schools' more accurate long-term evaluations. Basing employability on a single test is unrealistic, but industry has little choice, given the number of applicants for many jobs. If schools' grading systems were adequate and uniform and if an A clearly meant superior performance based upon an entire series of exams and other pertinent activities, employers would prefer to rely on the schools' data. Obviously, teachers are in a much better position to assess students' academic and general abilities, and their long-term evaluations can and should be more reliable than the results of a single college entrance or employability exam.

Another advantage of the ABCI system is that it permits students to learn at their own rates. They can work either faster or slower than the rest of the class without being unduly penalized. One of the main problems with gifted children is caused by the fact that they learn *faster* and move ahead of their classmates. Keeping them behind so that they can be with their age peers or moving them ahead to be with their intellectual peers both create problems. The ABCI system allows for many levels of learning and, to some extent, eliminates the need for grade levels.

Some high achievers may resent the fact that students who do not perform as well are allowed to take a test several times and thus may eventually end up with the same grade. It must be stressed, however, that slower students must put more work into achieving the same grade, so that brighter students have the reward of earning the grade sooner, often with less work. Unfortunately the ABCI system might also cause some of the better students to feel that they don't need to work as hard because they will eventually get an A anyway. These youngsters should be encouraged to view the system as somewhat like a cross-country race—most can cross the finish line, but some cross first, and that is where the honor lies. This time factor may, to some degree, be as discouraging as a D or an E to some students, but the point is that everyone *can* succeed. Every student can achieve many of their goals if they work at them. Under no system could we expect everyone to be truly equal, for in reality, of course, each individual is unique. The goal of the ABCI system is not to give the illusion of complete equality, but to remove some of the roadblocks to achievement.

Explaining the ABCI System to the Public

Anytime the schools adopt a new method of dealing with any educational issue, they face the problem of explaining it to parents and the community. When the ABCI system is introduced, parents will probably raise many of the same questions we have already discussed. Thus, it is important that administrators and teachers implementing this system, or limited aspects of it, be fully aware of both its advantages and disadvantages. Many teachers, especially in junior high school and above, already have the option of giving a student an I, and teachers, in some school systems could use this system on an individual basis, regardless of whether the other teachers use it.

A Comparison with the ABCDE System

Under the ABCDE system, students with D averages are often passed to the next grade year after year, and many times the D's are actually F's, but are given because the teacher hesitates to fail students. The problem of passing students with D's is that they get further and further behind. They never really achieve appropriate levels of performance (assuming the grading and testing systems are accurate) and are less and less able to compete. Eventually they drop out of school or graduate with serious academic shortcomings. The ABCI system would enable schools to ensure specified minimum levels of performance for *all graduates.*

Another problem is that some students are quite content to earn D's because it is the minimum necessary to pass. Actually, of course, D-level performance is far below minimum standards in most systems. Under the ABCI system, such students would receive I's and be required to meet *acceptable standards.* With D's they could move on, but with I's they cannot. Thus, the ABCI system upgrades standards performance. As one teacher put it, "Under the ABCI system, D level students are no longer allowed to glide through their educations to eventually graduate into a lifetime of mediocre illiteracy."

Flexibility may be built into the ABCI system by allowing students to graduate with one or two I's. Instead of having D's on their records to lower their grade point averages, they would have merely I's, which would have no effect. Furthermore, if a student later wishes to improve in an area of weakness, an I enables him or her to do so, while a D or an F, in most cases, would not. Students who later develop an interest in an area in which they at first did not do well, or who realize their weaknesses in a given area, are thus encouraged to improve these skills.

The ever present threat of low grades can be an important reason for many students' studying, and the ABCI system may remove some of this motivation. Nonetheless, students should still be motivated to earn an A, a B, or a C, and they should come to appreciate the ideal that studying should be for reasons other than grades. This system may force teachers to teach ways that emphasize the intrinsic worth of knowledge and the value of knowing. In addition, rewards such as praise, encouragement, and public recognition may come to replace threats of failure as motivators of learning.

The sorting function of the ABCI system would, in the long run, save time and energy. Most students in a group or grade would clearly belong there, and few would encounter problems of being seriously behind or ahead. Teachers must first be thoroughly educated in the system, however, and students and parents must also understand its purposes. Inevitably, at first, there will be resistance, for a system that is new most always engenders such a reaction. For example, if a child continually receives I's, his parents may become upset. But if these I's force *both* parents and the school to examine the child's performance more carefully amd correct what is wrong, the upset may end up benefiting all involved. It forcefully points out that a student is not performing adequately and that remedial steps will be taken. Parents may allow their child to continue earning D's, but I's more or less force them to take action to ensure that he or she will pass to the next level.

A possible objection to the ABCI system is that it may increase parental pressure on children. Youngsters can no longer receive mere D's and pass, but must perform at higher levels. The parents, realizing this, may push their children. The problem of misdirected parental pressure is also common under the present system, but all too often, D students have parents who lack interest in their children's academic performance. If their youngsters receive I's and are thus in jeopardy of not passing, such parents may be jolted into taking a more active role in the educational process. Ideally, the schools should work with parents to help them understand that if a student is *not* working up to capacity, there are definite ways to deal with the problem and that applying more pressure is usually not one of them. Giving a child's work a great deal of personal attention, employing an individual tutor, and encouraging that an hour or so per day be spent on any type of reading, thinking, writing, or problem-solving activity, including working puzzle or game books, tend to be very productive ways of helping a child overcome academic problems.

Removing the Threat of Failure

Probably, the foremost advantage of the ABCI system is that the threat and stigma of failure can be totally removed. School then becomes a place where one can *only do better*, or improve, and need never fail. One can continue trying—constantly going over the material until it is mastered—and one is not punished, stigmatized, or labeled along the way.

An E tends to be very final and defeating and, in effect, says to a student, "You cannot do this and will never be able." In reality, school performance should be viewed as a continuum of growth and experience and never as a single point at an absolute level. An I is an outgrowth of this philosophy: it means that a student has not yet accomplished the desired level of achievement. It does *not* say he or she will not, should not, or cannot do well in the future.

Thus, the ABCI system can be seen to distinguish between intellectual output and intellectual abilities. An E implies that a student *cannot* produce, when most often it really indicates that a student is *not* producing, or at least is not *yet* producing.

Some Problems in the ABCI System

Some students will stay at the incomplete level for a long time and will simply not produce the effort needed to receive a C. Others may not be capable of earning a C or better. Under the standard ABCDE system, such youngsters might be given D's and moved ahead, but this isn't possible under the ABCI system.

Another possible disadvantage of the ABCI system is that it places more demands on teachers and paraprofessionals. This is actually an advantage in disguise in that it forces teachers to develop the resources necessary to help *all* (or at least *most*) students to achieve minimum levels of performance. It is also likely that more paraprofessionals will be needed to tutor students. The need for record keeping may increase, but the records should *help* students and aid them in their progress. In the long run, all of these factors will clearly work to the advantage of students.

If a number of students accumulate many incompletes, it will call the administration's attention to the possibility that the teachers may not be able to cope with their students. Students who perform below a C level are usually not grasping the material and need help. If many I's are given, the administration would have to take remedial action. They may thus discover any number of underlying problems, such as classes that are too large or inappropriate grouping of students.

Students must be constantly reminded that an I is not the same as an E so that they will not think that they are failures or that their efforts don't count. This problem can be avoided if the teacher develops a system by which students can track their progress, such as a checklist of completed and uncompleted tasks. This encourages a sense of accomplishment while simultaneously emphasizing future goals.

Benefit for Poor Performers

Perhaps the strongest argument in favor of the ABCI system lies in its benefit for poor performers. For these students, the self-fulfilling prophecy of failure is avoided. Furthermore, it can help them better channel their efforts.

For example, if certain courses are required for graduation, students can quickly complete the courses that are easiest for them and then spend more time on those in which they are having difficulty. At the same time, students who are able to complete most or all of their required classes more rapidly can take additional courses and graduate with more credits than required. Slower students would achieve less in terms of quantity but more in terms of quality than they might under the ABCDE system. The differences would be evident on students' transcripts if one student completed 15 credits and another 19, the relative levels of achievement would be discernible, but the better student would not have been rewarded at the expense of the slower one. In fact, an excellent and a slow student (D and F students) may have the same grade point averages when they graduate, only the better one will have completed more classes and can thus still be seen as outstanding. The ABCI will have been beneficial to both of them.

Grading According to Effort

Teachers are prone to give good grades to almost any student who seems to be doing his or her best, but it is actually very difficult to judge exactly what a student's best effort is. In fact, research has shown that many people are capable of doing *far more* than they believe they can. Educator Aaron Stern (1979) thinks that the vast majority of students are not doing even a fraction of their best. In order to demonstrate the validity of his theories, he decided that he would make his new-born daughter into a genius. Twelve years later she entered undergraduate school, and at age 15 she began teaching college—the youngest faculty member on record. Stern claims that his daughter was not born with genes that predisposed her to genius but that his "total educational submersion method" was responsible for her accomplishments and her estimated I.Q. of 207. He further claims that these accomplishments are possible for almost everyone, and a number of educators agree with him. Other well-known examples of similar educational techniques include economist John Stuart Mill, mathematicians William Sidis, Norbert Wiener, and inventor Thomas Edison.

Central to the method are a great deal of one-to-one attention, many rewards for the smallest accomplishments, and innovative ways of teaching. Since discerning a student's true potential is both difficult and highly subjective, grading according to effort is bound to be unfair and inaccurate. An absolute approach, such as the ABCI system, offers more reliable results.

Probably one of the greatest impediments in implementing the ABCI system is tradition. The ABCI system is new and different (even though only slightly so), and many teachers would fear that you need the hammer to punish students with D's or F's. Actually, other more creative methods would have to be utilized as a means of "punishing" students. And hopefully, some would question whether or not it is necessary to look for other ways of "punishing" students. If punishment is deemed necessary, surely other ways could be found. The fact is that the failure system has a detrimental effect on so many students that it is doubtful that dropping it would have many negative effects.

An advantage of this system is that it to some degree reduces the barriers between elementary, junior high, high school, and, probably even college students. Breaking down these barriers probably will be functional towards helping our schools achieve their real goal, that of educating students. These barriers impede learning for many reasons. The trauma the children sometimes undergo in transferring from one school to another and the highly nonfunctional norms that develop within each individual school are two examples.

Summary

There are perhaps more grading options available to today's teacher than are immediately apparent. In addition to familiar letter grades, the pass-fail system has viable application, as do checklists, letters to parents, and parent-teacher conferences. A teacher can judge student performance by determining grades according to absolute value, a curve or distribution of scores, or a criterion-referenced system. Validity and reliability will perhaps always be called into question in many grading systems, but a thorough understanding of common biases in grading, the effects of grades, both positive and negative, on student performance, and the overall motivational effect of grading as a gauge for performance can help an educator weigh the issues. The ABCI system is an alternative grading program designed for flexibility for the teacher and encouragement in learning for the student.

Suggested Readings

Cleary, T. Anne et al. "Educational Uses of Tests with Disadvantaged Students." *American Psychologist,* January 1975, 15-40.

Cleary, T. Anne and Thomas L. Hilton. "An Investigation of Item Bias." *Educational and Psychological Measurement,* vol. 28 (1968), 61-75.

Cronbach, Lee J. "Equity in Selection—Where Psychometrics and Political Philosophy Meet." *Journal of Educational Measurement,* vol. 13 (1976), 31-41.

Darlington, Richard B. "Another Look at 'Cultural Fairness' " *Journal of Educational Measurement,* vol. 8 (1971), 71-82.

Eagle, Norman and Anna S. Harris. "Interaction of Race and Test on Reading Performance Scores." *Journal of Educational Measurement,* vol. 6 (1969), 131-35.

Echternacht, Gary. "A Quick Method for Determining Test Bias." *Educational and Psychological Measurement,* vol. 34 (1974), 271-80.

Feldmesser, Robert A. "The Positive Functions of Grades." In *Readings in Measurement and Evaluation in Education and Psychology,* William A. Mehrens, ed. New York: Holt Rinehart and Winston, 1976.

Kallingal, Anthony. "The Prediction of Grades for Black and White Students at Michigan State University." *Journal of Educational Measurement,* vol. 8 (1971), 263-65.

Lien, Arnold J. *Measurement and Evaluation of Learning.* 3d rev. ed. Dubuque, Iowa: W.C. Brown, 1976.

Lindeman, Richard H. and Peter F. Merenda. *Educational Measurement.* Glenview, Ill.: Scott, Foresman, 1979.

17   Rating Scales

Humans from a very early age are concerned with making comparisons, be they about which piece of cake is bigger, which person makes more money, or which political candidate is better. One way of expressing comparisons is through **rating scales**.

Making Comparisons Through Rating

A rating scale is a method of judging a specific aspect of someone or something. Grades are the most common example of a rating scale. Five rating positions are usually used: A, B, C, D, and E. Numbers or words may also be used in a rating system. For example, instead of letter grades, a school might issue report cards based on the following ratings:

1 = outstanding accomplishment
2 = excellent progress
3 = progressing satisfactorily
4 = needs to improve
5 = failure (or very poor progress)

Frequency of observation scales, such as the following, are also often used:

How often does the student turn in his or her homework?
0. not observed   3. sometimes
1. never   4. usually
2. seldom   5. always

Somewhat similar is a **normative rating scale**:

Compared to the average fifth-grader, the student's handwriting is
0. not observed   3. average
1. inferior   4. above average
2. below average 5. outstanding

Frequency of observation scale
Normative rating scale
Value judgment rating scale
Trait rating scale
Ability judgment scale
Performance scale
Personality scale
Agreement scale
Similarity scale

Bipolar adjectives
Bias
Generosity error
Severity error
Central tendency error
Halo effect
Stereotype error
Logical error
Feeling error

A **value judgment rating scale** might be as follows:

The student's art ability is:

    a. poor   d. superior
    b. fair   e. excellent
    c. good   f. not observed

Trait rating scales are used to evaluate personality. For example:

The student's attitude toward authority is

    a. rebellious   d. very cooperative
    b. resistant   e. extremely cooperative
    c. average   f. not observed

Other rating scales include:

1. **Ability judgment scales** based on ratings of excellent, very good, good, fair, poor, very poor.
2. **Performance scales** based on ratings of not able, minimum ability, adequate ability, highly capable.
3. **Personality scales** based on ratings such as arrogant, irritating, moderate, pleasing, cooperative.
3. **Agreement scales** based on ratings such as strongly disagree, disagree, neutral, agree, strongly agree.
4. **Similarity scales** based on ratings such as very similar, somewhat similar, similar, different, very different.

A rating scale for students' evaluations of a classroom teacher could include:

1. Knowledge of material
    excellent   very good   good   fair   poor   very poor
2. Ability to convey information in an understandable manner
    excellent   very good   good   fair   poor   very poor

3. Enthusiasm and interest in subject
   excellent   very good   good   fair   poor   very poor

4. Ability to motivate and interest students in the subject
   excellent   very good   good   fair   poor   very poor

5. General attitude towards students as individuals
   excellent   very good   good   fair   poor   very poor

6. Willingness to help students
   excellent   very good   good   fair   poor   very poor

7. Demonstrates knowledge of current developments in the field and integrates it with classroom materials
   never   seldom   sometimes   usually   always

8. Integrates other disciplines and schools of thought with assigned topics
   never   seldom   sometimes   usually   always

9. Displays open-mindedness toward student ideas
   never   seldom   sometimes   usually   always

10. Brings student ideas to the attention of the class
    never   seldom   sometimes   usually   always

Rating scale for a teacher's evaluation of students' reports could include:

1. Ability to organize thoughts and ideas into clear and understandable terms
   excellent   very good   good   fair   poor   very poor

2. Understanding of material
   excellent   very good   good   fair   poor   very poor

3. Ability to integrate own ideas and personal thoughts
   excellent   very good   good   fair   poor   very poor

4. Interest level of content
   excellent   very good   good   fair   poor   very poor

5. Content's pertinence to assignment
   excellent   very good   good   fair   poor   very poor

6. Overall effectiveness of report
   excellent   very good   good   fair   poor   very poor

7. Vocabulary
   excellent   very good   good   fair   poor   very poor

8. Writing style
   excellent   very good   good   fair   poor   very poor

Bipolar Adjectives

Another rating technique presents opposite pairs of descriptive words or phrases and asks students to judge something in terms of the dichotomies. Only two words are listed, but the students' judgments usually fall somewhere in between. In the following examples, note that the positive traits do not consistently occur in the same position. Depending on the purpose of the scale, similar quality traits may occur in the same position or be mixed.

Fast __ __ __ __ __ Slow
Poor __ __ __ __ __ Excellent
Cooperative __ __ __ __ __ Uncooperative
Performing adequately __ __ __ __ __ Performing inadequately

The Neutral Position

An *odd* number of rating positions are usually used if the respondent will be allowed to take a neutral position. To *force* students to decide one way or the other, an *even* number of choices is commonly used. An *odd* number of choices yields the following:

a. strongly agree
b. agree
c. neutral
d. disagree
e. strongly disagree

But an even number of choices eliminates the neutral choice:

a. strongly agree
b. agree
c. disagree
d. strongly disagree

Variations on the neutral choice format may include such ratings as *strongly like, like, neutral, dislike, strongly dislike* or *strongly favorable, favorable, neutral, unfavorable, strongly unfavorable.*

A problem with all rating scales is that terms can be quite difficult to define. Most words are not precise, and one person's interpretation of a word may differ greatly from another person's interpretation. This can lead to lower reliability, or another problem, errors in rating.

Errors in Rating

A number of common errors can affect the results of rating scales. Most errors in rating are made by the person doing the rating. Many ratings tend to be consistent; that is, they consistently give high ratings or low ones. The following errors in rating typify the pitfalls of rating scales.

Bias Bias is the tendency to rate high or low because of factors other than the trait being rated. For example, Teresa could be rated high in reading skills because she works hard and has good penmanship, clear pronunciation, and a pleasing personality. Judged objectively, she is actually quite weak in reading comprehension, but she was given a high rating because of the other factors. Several studies have found that attractive, pleasing, clean, polite students consistently earn higher grades, regardless of their actual performance. Other studies have found that the same term paper submitted in two forms—one hand-written and one typed—earned different grades. That the typed version tended to be given a grade higher than the untyped one is an example of bias. Bias is extremely common and very difficult to eliminate. Since bias tends to be subconscious, most people do not realize when their decisions are based on inappropriate criteria.

Generosity Error Generosity error is the most common form of bias and occurs when consistently high ratings are given on most scales (Bergman 1980). Students who are happy, well-adjusted, self-confident, outgoing, and are successful in school tend to give everything very high ratings. For example, note Merle's assessments in the following conversation

NICKY: What do you think of school this term?

MERLE: Great, I've got some really good classes. I have Jones for English, Thomas for Spanish, and Bronowski for algebra.

NICKY: You have Bronowski for algebra? What do you think of her?

MERLE: I like her. I know some of the other students don't, but I think she's really good. She expects a lot out of you, and I may not pull an A in that class, but still, it's a good class. She keeps you on your toes and makes you work.

NICKY: What did you think of your last test?

MERLE: Boy, that was a bear! Tests like that keep me on my toes, though. I like challenging tests occasionally, although I never thought I'd get a D! Me with a D—can you believe it? Oh well, I can't get A's all the time.

TOM: What do you think of Reginald? Isn't he in that class?

MERLE: Yes, he is. Some of the kids don't like him, but I think he's all right. Just because he isn't like everyone else, people criticize him. I think that's dumb. In fact, I sit next to him and we get along great.

Those kids should realize that everybody doesn't have to be just like them.

This student generally has a very positive orientation, even towards teachers and students that others dislike. For this reason, it is often said that a students' ratings of a teacher may often tell more about the students than it does about the teacher. If a teacher receives high ratings, it may not reflect on his or her teaching skills as much as it does on the self-concepts of the students themselves. In large classes, of course, students' ratings should balance out, with predictable numbers of students giving ratings at each level.

Severity Error Severity error is the opposite of generosity error and occurs less commonly. Severity error occurs when consistently low ratings are given on most scales. Most people who consistently give low ratings tend to have many social, personal, family, and/or school problems (Bergman 1980). Other low raters simply seem to be negative out of habit or background. Note the following conversation:

DON: How do you like your classes?

JULIUS: They're lousy. I have that dumb Mr. Taylor. Boy, that guy annoys me. I sure can't wait to get out of school.

DON: Are you still dating Shirley?

JULIUS: Yeah, but I don't know why. Girls really bother me. It seems you can give them everything you've got and they still want more. All she is giving me is trouble.

DON: Isn't she in your political science class?

JULIUS: Yeah, don't mention that dumb class. All we talk about is how corrupt government officials are. Boy, I'll tell you, our government is really messed up. Politicians are all crooks looking for a fast buck.

Central Tendency Error Central tendency error, the second most common form of bias, occurs when a rater consistently gives average ratings. People who are feeling rather neutral about themselves and the course of their lives will tend to give average ratings to everything, much as Char does in the following conversation:

VERN: How's your French class coming along?

CHAR: Okay.

VERN: How's your sister Gayle doing?

CHAR: She's doing all right.

VERN: How do you like Mr. Rogow?

CHAR: He's not bad for a teacher.

VERN: I hear you're going to the football game Saturday. Sounds exciting.

CHAR: Oh, I never get excited about football. It's okay, I guess.

VERN: Say, you'll be graduating soon, won't you?

CHAR: Yeah, I will.

VERN: What are you going to do when you get out of school?

CHAR: Oh, I don't really know. I suppose I'll go to college.

Although this type of person would tend to rate most of his or her teachers as average, regardless of their performances, he or she would rate teachers that are clearly excellent *higher* than average, but still close to average. Likewise, teachers who are clearly poor would be rated *lower* than average, but again, close to average.

The Halo Effect and Stereotype Error The halo effect occurs when a rater allows a single preliminary impression, whether good or bad, to affect all or most subsequent ratings. The saying "A first impression is a lasting impression" illustrates this concept. First impressions color all other impressions and are difficult to change. This bias is often unconscious, but has a strong influence on a person's likes and dislikes.

Where a previously learned sterotype affects ratings, **stereotype error** occurs. For example, a common stereotype is that women medical students are not as serious as male medical students. Thus, a young man may end up with higher grades than a comparable woman *not* because he has demonstrated better performance but because he is perceived as a better student because of his gender. A science student in a social studies class may end up with a lower grade, not because he is in fact lower in performance, but because he is seen as lower as a result of a stereotype error influencing the teacher's judgment. There are thousands of stereotypes in operation about every kind of people.

Logical Error A logical error occurs when two characteristics are rated alike because they are *assumed* to be related. For example, when a teacher is asked to rate students according to their creativity, he is likely to give high creativity ratings to those who have high I.Q.'s because of the incorrect assumption that high I.Q.'s and high creativity are related. There are many traits that people assume to be related when in fact they aren't. For example, it is often assumed that gifted students are small and rather sickly (actually the opposite is true), that attractive, boy-crazy girls are dumb (again the opposite is often true), and that students involved in antisocial activities have no personal loyalty to friends (again, this is usually not true). Obviously, this form of bias is just as subtle and difficult to overcome as most other biases are.

Feeling Error When a rater reaches a conclusion based on a hunch rather than on logical proof, **feeling error** occurs. This type of error is sometimes the result of previous experience with similar circumstances. For example, if a teacher is unable to explain her dislike for a certain student, it may be that the youngster subconsciously reminds her of someone else whom she also dislikes. This is sometimes called **emotional error** because it results when judgments are based on emotions.

Summary

In this chapter, we have looked at a number of ways of rating student performance and performance in general. An important point to keep in mind is that all rating scales are subjective—ratings depend upon the rater. Ratings are always approximations—estimates, and sometimes guesses, rather than exact measurements. There are a variety of rating-scale formats, but all essentially consist of a series of descriptive terms that range from one extreme to the other. They can be useful in helping students as long as their limitations are taken into account.

Suggested Readings

Noll, Victor H., Dale P. Scannell and Robert C. Craig. *Introduction to Educational Measurement*. 4th rev. ed. Boston: Houghton Mifflin, 1979. Chapter 14.

TenBrink, Terry D. *Evaluation: A Practical Guide for Teachers*. New York: McGraw-Hill, 1974. Chapter 10.

Thomas, Murray R. *Judging Student Progress*. New York: David McKay, 1960. Chapter 11.

Thorndike, Robert L. and Elizabeth Hagen. *Measurement and Evaluation in Psychology and Education*. 4th rev. ed. New York: John Wiley and Sons, 1977. Chapter 12.

18   Social Measurement Tools

There are three basic types of social measurement tools: (1) **self-report tools**, with which students report or explain how they feel about a class, what they think they would like to study, or what they know about themselves; (2) **observational tools**, with which one person reports his or her perceptions about another person; and (3) **collective observational tools**, with which a group of persons rate a third party.

Self-report tools are probably, on the whole, the most common and economical of all the social measurement tools. Most information-gathering methods rely on some form of self-report in which individuals record information about themselves.

The Personal Interview

The oldest and, in many ways, the best self-report technique is the **personal interview**. This technique is based on the premise that the best way to find something out about someone is to ask him or her about it. Many teachers find that they can discover much useful information during semidirected, open-ended conversations with students. In the course of an interview, the teacher can ask about a student's interests, abilities, goals, drives, and problems. This information can then be used to individualize instruction. Personal acquaintance with each child is absolutely necessary to the planning of appropriate courses of study. Conducting a personal interview with each student also helps the teacher establish one-to-one contact with *each* student. There is a tendency for teachers to spend more time with certain kinds of students, such as those with behavior problems or ones who are extremely likable. Shy students, who tend to withdraw, are often ignored, even though they may need more attention than the average student.

When arranging personal interviews, the teacher may find it useful to list all students in an order that will be most beneficial to his or her objectives. Many teachers also find it helpful to prepare a set of questions (or at least an outline) to guide the conversation into specific areas and to ensure that necessary information is gathered. With older students, much preliminary data (such as interests, occupational goals, and the like) can be gathered by way of written questionnaire. The personal conference can then be used to discuss the results of the questionnaire or any related problems the student may have. It is usually best to emphasize that the purpose of the interview is to help the student. For this reason, the student should be encouraged to talk about *anything* he or she wishes. The mere act of spending time and listening carefully to each student can be very productive because it communicates that the teacher is *concerned* about each individual as a person. After a student leaves, the teacher may wish to make notes about what was learned.

While formal training in counseling can be helpful when conducting a personal conference, it is not necessary. The following suggestions should facilitate an effective and beneficial conference that will enable the student to express him- or herself and the teacher to understand the student.

1. A teacher should attempt to be a noncritical, accepting listener. Not liking what a student says or does should not cause the teacher to dislike the student as a person. Once a youngster is assured of acceptance, he or she is more apt to communicate honestly and to respond to guidance. Often what a teacher dislikes in a student is a result of cultural differences and values or other preconceptions that are less than objective. In order to be optimally effective, teachers should not make normative judgments about their students.

2. A teacher should offer advice and suggestions very sparingly. Most students have repeatedly heard that they should study more, play less, buckle down, and concentrate. Worn expressions such as "You can do better," "You don't apply yourself," and "If you wanted to, you could be an A student," mean little. Rarely will repeating these oversimplified cliches help a student, although specific, concrete suggestions sparingly presented *can be* helpful.

3. What is said is often not as important as *how* it is said. A teacher may correctly assess a problem and try to remedy it, but the student won't cooperate until he or she is convinced that the teacher is genuinely trying to help. In addition, the child must respect the teacher and have some desire to change before the advice will even be considered. Tone of voice and choice of words play critical roles during a personal interview and in the teaching process in general.

Some teachers never even begin to effectively relate with many of their students. Others are very effective in helping students grow and mature as a result of working on a one-to-one basis, but they are successful partially because they have trained themselves to be good listeners. In addition, they have a strong interest in people and try to learn more about human behavior by reading, taking university classes, and spending time with many different types of people.

It is more difficult for a teacher to work with individual students at the junior high and high school levels than it is in the lower grades. If a teacher has five classes of thirty students, it is difficult to spend time with each youngster on a regular basis. A teacher may thus be forced to spend time only with certain students. If time for individual attention is limited, it can usually be best spent with students who have C averages or below, those who rarely participate in class discussions, and those who give any indication whatsoever that they have problems or that they would benefit from talking with the teacher. In some schools, all teachers work together to ensure that every student has a personal conference with at least one or more teachers and alert each other if they discover something that could benefit the student in other classes.

With high school or college students, teachers often have the entire class vote on whether or not they would like to have individual personal conferences. This reduces the feeling that the teacher is infringing upon the students' rights. The author, in twelve years of teaching experience, has never had even one class vote against having personal conferences. The voting was almost always unanimously for this option and helped most students to feel a personal commitment to their conferences. In addition, it was always stressed that the purpose of the personal conference was primarily so the teacher could better help each student.

The length of an interview may vary with the circumstances. Often, even though only ten minutes have been allotted, it may be best to extend the time as necessary to reassure a student that he or she is speaking with a concerned listener. Students must be helped to recognize that the interview will be beneficial to them.

Becoming better acquainted with the students also helps direct the teacher's casual conversation with them. Casual student-teacher conversation can thus become more beneficial. For example, the teacher could ask about specific problems or events, such as, "How is your brother doing at West Point? Did he complete his tactics course successfully?"

A Case History At his personal conference, it was discovered that Billy, a ten-year-old fifth-grader, usually did not eat breakfast or dinner unless he bought a hamburger at a local fast food chain. His father did not live at home, nor did Billy know where his father was. His mother, who worked nights, slept during the day and did not have time to fix her son either breakfast or dinner. The lunch he ate at school and the chocolate milk he drank at the morning and afternoon milk breaks comprised his primary diet. He was a sickly looking child, small and underweight for his age.

When this problem was discovered, he and his teacher discussed possible ways in which he could obtain a good breakfast and dinner each day. When asked if someone from the school might talk to his mother in order to arrange proper meals, Billy eagerly responded affirmatively. The school social worker talked to the mother, who very politely pointed out that she worked full time because she had to support her family completely on her own. She worked at night because she could not find a day job that paid as well. She felt that since there was always food in the house, if Billy wanted breakfast, he was old enough to make it himself.

With Billy's mother's permission, the social worker arranged for Billy to eat breakfast at a neighbor's home each morning. Billy and the neighbor's son then walked to school together. This arrangement worked out quite satisfactorily, and Billy even gained a new friend. The child was thus guaranteed good breakfasts and lunches, and his mother was encouraged to ensure that he also ate some type of evening meal, whether a frozen dinner, something from a fast food chain, or a sandwich prepared before she left for work.

There are several important principles a teacher should keep in mind when using the personal interview method. First of all, a teacher is not a psychotherapist, nor is she a marriage counselor or a medical doctor. If there are any signs that problems should be referred to another person, the suggestion should be tactfully made: "I have a friend who might be able to help you with your problem." Or, better still: "That really is an area I am not competent to talk about. Possibly, you could contact . . . or have your parents contact . . . ." A teacher may not want to suggest, for example, that a third-grader see a psychiatrist, but may prefer to talk to the school psychologist, the school nurse, or another professional who is in a position to help the child.

Interest Surveys

Interest surveys can be indispensable aids in developing the school curriculum and individualizing instruction because they allow students to indicate what they would like to learn and what they perceive as being important to learn. These self-report instruments are usually designed to tap students' various interests, especially those related to the subject matter being taught. A case history: Mr. Jones was preparing to teach a tenth-grade world history class. Because of the wide variety of material he could cover, he decided it would be best to limit course content to topics that the students felt were relevant, useful, and related to their interests. Of course, Mr. Jones also had his own preferences in subject matter. In order to reach the best compromise, he decided to list 20 possible topics and have the students rank them in order of preference. He then averaged the ranks to find out which topics were most popular with the class as a whole.

The most common use of interest surveys is to determine common interests in order to please as many students as possible. Each student's interest survey can also serve as a guide for individualizing instruction. In addition, students with common interests may be grouped together to work on special projects and activities. This tool is also useful in helping students plan their other classes and think about possible careers or part-time work.

Several questions teachers have found helpful are:

1. What would you do during four hours time if you could do anything you wanted?
2. Would you rather read a book, write a letter, or paint a picture about your favorite subject?
3. If you were independently wealthy and could spend your money any way you wished, what would you do with your time?
4. What do you usually do when you get home from school?
5. What is your favorite recreation?
6. Name several of your favorite books or movies, and explain why they are your favorites.

Teachers have found that interest surveys can be quite useful in helping them design a course around their students' interests and needs. The interest survey is divided into two parts. The first part deals with various subject areas that the teacher can cover in class and the second part deals with general interests such as those previously listed.

When students are asked to complete an interest survey, they are given the important message that their teacher is concerned about them as individuals and hopes to direct course content to their personal interests. Students usually enjoy filling out such questionnaires, especially when they contain open-ended questions. To some degree they see it as a game, primarily because the questions stimulate an enjoyable thought process.

Self-Expressive Devices

Self-expressive devices are observation tools used to *stimulate students* to express their feelings, attitudes, and behavior traits without calling attention to the appraisal process. When filling out self-report tools, students are usually conscious of the assessment procedure and may therefore give answers that they believe will please the teacher. A self-expressive device, on the other hand, stimulates the actual behavior the teacher wants to evaluate and may even reveal traits that students themselves are unaware of or would not openly admit. Thus, it can be used to help students learn about themselves as well as to help the teacher learn about the students. In addition, this tool allows the teacher to evaluate his or her teaching and discover material that needs to be reviewed or retaught. The more common self-expression devices are listed here.

Role Playing

In **role playing** two to four students are given a situation to act out with the expectation that they will act and react in realistic ways. Usually they are presented with only a setting and assigned roles. They must then improvise appropriate conversation and action. Most often they role play in front of the class (an important aspect of role playing is audience response), but sometimes pairs of role-playing groups will alternate with each other.

One teacher found role playing to be extremely effective in teaching juvenile offenders. The youngsters she worked with often had a great deal of hostility toward police, some of which was justified, but most of which was unrealistic. To encourage better understanding, she set up a role-playing situation for the youngsters to work on in pairs. One youth was asked to play the role of a police officer while another played the role of a twenty-year-old male who had been convicted of breaking and entering two years previously, but whose record since then had been clean. The youngster playing the police officer was given the following instructions: "You recognize this person as someone who has been in trouble many times before and believe that he could be guilty of a crime that was recently reported. The description of a person seen running away from the scene of the crime perfectly fits the man before you. Your job is to arrest him, bring him to the station, and try to draw a confession out of him." Each participant was aware of the other's instructions and recognized that they were merely acting out parts. Yet many became so involved that several fist fights broke out. As the youngsters played their roles, the teacher was able to assess each one's attitudes, values, and needs. The participants also learned a great deal about themselves and their partners in the situation.

Examples of role-playing situations that can be quite productive include:

1. Student A plays a teacher who has given a very poor mark to an essay written by Student B. Student B's task is to convince the teacher that the grade should be much higher.
2. Student A plays the president of a real estate association who is against selling homes in a certain exclusive area to members of minority groups. Students B, C, and D are members of the real estate board. One supports the president's position, but the other two are against it. The four must reach a consensus on the issue.
3. Student A plays a person who has only 20 minutes left to live. During this time the student reminisces aloud about his or her life, including successes, failures, joys, regrets, hopes, and the like. This situation is highly flexible in that it may be restricted to a single student or elaborated to include a larger group. In any case, an audience is usually required. Most students do not perform well in a room by themselves.

Dramatization

Dramatization is similar to role playing except that the parts are more structured, as in a school play. A dramatization for sixth through twelfth grades might explore how a student would feel after being turned down for a date by a person he or she especially likes. Students would be instructed to present their feelings as if they were talking to a friend as they walked home from school. They must specifically express disappointment and anger and the belief that the opposite sex is exploitative and inconsiderate of others' feelings. The teacher would then carefully observe how each student reacts to the situation. The purpose of this exercise is to evaluate and gain understanding of both the students playing the parts and the class's maturity and developmental level. Findings may be useful in planning future lessons or as a focus for later discussion. Teachers can even use this technique to evaluate the effectiveness of their teaching, especially efforts directed towards the affective domain.

Free Discussion

Free discussion is probably the most commonly used method of evaluating how students feel about various issues. The teacher begins a class discussion on a topic of interest and bases assessments on students' comments and reactions. A problem with this method is that more verbal students tend to dominate the conversation, even though they may not express the majority opinion or attitude. For this reason, the teacher may systematically elicit comments from *each* student or divide the class into small groups so that each individual will have an opportunity to speak out. This is an essential technique for evaluating teaching aimed at the affective domain and for gauging attitudes and values. During free discussion, the teacher can openly raise the specific issues he or she is concerned with and evaluate the students' reactions and comments. It is not recommended that free discussion be used for purposes of grading, but it *can* be an effective gauge of student development. It is especially useful in the social sciences.

Autobiographies

Autobiographies, or students' accounts of their life stories, are another effective means by which teachers can gain understanding of their students. The personal information a youngster chooses to reveal, as well as that which he or she chooses to withhold, can be very telling, and the majority of students are quite open and honest.

A problem with the autobiography approach is that it is a self-report technique, and, as such, a teacher has no way of judging how honest and accurate the answers are. It is quite possible that a student may leave out some information because he or she may not want the teacher to find out about certain events or prefers not to talk about some topics because they are embarrassing. Teachers should therefore respect their students' privacy and use an autobiography's content only to help specific individuals. To avoid any possible negative effects, an autobiography should never be read aloud in class or shared with others without express permission from its writer.

Problems with Self-Report Devices

Probably the foremost problem with any self-report device is the ease with which the students can fake answers in order to create desired impressions. Extensive research has found that many students will try to guess what the teacher wants and then give answers that will create the best impression rather than those that express their true feelings.

For example, it was found that almost all subjects answer no to the question "Have you ever felt like you wanted to murder someone?" Subjects apparently think that it is not nice or proper to answer yes to this question, even though research has shown that a significant number of people have *felt* this way at one time or another. Since it is quite difficult to prove that a self-reported answer is accurate, steps must be taken to reduce the effect of falsified responses. Among the ways to reduce distortion on self-report tools are:

1. Two similar questions may be asked in different sections of the survey. For example, question 29 might ask "Do you occasionally feel bored?" and question 46 might be "How often do you feel bored?" The teacher could then check how well the two responses correspond.
2. The same information may be requested in opposite ways. For example, on a true-or-false survey, item 5 could be "I have never felt that I wanted to hurt someone," while item 68 could be "I have felt at times that I wanted to hurt someone." This provides a cross check for consistency.
3. A very large number of questions may be asked in the hope that respondents will grow tired of faking. If students know that they have many questions to answer in a limited amount of time, they are less likely to spend time thinking about which answers *look* best. When forced to answer quickly respondents will give more accurate responses.
4. Norms may also be used to gauge the accuracy of responses. Norms indicate that a certain percentage of students can be expected to answer in a given way. If a significant number of student responses don't correspond to the norms, it may *indicate* that the students are not being fully honest.
5. A forced-choice questionnaire may help to reduce faking. For example, if students have a set of equally complimentary terms to choose from (such as the brightest, the most beautiful, the most charming), they will choose the response that they feel is most accurate. Likewise, if forced to choose from a set of equally uncomplimentary terms (ugliest, stupidest, most boring), they are likely to choose in keeping with self-image.

Some teachers do not like to use questions that look at negative qualities because they believe that such questions force students to look at the worst aspects of themselves. Other teachers contend that in order to help students, they need to know what they feel about themselves, their work, and their performance as students and human beings. In the process, they may uncover some sore spots, but this is an unavoidable necessity if students are to be helped in the long run.

Summary

There are three basic types of social measurement tools: self-report, observational, and collective observational tools. One of the oldest and best self-report techniques is the personal interview, in which much useful information can be discovered. Interest surveys are another important self-report instrument designed to tap students' various interests. The most frequent use of interest studies is to determine common interests in order to please as many students as possible. Self-expressive devices are observational tools which stimulate the actual behavior the teacher wants to evaluate. Role playing, dramatization, free discussion, and autobiographies are some of the more common self-expressive devices. Certain steps can and should be taken to reduce the effect of falsified responses.

Suggested Readings

Ahmann, Stanley and Marvin Glock. *Evaluating Pupil Growth: Principles of Tests and Measurements*. 5th rev. ed. Boston: Allyn and Bacon, 1975. Chapter 13.

Gerberich, J. Raymond, Harry A. Greene and Albert N. Jorgensen. *Measurement and Evaluation in the Modern School*. New York: David McKay, 1962.

Mehrens, William A. and Irvin J. Lehmann. *Measurement and Evaluation in Education and Psychology*. 2d rev. ed. New York: Holt, Rinehart and Winston, 1978. Chapter 12.

Noll, Victor H., Dale P. Scannell and Robert C. Craig. *Introduction to Educational Measurement*. Boston: Houghton Mifflin, 1979. Chapters 13, 14.

Ross, Clay Campbell and Julian C. Stanley. *Measurement in Today's Schools*. Englewood Cliffs, N. J.: Prentice Hall, 1954. Chapter 2.

Thorndike, Robert L. and Elizabeth Hagen. *Measurement and Evaluation in Psychology and Education*. 4th rev. ed. New York: John Wiley and Sons, 1977. Chapter 12.

19 Sociograms and Other Sociometric Tools

What Is A Sociogram?

A **sociogram** is a method of measuring the interpersonal structure of a group of people. It is such a popular tool that in some school districts teachers are required to do sociograms of their classes two or more times per year. To construct a sociogram, a teacher simply finds out who likes who and graphs the information, which yields a representation of the social structure of the class.

A teacher making a sociogram often collects data and makes up a new seating chart at the same time. Students are asked to help with the new seating arrangement by writing their names and the names of three students they wish to sit by. So that students will rank order the names, they are asked to indicate the person they'd most like to sit with and their second and third choices, just in case the teacher cannot match all first preferences.[1] To counteract such reverse thinking as, "The teacher wants to know who we like so he can minimize talking during class by putting us on opposite sides of the room," many teachers stress that they will at least *try* to put each student by his or her first or second choice and make changes later if it doesn't work out.

Other reasons may be given for needing the data, but the reason should always be acted upon. For example, if a teacher tells students she is going to develop a new seating chart, she should do so; and the students should be in their new seats within a week. If the teacher does not plan to develop a new seating chart, a different approach should be used. Posing a hypothetical question usually works well. Among the most successful are:

1. If we were going on a field trip and you had to sit next to one person on the bus, who would that person be?

---

[1] Some teachers believe it is best that students *not* know a sociogram is being done, while others openly explain the process to the class.

Sociogram matrix
Stars
Co-stars
Neglectees
Isolates
Schematic diagram
Guess-who survey
Paired-comparison method

2. If we were going to do a lab experiment (work on a project, write a paper), who would you want to work with?
3. If you were stranded on an island, what student in this class would you choose as your one and only companion?
4. If you could choose a locker partner, who would it be?

The results of the completed sociogram depend somewhat upon the question asked. The previous questions ask for either a *social* preference or an *academic* preference. As a social preference, a student may select someone with whom he or she enjoys spending time, who is popular, or with whom he or she feels compatible. As an academic preference, a student may select the person he or she feels is most helpful, the brightest, or the most scholastically capable. Some teachers thus may develop two sociograms, one to find out *social* preferences and a second one to find out *academic* preferences. In many cases the results are not drastically different.

Table 19.1   Preparing a Sociogram: Listing of Students' Choices

	Selector	1st Choice	2nd Choice	3rd Choice
1	Andy	Donnie	Derrick	Katja
2	Joyce	Katja	Karen	Andy
3	Erwin	Abby	Donnie	Andy
4	Derrick	Andy	Abby	Katja
5	Donnie	Derrick	Andy	Scott
6	Abby	Katja	Derrick	Randy
7	Scott	Andy	Donnie	Derrick
8	Karen	Katja	Andy	Abby
9	Randy	Scott	Abby	Andy
10	Katja	Abby	Donnie	Scott

The collected data will consist of a sheet of paper from each student that contains the student's own name and three other names. This data can be compiled in the format shown in Figure 19.1. For illustration purposes, we will use ten names. Using such a small sample will distort our findings somewhat, but will simplify our explanation.

Figure 19.1 Sociogram Matrix

	Andy	Joyce	Erwin	Derrick	Donnie	Abby	Scott	Karen	Randy	Katja
Andy				2	3					1
Joyce	3							2		3
Erwin	1				2	3				
Derrick	3					2				1
Donnie	2			3			1			
Abby				2					1	3
Scott	3			1						
Karen	2					1				3
Randy	1					2	3			
Katja	0			2		3	1			
Total	15	0	0	8	7	11	5	2	1	11

Information from the list is charted in the form of a matrix, as shown in Figure 19.1. Both the horizontal and vertical columns list the students' names in identical order. Choices are then assigned a point value: first choices are given three points, second choices receive two points, and third choices earn one point. Andy's first choice is Donnie, so Donnie would be given three points. The points are placed below the person's name in the vertical column. The number of points a person in the vertical column gave a person in the horizontal column is indicated at the point where the two columns intersect. The entire table is completed in this manner. Then, column-by-column, the points are totalled from top to bottom and written below each name. In this case, Andy has 15 points, Joyce 0 points, Erwin 0 points, and so forth. Students are then placed in the following categories:

1. **Stars** are the students who were chosen most often. They are the most popular according to the number of points earned. Although there is no strict cut-off point between stars and the next category, co-stars, we usually try to limit the first group to the top three or four choices and make the difference as noticeable as possible. In the data we are considering, the stars would probably include Andy, Abby, and Katja.
2. **Co-stars** are the students who have received a goodly number of points, but not as many as the stars. In our example, Derrick and Donnie would be classified as co-stars. Some teachers might include Scott, others might not.
3. **Neglectees** are students who have received no more than one to three points. While these youngsters are not totally cut off, their classmates clearly assign them a socially inferior position. In our example, the neglectees would be Karen and Randy.
4. Because **isolates** receive no points whatsoever, they are considered to be totally cut off from the class. Sometimes the isolates are foreign students, new students, very shy students, or students who stand out as clearly different from the rest of the class.

This method only labels the students at each end of the continuum—the most popular and the least popular. Overgeneralizations about the meaning of these results, therefore, must be avoided. It is important to recognize that stars may still have many social or other problems and that neglectees and isolates need not necessarily have serious problems at all.

In the ideal class, every student would give 6 points: one first choice, or 3 points; one second choice, or 2 points; and one third choice, or 1 point, for a total of 6 points), and each would receive 6 points. If the class portrayed in Figure 19.1 were perfectly balanced, each child would have received a total score of 6 points. While such a situation would be rare, it is a goal most teachers work towards. The *greater the differences* between scores, the less social homogeneity there is among students and the more work there is for the teacher. Increased homogeneity makes a class easier to work with.

The Problem of Negativity

Sociograms may also be based on negative choices. Such information can be very helpful to a teacher. Some students are simply ignored and are neither liked nor disliked, but others are openly rejected. If a teacher can determine who these youngsters are, she can help them to become better integrated in the class. To gather the necessary data, the usual hypothetical questions are posed in reverse and students are asked whom they would least like to sit by, work with, and so forth. Results are also tallied in much the same way, but with negative values assigned to the rankings: −3 points for each first choice, −2 points for each second choice, and −1 point for each third choice. The student who has the greatest number of negative points would probably be *in most need* of special help.

A problem with this approach is that sometimes the students have not thought much about who they "dislike the most," and this technique may force a student to crystallize some vague negative feelings he or she may have. Also, some contend that a good teacher should know which students are unpopular, but study after study has found that teachers' and students' opinions often don't coincide. (Gronlund 1976) No matter how sensitive a teacher may be to his or her students, sociograms are still a more exact way of determining the social structure of a class.

Schematic Diagrams

A **schematic diagram** is a pictorial way of quickly assessing the total social structure of a class. Such a diagram is a trial-and-error process that takes time and patience to develop. Even at best, it remains merely a rough approximation of the actual situation.

The first step in preparing a diagram is to write the names of the students with the highest vote totals near the center of a large sheet of paper. Students with less points are placed progressively farther away from the center. The fewer points a student has, the farther away from the center he or she is placed. The names of males are usually placed in boxes, while names of females are placed in circles (see Figure 19.2). Then, for small classes, first, second, and third choices are diagrammed. For example, using the data collected, a line with an arrowhead would be drawn from Andy to Donnie and from Joyce to Katja. There are several ways to distinguish first, second, and third choices. Some of these are as follows:

1. First choice, three lines with one arrowhead ⟹ ; second choice, two lines with one arrowhead ⟹ ; and third choice, one line with one arrowhead ⟶.
2. First choice red, second choice blue, and third choice green.
3. First-choice indicators are marked on a piece of clear plastic taped on top of a large 8 1/2'' x 11'' card; second choices are diagrammed on a second piece of clear plastic taped on the right side; and third choices are marked on a piece of plastic taped on the left side. The names, boxes, and circles are drawn on the card or a sheet of paper

Figure 19.2 Schematic Diagram

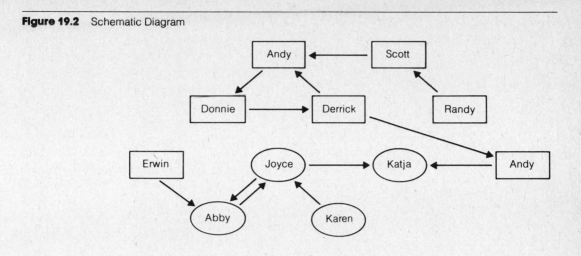

below. Any one, two, or all three of the sheets with indicators can be flipped over the base. This format enables the teacher to assess the class in terms of first choices, second choices, third choices, or any combination thereof. This system works quite well but can be time-consuming to prepare.

For larger classes, it is generally easier to diagram only first and second choices, or merely first choices. If too much information is included, the diagram becomes too cluttered and difficult to read.

During the diagraming process, the teacher should be particularly careful to look for cliques and cleavages. A **clique** is a small group of students who choose each other—for example, Fred chooses Larry, Larry chooses Tom, and Tom chooses Fred (Figure 19.3). One can usually determine if a clique exists by looking at first, second, and third choices. For example, Fred's first choice could be Larry and his second choice could be Tom (Figure 19.4). A clique made up of two people is called a **dyad**, and a clique made up of three people is called a **triad**.

A **cleavage** is a clear division between two groups. Among the most common cleavages are:

1. male—female
2. college prep—non-college prep
3. one race—another race
4. students from one geographical area—students from another geographical area
5. athletes—nonathletes
6. one ethnic group—another ethnic group

Figure 19.3   Figure 19.4

First Choice   Second Choice

A clique is a small group of students who stick together, while a cleavage splits a class roughly in half. Sometimes a class is cleaved in two ways, perhaps between blacks and whites *and* between males and females. The white males tend to choose other white males and *not* black males, black females or white females. Likewise, the black males choose mostly black males, and *not* white males, black females, or white females. Once this is discovered, the teacher can work on eliminating these artificial boundaries by helping students to select their friends for more relevant reasons, such as common interests or goals.

The Accuracy of the Sociogram

The level of accuracy of the sociogram increases in direct proportion to the age and maturity of the students. Sociograms are not as valid for the retarded, and sometimes even the handicapped, due to their traditional segregation. With very young students, the sociogram is extremely unstable. Their choices can change daily, depending on their moods and recent events. With third-, fourth- and fifth-graders, accuracy begins to increase, and with high school students, accuracy tends to be quite high. If a group of sixteen-year-olds were to complete two sociograms separated by one month's time, few differences would usually be found.

Using Sociometric Data to Improve Classroom Environment

The social structure of the classroom is an extremely important part of the learning experience. Once a teacher has determined that a change in social structure is justified, he or she must proceed with care. A sociogram can provide much useful information, but it should be used only as a *guide* to help teachers learn about students' present patterns of stated association preferences. To make optimal use of a sociogram, a teacher must combine his or her previous knowlege of the students with the information presented in the sociogram. If a teacher knows that Butch tends to be aggressive and pugnacious, she may not be surprised if he receives many negative choices on a sociogram. But discovering who Butch antagonizes, and who antagonizes him, can be useful in first understanding and then solving the problem.

Most teachers respond to the results of a sociogram by regrouping class members. The new groups are usually fairly subjective products of trial and error. In general, teachers try to attain balance by placing one star, several average students, and an isolate in each group. A group may be defined as a set of students at one table, one row of desks, a team for a special project, or some other classroom division. Sometimes it is quite functional to have students work in triads, with average students in one set of groups, stars in another, and isolates in a third. In addition, the teacher usually tries to match the students' personalities. Even though one student is an isolate and another is a star, they may have very similar personalities, interests, likes and dislikes.

Another technique is to arrange the seating chart so that each student is placed where he or she will gain the most benefit from the surrounding people or things. For example, seating an isolate next to the wastebasket, pencil sharpener, or door can be very effective because it puts the child in the spotlight as well as in a physical position to get to know others. Notice the following example:

According to a sociogram, Carey, a very shy, quiet fourth-grader, was an isolate. Having observed his behavior and talked with him and his parents, his teacher was convinced that he had no emotional, personality, or other problems. Although Carey was very shy, other students tended to accept him once they got to know him. The teacher decided to place Carey strategically in the front corner of the room by the wastebasket. Each time a student threw a piece of paper away, he or she and Carey would invariably notice each other. If a crumpled piece of paper thrown from a distance landed in the basket, Carey would often respond with a smile and, later, a little clap of his hands or admiring comments. In time, Carey became more integrated into the social structure of the classroom.

Sometimes a child is an isolate or rejectee because he or she is perceived as different from others. This problem can be reduced by encouraging students to understand and accept the differences they find in their peers. Sometimes a presentation about each culture is effective. One teacher invited representatives of local ethnic groups to give presentations about their cultures—Mexican, Italian, Vietnamese, Pakistani, Kenyan, and so forth. Each child has unique qualities, abilities, interests, attitudes, and values. It is the teacher's responsibility to identify the positive qualities in *all* students and encourage class members to appreciate them.

Obviously though, if individual children are singled out, or if only the qualities of a few children are displayed, problems could develop. It is much better to present the strong points of *each* and *every* student in front of the class. Sometimes, this could be done in groups, i.e., if there are three or four children of Spanish extraction, they, as a group could present a symposium. One student could cover Spanish history, another Spanish culture, and the last student scientific, social and cultural contributions of the Spanish people.

Other skills that the children have could be demonstrated to the whole class. One teacher learned that a student who was extremely shy had a strong interest in photography. The teacher had the student, an eighth grade boy, bring a Polaroid camera to class to demonstrate its operation. He even took apart a roll of film to show the students how the film worked. After this demonstration, the class warmed up towards him, and for the first time included him in several of their social activities.

Special team projects may also be used as a means of reorganizing classroom social structure. Studies have shown that in many cases personal contact reduces antagonism and facilitates acceptance (Secord et al. 1964). Since contact can at times increase antagonism, however, a teacher should carefully monitor such groups to ensure smooth progress.

An extremely successful technique is to use isolates and neglectees as tutors to help either peers or younger students. When cast in the role of tutor, the child becomes an authority and an expert, which highly facilitates social development (Bergman 1978). A tutoring relationship with a younger child can be especially productive in that the younger student is likely to look up to the older student, even though the older one may be shy and introverted among peers. Working with a younger child helps the shy boy or girl develop confidence, poise, experience in social relations, and enjoyable contacts with others.

Other techniques for integrating the class and reducing social barriers include role playing, problem discussion groups, and even T-groups. These, and sometimes other change-inducing processes, may be best implemented in cooperation with the school psychologist, social worker, counselor, or other specialist in human behavior. The teacher should take full advantage of available school and community resources.

The Sociometric Index

Teachers often wish to compare students' social acceptance in one class with their social acceptance in other classes for the same year or previous years. This can be done by using the **sociometric index**, a formula that gives each student a standardized rating for purposes of comparison. The sociometric index formula is as follows:

$$CS_j = \frac{\Sigma C_j}{N - 1}$$

CS_j = the choice status of individual j
ΣC_j = the sum (Σ) of the number of first choices a student receives (In the following example, Andy would have a ΣC_j of 3 because three people chose him first.)
N = the total number of individuals in the group ($N - 1$ is used because the individual being scored is not counted.)

Example: Andy received three first choices in a class of ten students. What would his sociometric index be? The calculation would be:

$$CS_j = \frac{\Sigma C_j}{N - 1} = \frac{3}{10 - 1} = \frac{3}{9} = .333$$

A score of 1.0 would means that everyone in the class chose the student first, while a score of 0 would mean that no one chose him or her first. For this index only *first* choices are used, not the total number of points. If every student in a class of ten chose Andy as their first choice and he did not choose himself, he would have a total of nine first choices. The calculation would then be:

$$\frac{9}{10 - 1} = \frac{9}{9} = 1.00$$

If a student does not receive *any* choices, the index would be:

$$\frac{0}{10 - 1} = \frac{0}{9} = 0$$

The Expansive Sociometric Index

It is usually preferable to include *all* choices rather than just first choices. Depending on one's purposes, this can be more accurate. If this technique is used, one would simply count the total number of times the student was chosen and proceed as before. For example, Andy received three first choices, two second choices and two third choices, or a total of seven choices. The same formula is used, but the number 7 is used in place of the number 3. Continuing to use Andy as an example, the formula (called SC_{ij} to differentiate it from the previous formula) is as follows:

$$SC_{ij} = \frac{\Sigma C_{ij}}{N - 1} = \frac{7}{10 - 1} = \frac{7}{9} = 7.7$$

The disadvantage of this formula is that it doesn't take into account how many first choices, second choices, or third choices a student received. If we add up the total number of points (3 points for each first choice, 2 points for each second choice and 1 point for each third choice,) we are able to consider not only the *number* of choices, but also, to some degree, whether the choices were first, second, or third. In this system, one first choice could be equivalent to three third choices. Calculation of Andy's score under this system would be:

Number of Choices	Point Value	Total
3	3	9
2	2	4
2	1	2
		15

$$\text{SC points} = \frac{15}{10 - 1} = \frac{15}{9} = 1.67$$

The last formula is the most commonly used because it takes into account the most information. When working with these indexes, it is important that the teacher compare only like data obtained from like formulas. It is not crucial which formula is used, as long as the teacher is *consistent* when making comparisons. Some schools make it a policy to use one formula consistently, often the third one. Then a teacher can easily compare students' results in various classes.

The obvious advantage of this technique is that it enables the teacher to assess each student's social growth. It is preferable to assess such progress on a long-term basis because social growth is typically slow. So many factors may come into play that the teacher must be very cautious in interpreting the results of a sociometric index.

Guess-Who Surveys

A **guess-who survey** is a peer-appraisal technique that helps the teacher assess students' perceptions of each other. This technique is very simple and forms of it can be used from first grade through college. The teacher presents a list of traits, behaviors, attitudes, and values and asks the students to supply the name of the person each trait most appropriately describes. For example, the teacher may ask:

In our class, guess who is the
1. friendliest _____
2. shyest _____
3. smartest _____
4. slowest _____
5. most popular _____
6. kindest _____
7. bravest _____

The teacher then tabulates the number of times each student is mentioned for each trait. For example, Reginald may receive 12 votes as the friendliest, 3 votes as the smartest, 9 votes as the most popular, and 2 votes as the bravest. Generally, the votes will be quite consistent, with only a few contradictions.

Some teachers prefer to list only positive traits, feeling that asking the class to focus on negative characteristics can only reinforce negative feelings. Others argue that in order to help students, the teacher has to know the perceptions of their peers. If the class as a whole perceives, for example, that Chuck is the slowest, then the teacher is able to work actively to reverse this perception.

As with sociograms, some teachers may be surprised by some of the results of a guess-who survey. This may be caused by the fact that teachers tend to judge students according to their own values and assume that students judge their peers according to similar criteria. Students' perceptions of each other are generally quite different from the teacher's perceptions of them. Furthermore, it is important to recall constantly that guess-who surveys deal *only* in perceptions, not reality.

Some teachers attempt to quantify the results of a guess-who survey by deducting 1 point for each trait that is considered negative and adding 1 point for each that is considered positive. Under such a system, neutral traits are also classified as positive. Some teachers even attempt to give each trait a weighted point value. For example, *shyest* might be weighted as −3 points and *most popular* as +10 points. Assigning point values is a difficult and highly subjective process. Nonetheless, as long as the teacher is consistent, some rough comparisons can be made.

Paired Comparison Method

When the **paired comparison method** is used, a rater considers only two students at a time and indicates which member of the pair is superior for the trait being measured. Raters may be teachers, peers, members of the counseling staff, or other relevant parties. The number of times each student is checked for each trait is then tallied.

Example: For *each* pair, circle the name of the student in our class who you feel is the *most honest*.

1. Reginald — Marcus
2. Reginald — Al
3. Jeri — Sally
4. Sue — Marci
5. Jeri — Al
6. Sue — Al
7. Reginald — Sally
8. Reginald — Sue

The problem with this approach is that its use in larger classes is more difficult because of the large number of *possible combinations*. In smaller classes, however, the teacher can compare each student with each other student. If there are ten students, each name could be listed nine times so that it would occur once in combination with each other student.

Invasion of Privacy

Most teachers find they need *many* kinds of data in order to help students realize their potential. This may entail delving into areas that some people may consider highly private. Every teacher should thus be very sensitive to students' personal feelings when using sociometric and self-report tools. The information-gathering process should be treated with seriousness, and much emphasis should be placed on the fact that the data gleaned will be used only in the most constructive ways possible. Furthermore, students should clearly understand that they need never answer if they prefer not to. For example, while passing out an interest survey, a teacher might say:

> Every year my class fills out an interest survey to help me develop activities around their specific interests. I'd like you to fill one out for me too. That way I can plan to do things I think you'll enjoy, and, in addition, I'll get to know each of you a little better. Feel free to add any comments you wish, and if there is something you prefer not to talk about, or prefer to talk about privately, that's okay too. Most of the questions ask about things you like to do, so

you might find that they're actually fun to answer. Obviously this won't be graded, and nothing you say will be held against you.

With an introduction such as this, there are rarely any problems, and the students accept the interest survey as a matter of course.

Like all feedback tools, sociometric measures should be used with *caution, skill, and a keen awareness of their limitations.* All information teachers obtain about their students, including their academic progress and their intelligence scores, is confidential. A teacher does not have the right to tell *anyone* about a student's academic progress or about his or her placement on a sociogram. Generally, within the school, it is acceptable practice to convey necessary information to other professionals who have a clear need for it. This includes other teachers, the guidance staff, principal, school nurse, and similar concerned parties. In all cases, respect for students' privacy and dignity should be the uppermost concern.

Many teachers obtain permission from the school administration before using such tools as sociograms, interest surveys, or attitude surveys. If any parents do object, which is bound to happen from time to time, most teachers find that if they stress that the main function of these tools is to help the students, most parents are supportive. Within the classroom, if the tools are introduced as a routine part of the curriculum and as a way of helping individuals and the class as a whole, most youngsters accept them without reservation.

Summary

In this chapter, we have looked at sociograms and how they can be used to facilitate a student's social adjustment in the classroom. Social integration is a key factor in the learning process. Students who are happy among their peers will learn much more effectively than those who are rejected or have a difficult time relating to others. Sociograms help identify strengths and weaknesses in the class's social structure and facilitate their remediation. They are a limited but useful first step in helping the teacher understand and help students.

Suggested Readings

Mehrens, William A. and Irvin J. Lehmann. *Measurement and Evaluation in Education and Psychology*. New York: Holt Rinehart and Winston, 1978. Chapter 12.

Noll, Victor H., Dale P. Scannell and Robert C. Craig. *Introduction to Educational Measurement*, 4th rev. ed. Boston: Houghton Mifflin, 1979. Chapter 14.

TenBrink, Terry D. *Evaluation: A Practical Guide for Teachers*. New York: McGraw-Hill, 1974. Chapter 11.

Part IV
Statistics

20   Introduction to Statistics

Statistics are *tools* that help us to state and understand test data. The primary purpose of these chapters is to introduce some basic information about the meaning of statistics and how and why they are used.

It is quite true that statistics are commonly abused and can sometimes be manipulated to "prove" contradictory ideas. A person who understands the use of statistics, however, will generally not be fooled by this misuse. Any tool can be abused, including both standardized and teacher-made tests. But understanding statistics can help the teacher better interpret test data and thereby better help students.

When considering statistics, it is important to keep in mind that they tell something that is true for a specific group as a whole, but not for every individual, or even for most individuals, in the group. For example, statistically speaking, the gifted child is taller, more socially aware, and more athletic than the nongifted child. This does not mean that *every* gifted child is taller than average, or even that most are, but only that the *average* gifted child is taller. (Spence et al. 1968) Thus, the chances are that any one gifted child, when compared with a nongifted child, will be taller. For example:

Heights of Two Groups of Teenage Males

Gifted		Nongifted	
Bill	5'11'' (71'')	Tom	6'1'' (73'')
Larry	5'8'' (68'')	Mark	5'2'' (62'')
Telly	5'7'' (67'')	Anatole	5'9'' (69'')
Aaron	6'3'' (75'')	Gregg	5'11'' (71'')
Terry	5'10'' (70'')	Harold	5'5'' (65'')
Mikal	5'11'' (71'')	Milton	5'10'' (70'')
Average = 5'10'' (70'')		Average = 5'8'' (68'')	

The gifted boys are, *on the average,* taller than the nongifted boys. Nonetheless, there are still several in the gifted group who are shorter

Key Concepts   Descriptive statistics
                        Inferential statistics
                        Nominal scale
                        Ordinal scale
                        Ratio scale
                        Raw score
                        Derived score

than the *average* for the nongifted group. On an individual basis, a number of the gifted boys are also shorter than specific nongifted boys. The fact that individual cases vary from the average is to be expected and does not detract from the veracity of the statistic.

Classification of Statistics

Descriptive Statistics

To illustrate how statistics can help us use and understand a group of test scores, consider the case of a teacher who has just given her class an exam covering a unit of material that she had presented in an innovative way. Other teachers, curious about the effectiveness of the new technique, have been asking how the students did on the exam. In reply, the teacher could say, "Johnny got an 87, Larry a 52, Michele a 94, Aaron an 87, Tony a 93, Katja a 69, Norbert a 62. . . ." If it were a large class, few would want to hear the score of every student, and even those who did listen to the full report would probably still not know how well the class did as a whole. If this teacher knew statistics, she would know that the easiest way to *organize, describe, or summarize* a class's performance is to *average* all the individual scores. In this case, the teacher might find averages of 78 percent correct for the innovative class and only 54 percent correct for a noninnovative class. She then could compare this with the innovative class's previous average, which was 62 percent. A possible comparison between the two groups then becomes obvious. The data are immediately useful because they indicate that the innovative method probably is better. This type of statistic is called a **descriptive statistic** because it attempts to describe a population, usually by summarizing a large set of data. This is an important branch of statistics that will be examined more closely in the following pages.

Inferential Statistics

The other basic type of statistic is an **inferential statistic**. Inferential statistics attempt to predict or infer something about a large group, the population, by looking at a representative small group, the sample. For example, assume that we measure the height of every tenth male who walks into a high school between seven and nine o'clock in the morning. From this group (the sample), we find an average height and then *infer* that this average height would apply to all boys in that school (our population). That is, if the average height of the boys in our sample was 5'10'', we could reasonably infer that the male population at that high school averages 5' 10'' in height. From a fairly large sample, we can make specific predictions about an entire school population. If we measured the height of every student and found the average, we would have a **descriptive statistic**. We would not need to *infer* from a sample to the entire population because we have measured the entire population.

There are several problems inherent in using inferential statistics. One is that members of the original sample may differ in some way from the whole population. If this occurs, it is called **sampling error**. Assume, for instance, that I measure only the first 20 male high school students who enter the school. I may obtain a **biased** sample if the basketball team is practicing early and the students who happen to come in are mostly members of the team. Such a sample would *not* be representative of the whole school, and any inferences based on it would most likely be inaccurate.

The Mathematical Bases of Statistics

In order to understand the statistics discussed in this book, one need only know how to add, subtract, multiply, and divide and understand three other operations: signed numbers, squaring, and square roots. These three operations will be discussed below. Readers who are familiar with negative numbers can skip to page 247.

Signed Numbers

Signed numbers are numbers that are accompanied by either a positive sign (+) or a negative sign (−). Usually a sign is written only if the number is negative. If there is no sign by a number, we assume that it is positive; thus, $3 = +3$. In working with signed numbers, there are several rules to remember:

1. When numbers with *like* signs are added, the answer has the same sign as the original numbers. The sum of positive numbers is always positive, and the sum of negative numbers is always negative:

$$(+2) + (+2) = (+4) \quad (-2) + (-2) = (-4)$$

2. When numbers with *unlike* signs are added, the smaller number is subtracted from the larger number and the sign of the *larger* number appears in the answer:

$$(+4) + (-3) = (+1) \quad (+4) + (-20) = (-16)$$
$$(-20) + (+10) = (-10)$$

3. When numbers with unlike signs are subtracted, the sign of the number being subtracted is reversed and the numbers are then added:

$$(+7) - (-7) = (+7) + (+7) = (+14)$$
$$(-7) - (-7) = (-7) + (+7) = (0)$$

4. When signed numbers are multiplied or divided, if the signs are the *same*, the answer is always a positive:

$$(-4) \times (-4) = (+16) \quad (+6) \times (+6) = (+36)$$
$$(-8) \div (-2) = (+4) \quad (+12) \div (+4) = (+3)$$

5. When numbers with unlike signs are multiplied or divided, the answer is always a *negative* number:

$$(-3) \times (+4) = (-12) \quad (-8) \div (+2) = (-4)$$

Squares

To square a number is to multiply the number by itself. Thus, $2^2 = 2 \times 2 = 4$, $9^2 = 9 \times 9 = 81$, and $10^2 = 10 \times 10 = 100$. When a positive number is squared, the answer is positive. Likewise, when a negative number is squared, the answer is positive. Thus, whether a number is positive or negative, its square is *always* positive: $4^2 = 16$ and $-4^2 = 16$.

Square Roots

The square root of a number is the number that multiplied by itself equals the original number. For example, to find the square root of 9 ($\sqrt{9}$), one determines what number times itself equals nine. In this case the answer is 3 ($3 \times 3 = 9$). There is a trial and error formula that can be used to determine square roots, but an easier method is to consult a square root table or use a hand calculator that computes square roots. In this book, most of the square roots will be easy to calculate, such as $\sqrt{25}$, $\sqrt{49}$, $\sqrt{144}$, and so forth.

Discrete and Continuous Numbers

Discrete numbers are numbers arrived at by counting individual items. For example, the number of people in a room is represented by a discrete number. Discrete numbers are always whole numbers and can take on only designated values: there can be only a fixed number of people in a room and, of course, there would be no fractions of people.

Continuous numbers are numbers that result from *measuring*. They may fall *anywhere* along the scale being used. For example, a student may be measured as 5 feet, 11.5 inches tall. To be more accurate, one might measure again and find that the student is 5 feet, 11.53 inches tall. Theoretically, there is *no limit* to the accuracy of the measurement. One can always measure more accurately, reaching even millionths of an inch or beyond.

Since the accuracy of any measurement can always be increased, all continuous numbers are *estimates*. The estimate may be very close, and there may be no need for more accuracy; nonetheless, this type of number is *always* an estimate.

Some numbers that are continuous may *appear* to be discrete. For example, one might assume that one two-pound weight would be equal to another two-pound weight. However, if the two objects are weighed on a very accurate balance, one may find that the first weight actually weighs 2.0047 pounds, whereas the second weight actually weighs 2.0091 pounds. There is clearly a difference, even though it is very small. The more accurate a measuring instrument is, the *more likely* it is to show differences on a continuous scale. This is *not* true for discrete, or counting, numbers. If there are four students in a room, no matter how many times we count them, we will always arrive at the same number. If our original count is correct, we cannot count more accurately.

Discrete numbers are thus very easy to work with. We do not need to estimate, but can simply count the number of answers wrong, the number of students in a room, or the number of books in a library. On the other hand, because continuous numbers are *always estimates*, they can create problems.

For example, when Jay measured his classroom, he found that it was 26 feet long. Since he was measuring only whole feet, the measurement may not be very accurate. If the room actually is 26.7 feet long, 27 feet would be a more accurate measurement. But in order to know that the number is closer to 27 than 26, Jay would have had to measure one decimal point *beyond* the number that he needed. In this case, he should have measured to the first decimal place and then rounded back to a whole number. If this procedure had been followed, one could assume that the measurement of 26 feet actually indicates that the room might be from approximately 25.5 to 26.4 feet in length.

Thus it can be seen that when several measurements are used in combination, normal error is multiplied. For example, consider a room that is measured in whole feet as 16 feet by 19 feet. The minimum area of the room could actually be as small as 15.5×18.5, or 286.75 square feet. The maximum area, on the other hand, could be as much as 16.4×19.4, or 318.16 square feet, a difference of 31.4 square feet. If the room had not been measured one decimal beyond the number needed and rounded off, the error could be much greater. The less precise a measurement is, the greater the possible error it can lead to.

The Form of Estimated Numbers

We can tell certain things about a number just by looking at it. For example, zeros are often used as placeholders for numbers that are arrived at through estimation. It is unlikely, for example, that a student would score an even 400 points on a series of tests unless each test was worth exactly 50 or 100 points and she scored 100% on each test. The most likely total score for most students would be a number like 423 or 397 points. Numbers such as 400 come up occasionally, but not nearly as often as the combined sets of all other combinations, i.e, 461, 392, 403, and so forth. Accordingly, when we see numbers such as 400, 500, 700, and 1,000, we can assume that they are most likely rounded numbers or estimates, while numbers such as 268, 381, 530 and 1,183 are probably *not* rounded. Thus, numbers ending in several zeros, although they may be correct, are likely to be estimates, and sometimes very rough estimates.

Number Scales

Numbers may convey a great deal of information if they are arranged into scales. These scales, in order from the simplest to the most complex, are nominal, ordinal, interval, and ratio.

Nominal Scales

A **nominal scale** is used to *distinguish* one individual or one thing from another. It uses only discrete numbers and conveys the least information of any scale. Essentially, it is used to label or name. An example of a nominal scale is the number on a football player's jersey; this number is used primarily to distinguish one football player from another. Another example is the license plate numbers that are used to distinguish automobiles from each other. Little other information is conveyed by such a number. For instance, larger numbers do not mean that a car is faster or more expensive. Zip codes and social security numbers are also nominal scales.

In these examples, the numbers are used only to name an item or a category. One could easily use a combination of letters to accomplish the same thing. Instead of football player number 22, one could have football player BB.

Ordinal Scales

An ordinal scale distinguishes and names, as does a **nominal scale**, but in addition it assigns a general **rank**, or orders the data. An ordinal scale uses discrete numbers to rank from high to low or vice versa, but the ranking is *general*. We do not know how *much more* a rank of 2 is than a rank of 1; we only know that it is more or greater. Examples would include:

1. Runners cross the finish line in the order of first, second, third, and so forth. The runner who crosses first is not automatically twice as fast as the runner who crosses second. The second place finisher could be a tenth of a second slower than the first, and the third-place finisher could be seven hundredths of a second slower than the second, as shown below:

Place	Name	Time
1	Sandy	8.70 minutes
2	Debbie	8.80 minutes
3	Linda	8.87 minutes

2. Academic rankings of students are almost always ordinal. Ordinal scales are probably the most useful and common type of scale in the field of education. Most statistics used in education, including virtually every test score, are actually only estimates. If Donna receives 100% on a social studies exam and Wally receives 50%, it does not mean that Donna knows twice as much as Wally. It only indicates that she *probably knows more* than he does, at least according to this particular test. Achievement tests and I.Q. scores are actually both ordinal scales.

Interval Scales

An **interval scale** has all the features of nominal and ordinal scales, but in addition to ranking, this scale incorporates uniform units of measurement. For example, there is the same amount of increase in temperature between 1 degree Fahrenheit and 2 degrees Fahrenheit as there is between 101 degrees Fahrenheit and 102 Fahrenheit. An interval scale uses *continuous* numbers. Unfortunately, very few scales in education are this sophisticated—most are only nominal or ordinal. There is not the same degree of "I.Q." difference, for instance, between I.Q.'s of 100 and 110 as there is between I.Q.'s of 150 and 160. Nor is there usually the same difference in achievement between the two scores of 65 and 70 as there is between the scores of 85 to 90.

Ratio Scales

A **ratio scale** has all the characteristics of nominal, ordinal, and interval scales, and, in addition, it starts at zero. A ratio scale is by far the most versatile scale because it is the most flexible and conveys the most information. For example, 20 degrees Kelvin (a system of measuring temperature that begins at absolute zero, or no temperature, i.e. the molecules do not move from their own energy) is exactly *twice* the heat as 10 degrees Kelvin. On an interval scale, on the other hand, 20 degrees Fahrenheit is *not* twice as much heat as 10 degrees Fahrenheit; the two temperatures are actually quite close together. This occurs because the Fahrenheit scale does not begin at absolute zero. Zero degrees Fahrenheit is fairly warm compared to absolute zero. The measurements of weight, time, length, and number wrong on a test are also ratio scales.

Ratio scales are used primarily by physical scientists when the absolute zero of a quality can be measured. Obviously, it is difficult to measure educational concepts in terms of absolute zero. It is the goal of some educators to develop ratio scales for use in the classroom, but many doubt that this is possible.

Raw Scores and Derived or Transformed Scores

After a test is administered and corrected, the teacher assigns it a score based on the number wrong, the number right, or the number of points earned or lost. This is called a **raw score**.

When a raw score is converted into a percentage, a ranking, or a similar statistic for purposes of comparison, it is called a **derived**, or **transformed, score**. The new score is *derived* from the old score, or the old score is *transformed* into a new score. Scores are transformed to make them more meaningful. Instead of reporting that Matt earned 34 points out of 42 or that Kay earned 98 out of 131, we often convert these scores into numbers that are more easily comparable. As is, it is not readily apparent which student performed better; but if both scores are changed to percentages (a fraction with the denominator of 100), we would find that Matt had 76.2% correct and Kay 74.8% correct. When scores are expressed as percents, comparisons are easier to make. Other transformed scores include z-scores and their derivatives, including T-scores and stanines, which will be discussed in Chapter 23.

Summary

Statistics are *tools* that help us to state and understand test data. Statistics tell something that is true for a specific group as a whole, but not for every individual, or even most individuals in the group. There are different classifications of statistics. Descriptive statistics attempt to describe a population by summarizing a large set of data. Inferential statistics try to predict something about a large group by looking at a sample group. In order to understand the statistics discussed in this book, one need only know how to add, subtract, multiply, and divide and understand signed numbers, squaring, and square roots. Numbers may convey a great deal of information if they are arranged into scales. Nominal scales are used to distinguish one individual or thing from another. Ordinal scales not only distinguish or name, but assign a general rank. Interval scales have all the features of nominal and ordinal scales, but also incorporate uniform units of measurement. Ratio scales have all the characteristics of the three other scales and, in addition, start at zero. When a raw score is converted into a percentage, a ranking, or similar statistic, it is called a derived or transformed score. Some transformed scores are percentages, z-scores, T-scores, and stanines.

21   Presenting Data for Ranking and Graphing

When an educator is working with a set of scores, especially a large number of scores, it is often convenient to *rank* them. Ranking scores entails arranging them in a specified order. By tradition, we usually place the highest score at the top, and the lowest score at the bottom. Although the scores could be ranked from lowest to highest, it is so uncommonly done that it could be confusing. If larger numbers relate to higher performance the scores 24, 18, 29, 32, 17, 38, and 14 would be ranked as follows: 38, 32, 29, 24, 18, 17, and 14. On the other hand, if the numbers represent the points *lost,* then the rank would be −14, −17, −18, −24, −29, −32, −38. After a set of scores is rank ordered, it is often helpful to divide it into groups. Several of the many ways this can be done are discussed in the following pages.

Halves, or Bitiles

The simplest way to group scores is to divide them into halves, called **bitiles**. To obtain bitiles, one would, after ranking the scores, split them into two equal sets so that the highest scores would be in the top half and the rest in the bottom half. If there are 30 scores, the best 15 would be in the top bitile and the lowest 15 would be in the bottom bitile. High school graduation classes are often divided this way. Each student is reported as being in either the top or the bottom half of his or her graduating class.

With an even number of scores, one can always divide the set perfectly in half, but with an odd number, there is always one score that falls in the middle. When this occurs, the most common procedure is to put the leftover score in the group to which it is numerically closest. For example, in the set of scores 36, 33, 32, *31,* 26, 24, and 21, the middle score of 31 is only 1 point away from 32 but is 5 points away from 26. Thus it would be placed in the top half of the group. If the distance between the score is equal, it is common practice to put the middle score in the top half. As will be discussed later, there is *no* satisfactory method of dealing with borderline scores. They are almost always a problem.

Quartiles and Quarters

Another convenient way of dividing a set of scores is to split them into four equal groups, or quarters. To find quarters:

1. Rank order the scores from highest to lowest.
2. Count the total number of scores. In statistics, such a total of scores, students, or cases is often signified by the symbol N.
3. Divide N by 4 to see how many students will fall in each group. For example, if there are 100 scores, the number in each group would be $100 \div 4 = 25$.
4. Starting with the highest score, divide the rank ordered list into four groups of 25 scores each. In this case, the top 25 scores would be in the highest, or fourth, quarter; the next 25 would be in the third quarter; the next 25 would be in the second quarter; and the bottom 25 scores would be the lowest, or first, quarter.

For example, consider a set of eight scores: 83, 82, 90, 74, 80, 85, 87, 72. We first rank order them: 90, 87, 85, 83, 82, 80, 74, 72. Since $8 \div 4 = 2$, there will be two scores in each quarter. The two highest scores would be in the fourth quarter, the next two in the third quarter, the next two in the second quarter, and the last two in the bottom, or first, quarter, as follows:

$$\left.\begin{array}{l} 90 \\ \\ 87 \end{array}\right\} \text{fourth quarter}$$

Third quartile (Q_3), 75th percentile

$$\left.\begin{array}{l} 85 \\ \\ 83 \end{array}\right\} \text{third quarter}$$

Second quartile (Q_2), 50th percentile

$$\left.\begin{array}{l} 82 \\ \\ 80 \end{array}\right\} \text{second quarter}$$

First quartile (Q_1), 25th percentile

$$\left.\begin{array}{l} 74 \\ \\ 72 \end{array}\right\} \text{first quarter}$$

Technically, **quartiles** are *points* on a distribution. The first quartile is equal to the twenty-fifth percentile, or what would be the 25th score from the bottom if we had 100 scores. The second quartile is equal to the fiftieth percentile, or the median (the middle score), and the third quartile is equal to the seventy-fifth percentile. The *three* quartiles in a distribution divide it into four equal parts. Technically, each *group* is called a quarter. Sometimes, though, a *quarter* is referred to as a *quartile*. Thus, care must be taken to define terms when speaking of quartiles and quarters. One must also ascertain that there is no confusion about which quarter is the highest: the first quarter contains the lowest scores while the fourth quarter contains the highest ones. To avoid confusion it is probably best to refer to the first quarter as the *bottom* quarter, the second quarter as the *second-from-the-bottom* quarter, and so forth.

Finding Quarters for an Uneven Number of Scores When a set of scores that is not evenly divisible by four (as *are* 8, 12, 16, 20 etc.) is divided into quarters, the same reasoning that is used with bitiles is applied. For classroom purposes, the scores that are closest are usually grouped together. For example, note how the following set of nine scores is divided into quarters:

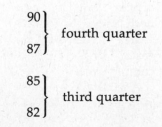

$$\left.\begin{array}{l} 80 \\ \\ 74 \end{array}\right\} \text{ second quarter}$$

$$\left.\begin{array}{l} 72 \\ \\ 70 \end{array}\right\} \text{ first quarter}$$

Once again, when an odd score is an equal amount away from two different groups, it is usually placed in the higher group. When two identical scores would normally fall into two different quarters, adjustments are made so that they are put in the same group, usually the higher one. Like bitiles, quarters are only a rough way of grouping, so subjective factors may enter into final grading, such as class attendance.

The problem of duplicate scores also occurs when scores are ranked from highest to lowest. Consider, for example, the following ranked scores: 90, 88, 87, 85, 85, 82, 80, 78.

Score	Rank	Adjusted Rank
90	1	1
88	2	2
87	3	3
85	4	4.5
85	5	4.5
82	6	6
80	7	7
78	8	8

Percentiles

Percentiles (also called *centiles*) are one of the most common performance reporting methods used in testing and education. They are easy to use, and often convey more information than ranks and many other kinds of scores. Ranks are useful only when two groups of similar size are compared. A rank of 15 out of 30 may easily be compared to a rank of 30 out of 30, but a rank of 15 out of 45 is difficult to quickly compare with a rank of 10 out of 32. When we can mathematically transform scores' denominators to a given standard, comparisons become much easier. Ideal standards are 10, 100, 1,000, and so forth, but the most common is 100.

A **percentile** indicates the position any one score would have *if* there were exactly 100 scores. Under a percentile system, if a student scores in the 92nd percentile, there would be 92 scores below. Rarely, though, do we have exactly 100 scores. Therefore, the number of scores we actually have must be converted to percentiles.

There are few problems calculating percentiles, except when we have a small sample of scores, usually less than 50. When we have more than 50 scores, we can simply divide the total number of scores into the number of scores that ranked below the score for which we want the percentile rank. Then we multiply by 100 to eliminate decimals. This same process is repeated for each score.

For example, Helen's test score of 36 ranked 11th from the top in a class of 60 students. There are thus 49 scores below hers. To calculate a percentile for Helen's score, we would first divide 49 by 60 and then multiply the result by 100:

$$49 \div 60 = .8166 \times 100 = 81.67 = 82$$

Thus Helen would be in the 82nd percentile of her class; or 82 percent of the class scored lower than she did.

In summary, percentiles for 50 or more scores are calculated by dividing the total number of scores into the number of scores that rank *below* the score we are examining. The result is multiplied by 100 to eliminate decimal points. The formula for calculating percentiles is:

where
P_x = percentile rank
B = number of scores or persons below the score for which the percentile is being calculated
N = total number of scores or persons who took the test

$$P_x = \frac{B}{N} \times 100$$

If there are less than 50 scores, problems occur because each score takes up a significant percent of the total distribution. For example, if we have a class of ten students and George's score is higher than the scores of five other students, we would have the following situation:

$$\underset{50\%}{\underline{1 \quad 2 \quad 3 \quad 4 \quad 5}} \quad \underset{10\%}{\underline{6}} \quad \underset{40\%}{\underline{7 \quad 8 \quad 9 \quad 10}}$$

In this case, because we have a small number of scores, the formula is distorted somewhat in that George's score actually takes up 10% of the total sample. Therefore we could place George at the lower end of his score range (51st percentile), in the middle (55th percentile), or at the upper end (59th percentile). Probably the most accurate is the middle part of his score. The above formula, which is fairly accurate for most purposes when a *large* number of scores is to be ranked, would place George at the 50th percentile.

A percentile for a small number of scores is determined by adding the *sum* of scores in the distribution below the score we are concerned with, plus *one-half* of the percent this score comprises in the distribution. For example, since George's score was higher than those of five students and lower than those of four students, 50 percent of the total class would rank below him and 40 percent would rank above. His score range or area would account for 10 percent of all scores if there were 100 scores. Utilizing the formula—the percent of scores below him plus one-half of the percent of the area that his score comprises—would lead to the following calculation:

$$50\% + \frac{10\%}{2} = 55\%$$

Thus, George ranks in the 55th percentile for his class.

Test scores are usually distributed in such a way that most of the scores cluster around the mean, with fewer scores occurring the farther we go in either direction from the mean (see Figure 21.1).

Figure 21.1 Positions of Percentiles on the Scale of Measurement for a Normal Distribution

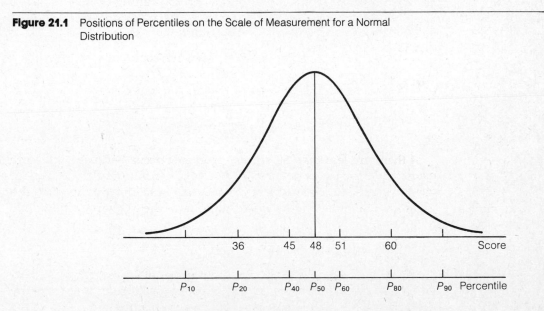

Thus, when percentile ranks are used, small score differences near the center of the distribution produce large differences in percentile ranks, but larger score differences at the extremes produce only small differences in rank. Thus, in the center of the distribution, two scores that are 15 percentiles apart may indicate only insignificant differences in actual performance, while at the top extreme, two scores only five percentiles apart may indicate significant differences in performance.

Summary of Percentiles

Percentiles represent the rank a score would have if there were 100 scores. When a student is characterized as ranking 25th, out of a group of 50, we are speaking of his absolute rank. The same student would have a percentile rank of about 50. The 50th percentile is always the median (middle number), or the second quartile.

If several students earn the same score, their percentile rank is determined by averaging, as with other systems. For example, if three students earned scores of 70, they would fall in the same percentile, which would be the mean of the three ranks. If there were 100 scores and the three scores of 70 ranked 87th, 88th and 89th, respectively, all three scores would have a percentile rank of 88.

One disadvantage of percentile ranking is that the difference in the raw scores between one percentile and another may be great but the percentile may not express this. In the distribution of scores in Table 21.1, the raw scores show a difference of 28 points between the 35th and 45th percentiles, yet there is only a one-point difference in raw scores between the 85th and 95th percentiles.

Table 21.1 Transforming Raw Scores into Percentiles

Raw Score	Percentile
99	95
98	85
92	75
91	65
89	55
88	45
60	35
59	25
52	15
50	5

Another potentially misleading characteristic of this ranking system is that a percentile score of 98 in one class may be very different from the same percentile rank in another class. In the two hypothetical distributions shown in Table 21.2 the *top* score in each would be in the 95th percentile, yet there is a vast difference between the percentages of correct responses. Assuming that this is the same test given to two different classes, we must explain that a 95th percentile in one class equals 98 percent correct and a 95th percentile in another class equals 64 percent correct. Nonetheless, as long as we provide all the data— preferably the raw scores, the explanation that one class did considerably better, and perhaps a percentile distribution for both classes combined—percentiles can be useful. The problem occurs when statements such as "Nancy's in the 98th percentile" are made and no additional data is given. We should ask, "The 98th percentile compared to whom? All fifth-graders in the nation, just her class, or just her reading group?" If the comparison is made with a small group, the raw scores, the average (usually the mean), and the range of scores should also be given.

Table 21.2 Transforming Percent Correct into Percentiles

Percent Correct	Percentile	Percent Correct	Percentile
98	95	64	95
96	85	63	85
92	75	60	75
87	65	59	65
84	55	57	55
82	45	56	45
80	35	53	35
79	25	50	25
77	15	48	15
76	5	47	5

One of the strongest handicaps of percentile ranks is that one set of ranks cannot be averaged with another set unless the score distributions of the two sets are identical. Nonetheless, rough comparisons may be made if the two sets of scores are very similar. The difficulty with averaging percentile ranks stems from the fact that a 98th percentile in one case may reflect clearly different performance from a 98 percentile in another, as discussed previously.

Frequency Distributions

A set of scores, especially from a *large* class, is sometimes difficult to work with. One way to condense a set of data to make it easier to work with is to develop a **frequency distribution**. Each different score is listed according to rank and the number of times that score occurred is tallied, as illustrated in Table 21.3. This data can be even further condensed if the scores are grouped by ranges, as in Table 21.4.

If fewer groups are used, some precision is lost because larger ranges result in more scores being massed together. Nonetheless, using fewer groups makes the data easier to handle. We usually try to strike a balance between a manageable number of groups and a high level of precision.

Table 21.3   Tallying Scores for a Frequency Distribution

Score	Tally of Occurrences
39	I
37	I
34	II
33	I
32	I
29	I
28	II
27	I
26	IIII
25	III
24	II
23	IIIII
21	II
20	I
19	II
17	II
16	I
15	II
14	II
13	I
12	II
11	I
10	I
9	I
7	I

Table 21.4   Frequency Distribution of Scores Tallied in Table 21.3

Range	Tally	Frequency	Midpoint
37—41	II	2	39
32—36	IIII	4	34
27—31	IIII	4	29
22—26	IIII IIII IIII	14	24
17—21	IIII II	7	19
12—16	IIII III	8	14
7—11	IIII	4	9

Graphs

To diagram frequencies, we usually produce some type of graph. One of the most common and useful is a **frequency polygon**. The vertical axis shows the number of scores in each group, while the horizontal axis shows each group's midpoint. Figure 21.2 presents the data in Table 21.1 graphed as a frequency polygon. These and other types of graphs arrange data visually so that it can be readily understood by other teachers, the class itself, parents, and administrators.

Figure 21.2   Frequency Polygon

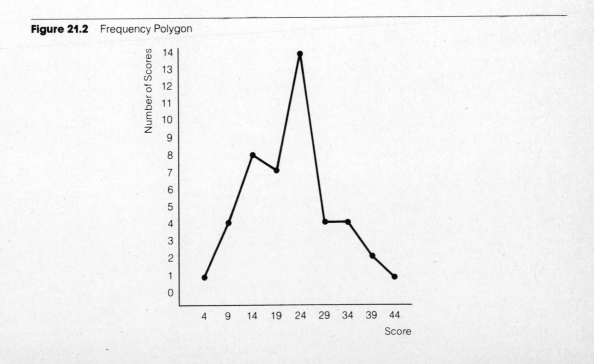

Figure 21.3 Base for a Frequency Polygon

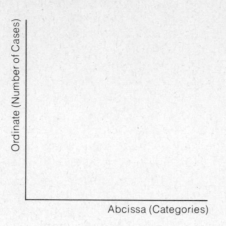

Figure 21.4 Effects of Increased Sample Size on Graphed Line

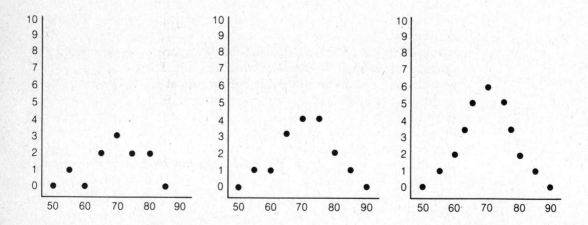

Constructing a Frequency Polygon

Frequency polygons are especially useful for illustrating relationships and trends. Most are based on two lines that intersect at the lower left corner. The horizontal line is called the **abscissa** and the vertical line is called the **ordinate**. The ordinate usually tells the number of cases in each category, while the categories themselves are listed on the abscissa. Thus, in Figure 21.3, to show how many students fell in the group whose midpoint score was 19, one plots a point that aligns with 19 on the abscissa and 7 on the ordinate.

When small amounts of data are graphed, the resulting shape is often quite irregular. But, as the number of cases increases, the shape becomes smoother because the extremes tend to balance out. The more cases we have, the easier it is to see the true pattern of the distribution. Figure 21.4 shows the effect of increasing the sample size. Generally, the more cases there are, the more the graph will resemble a normal curve (see Chapter 23). Note that before a graphed line is smoothed it is called a frequency polygon, and after it is smoothed it is called a curve.

Ogives

Instead of showing each individual performance separately, as in Figure 21.5, an **ogive** shows accumulated progress, as in Figure 21.6. An ogive is also called a **cumulative frequency diagram** because it accumulates frequencies, or numbers of cases. For example, assume that a student receives the following scores on a series of ten spelling tests of ten words each: 2, 4, 7, 5, 4, 5, 6, 5, 6, 7. If each score were recorded separately, the graph in Figure 21.5 would result. From this graph, one would assume that the student is performing at a steady rate, but not doing particularly well. In fact, the student is clearly progressing. Assuming that he did not know any of the words on any of the tests, in the space of ten tests he has learned a total of 51 words. Even though he may not perform equally well on all tests, he is still learning new words and is thus moving ahead. Progress does not require that he earn a higher score on each test, but this fact is not always obvious. If the same data is presented in the form of an ogive, however, the growth becomes more apparent (see Figure 21.6).

When plotting an ogive, we accumulate the frequencies, or add each new score to the total of all previous scores, as shown in Table 21.5. We then graph these totals in the usual way. The steadily rising slope of the line clearly indicates the student's continuing progress.

Figure 21.5 Graph of Ten Separate Scores on Ten Separate Spelling Tests

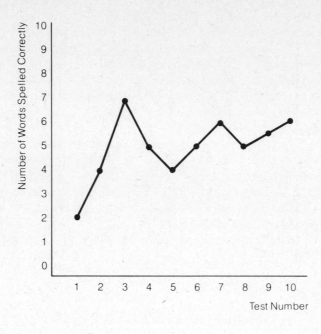

Table 21.5 Accumulated Frequencies for Use in an Ogive

Test	Number Correct	Cumulative Total
1	2	2
2	4	6
3	7	13
4	5	18
5	4	22
6	5	27
7	6	33
8	5	38
9	6	44
10	7	51

Figure 21.6 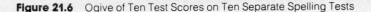 Ogive of Ten Test Scores on Ten Separate Spelling Tests

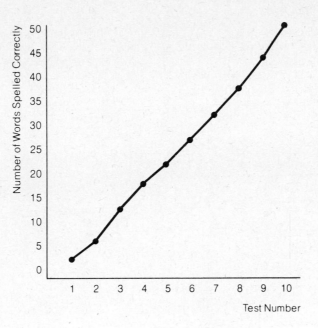

Pie, or Circle, Graphs

Pie, or **circle, graphs** may be used to illustrate proportions or percents. To make a circle graph such as the one in Figure 21.7, we divide the number 360 (the number of degrees in a circle) by the percent we wish to show on the graph. For example, if 15 percent of a class earned A's, 39 percent B's, 37 percent C's, and 9 percent D's, one would calculate the proportion of the circle graph each grade would occupy as shown in Table 21.6. Note that the total number of degrees should add up to 360. A protractor is then used to draw the angles that will appropriately divide the circle. Such a graph helps us to quickly visualize relative proportions and is thus an especially good way of presenting grade distributions. Figure 21.7 shows the data in Table 21.6 first as it would be divided with a protractor and then as a finished product.

Table 21.6 Calculating Segments of a Circle Graph

Grade	Percent of Class	
A	15%	$360 \times .15 =$ 54.0 degrees
B	39%	$360 \times .39 =$ 140.4 degrees
C	37%	$360 \times .37 =$ 133.2 degrees
D	9%	$360 \times .09 =$ 32.4 degrees
	Total	360.0 degrees

Figure 21.7 Circle Graph of Data Presented in Table 21.6

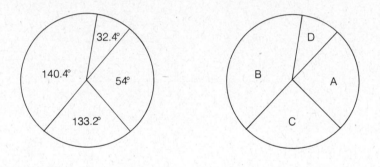

Summary

When working with a set of scores, it is often convenient to rank them. After a set of scores is ranked, it can be grouped into bitiles or quartiles. Percentiles are one of the most common performance reporting methods. They indicate the position any one score would have if there were exactly 100 scores. Some disadvantages to percentile ranking would be that the percentile may not express a great difference between one percentile and another; a percentile score in one class may be very different from the same rank in another class; and finally, that one set of ranks cannot be averaged with another set unless the score distributions are identical. One way to condense a set of data to make it easier to work with is to develop a frequency distribution. To diagram frequencies, we usually produce a graph; one of the most common being a frequency polygon. An ogive or cumulative frequency diagram shows accumulated progress. Pie or circle graphs are used to illustrate proportions or percentiles.

Suggested Readings

Karmel, Louis J. and Marylin O. Karmel. *Measurement and Evaluation in the Schools*. 2d. rev. ed. New York: Macmillan, 1978. Chapter 3.

Lindvall, C. Mauritz and Anthony J. Nitko. *Measuring Pupil Achievement and Aptitude*. 2d. rev. ed. New York: Harcourt Brace Jovanovich, 1975. Chapter 5.

22   Measures of Central Tendency and Dispersion

Now that we have reviewed some basic statistical concepts, we will discuss several statistical operations that are especially useful to educators. These are all descriptive statistics and they describe or summarize information about a population or set of data. We will first look at the three most common measures of central tendency and then at measures of spread or dispersion.

Measures of Central Tendency

When examining a large set of data, such as test scores, it is often desirable to determine a single score that typifies the whole group. This number usually falls near the middle when the scores are ranked from highest to lowest.

A measure of central tendency is similar to the focal point of a balance. When balanced, there are equal amounts of weight on each side. It is largely for convenience and to make comparisons that we want one number to represent a whole set of scores. It may also serve as a reference point in comparing one score with another. Note how scores are compared in the following conversation:

ADAM: How well did you do on your test yesterday?

MELANIE: I scored 48.

ADAM: Is that a good score?

MELANIE: Well, the class average was 29 and the top score was 50.

Thus, the average score and, in this case, the top score, are reference points that help the two students understand the value of a single score. Obviously, Melanie did quite well.

Means

The most common measure of central tendency is the **mean** (μ). The mean is commonly referred to as the average, but it is actually only *one* of *many* kinds of averages. To find a mean, all scores in the set are added and their sum is divided by the total number of scores. The formula for the mean is:

$$\mu = \frac{\Sigma X_i}{N}$$

where

μ (mu) = the mean
Σ = sum of
X_i = each of the scores in turn
N = the total number of scores

For example, to find the mean of the scores 10, 12, 8, 6, 11, and 13, find their sum (Σ) and divide by 6 (N):

$$10 + 12 + 8 + 6 + 11 + 13 = 60$$
$$\frac{60}{6} = 10 = \mu$$

Advantages and Disadvantages of Means The mean is, for most purposes, the most accurate measure of central tendency and therefore the most common. It takes into account the value of *each* number. Thus, a change in the value of any of the numbers will cause a change in the mean, although in some cases, this change may be very small. Not all measures of central tendency have this advantage, as we will discuss later. Another quality of means that other measures of central tendency lack is that means can be averaged. The mean lends itself well to use with other statistics, such as standard deviations and correlations.

The main disadvantage of the mean is that extreme values will distort the data. For example, suppose an entrepreneur wants to open a hot dog stand in the center of a large college campus. Since she will not accept checks or credit cards, she wants to be sure that students carry enough pocket money to purchase her product. To determine this, she asked the first nine students she encountered how much money they were carrying. The nine responses were: $11, $5, $2, $1, $4, $1, $10, $3, $250. Based on this data, she calculated that the mean (average) amount of pocket money students carry is $31.89. Note that in this case the mean is far above the amount of money carried by every student in the sample except one. This occurred because of the presence of one extreme amount, $250. If this student weren't in the sample, the mean would be only $4.62. When this occurs, it may be desirable to use a different measure of central tendency that is *not* distorted by extreme scores.

Medians

A very informative statistic that is *not* influenced by extreme scores is the **median**. The median marks the center of a ranked set of data, or the 50th percentile. Exactly half the scores fall above the median and exactly half fall below.

To determine the median, rank order the scores either from lowest to highest or from highest to lowest. Then find the *middle* number, or the one that half of the scores are above and half are below. Here is how the hot dog stand owner would find the median of the data she gathered:

Rank Order of Amounts of Pocket Money

$250
11
10
5
4 ← Median
3
2
1
1

When a set contains an odd number of scores, the median may be found simply by counting. When the set contains an even number of scores, the median is the mean of the two middle numbers. For example, the median of the numbers 1, 4, 5, and 8 is 4.5 (the mean of 4 and 5). The median is also called the **counting average**.

Advantages and Disadvantages of Medians Returning to the example of the college students' pocket money, note that the median gives a much more accurate indication than the mean does of the amount of money most students carry. This occurs because the median is not affected by extreme scores. Because of this quality, the median is most useful when extreme scores might distort the interpretation of data. The main disadvantage of medians is that there are problems averaging them or using them with most other statistics.

Modes

The **mode** is the most frequently occurring number or score in a set of data. It is determined simply by counting how many times each score appears. In the following example, the mode is 7 because it occurs more frequently than any other score:

$$1, 3, 7, 7, 9, 12, 14, 18$$

Like a median, a mode is not affected by extreme scores and tends to give a good indication of the range of the most common scores. There are difficulties in averaging modes or using them with most other statistics.

If two different scores each occur an equal number of times, the distribution has two modes, or is **bimodal**. A distribution with three modes is **trimodal**. Unimodal and bimodal distributions are most common, and very few distributions have more than three modes. A mode is usually used when a teacher wants to find an average in a short amount of time, and when the mean is not necessary.

Using Averages

A mean, a median, and a mode, while all measures of central tendency, each measure different qualities of a distribution. Thus, when analyzing and interpreting data, one must be careful to choose the measure that is most appropriate. For example, based on the data collected by the hot dog purveyor, all three of the following statements could truthfully be made:

1. The students at our university have a great deal of money at their disposal. The average student carries $31.89 in pocket money (based on the mean).
2. On the whole, students at our university carry just enough money to cover incidentals. According to a recent survey, students had an average of $4.00 in pocket money (based on the median).

3. Students at our university live in shocking poverty. Most commonly, a student has only $1.00 in pocket money (based on the mode).

Depending on her purposes, the store owner can choose the average that will help her prove her case. The only way a listener could discern which average she used would be by asking for more information. It would be most informative if all three measures of central tendency were presented. Other statistics, such as the standard deviation and the range (to be discussed later), would also clarify the matter.

Actually, most distributions do *not* contain scores as extreme as the example we have been using. In most cases, the median and mode are the *same* or *very close to the mean*. In a perfectly symmetrical distribution (a curve in which both sides are mirror images of each other) these three statistics are always *identical*. Only when scores are extremely skewed is there a large difference between the mean, mode, and median. In addition, the larger the number of scores, the more similar the mean, the mode, and the median generally become.

Measures of Dispersion

After looking at one or more measures of central tendency, we typically want to know the *spread* of scores—that is, how they are grouped around the measure of central tendency. Whether most of the scores are clustered closely together or show wide variety has important bearing on the interpretation of a set of data.

Ranges

The simplest measure of spread is the **range,** which is equal to *the highest score minus the lowest score* + 1. The formula for the range is:

$$R = (H - L) + 1$$

where

R = range
H = highest score
L = lowest score

For the hot dog vendor's set of data, the range is 250, or $(250 - 1) + 1 = 250$). This gives us some idea of the spread of scores, but, like the mean, the range is highly affected by extreme scores. If the high score of 250 were eliminated, the range would be only 11, or $(11 - 1) + 1$, a vast change that conveys quite a different impression of the data.

The advantages of the range are that it provides a quick estimate of the spread of scores, indicates the difference between the upper and lower scores, and is affected by *all* scores, even extreme ones (which can sometimes be useful).

Disadvantages of the range include that extreme scores can grossly distort it and that the addition or subtraction of a single score can grossly change it. Thus, with the range (as with the mean), a preferable statistic might be one that indicates *general spread* but *excludes extreme scores.*

Interquartile Range Use of the interquartile range minimizes or eliminates most of the effects of extreme scores. To quickly determine the interquartile range:

1. Rank order the scores from lowest to highest or highest to lowest.
2. Disregard the *top* and *bottom 25 percent* of the scores.
3. Subtract the lowest remaining score from the highest remaining score.

For example, to find the interquartile range of the scores 24, 34, 29, 23, 16, 20, 19, or 15, one would follow these steps:

Rank Order

$\left.\begin{array}{l} 34 \\ 29 \end{array}\right\}$ Top 25%

$\left.\begin{array}{l} 24 \\ 23 \\ 20 \\ 19 \end{array}\right\}$ $24 - 19 = 5 =$ Interquartile range

$\left.\begin{array}{l} 16 \\ 15 \end{array}\right\}$ Bottom 25%

Semi-Interquartile Range Sometimes the semi-interquartile range is useful. This statistic is determined by dividing the interquartile range in half. To find the semi-interquartile range, find the interquartile range and divide it by two. The semi-interquartile range usually corresponds roughly to the standard deviation, a statistic that will be discussed shortly. The semi-interquartile range for the immediately previous example is $5 \div 2 = 2.5$. It is used as a quick estimate of standard deviation, much like the mode may be used as a quick estimate of the average.

The teacher of a small elementary school class will probably not have enough scores to make full use of interquartile and semi-interquartile ranges, because the distribution can be understood without transforming the scores. But for high school classes, or for several elementary school classes combined, they can be quite useful. Because these are standard ways of eliminating extreme scores, it is possible to compare the interquartile or semi-interquartile range of one set of scores with the interquartile or semi-interquartile range of any other appropriate set of scores.

Kelly's Range Kelly's range is the distance between the 10th and 90th precentiles. In this case we eliminate the top 10 percent and the bottom 10 percent of the scores and subtract the lowest remaining score from the highest remaining score. For example, to find Kelly's range for the scores 1, 2, 3, 4, 5, 6, 7, 8, 9, and 10, one would follow these steps:

Rank Order

$$
\left. \begin{array}{l} 10 \\ 9 \end{array} \right\} \text{Top 10 percent}
$$

8
7
6
5
4
3

$$
\left. \begin{array}{l} 2 \\ 1 \end{array} \right\} \text{Bottom 10 percent}
$$

9 − 2 = 7 = Kelly's range

Kelly's range is useful for small classes when using quartiles or quarters would remove more scores than is necessary. It enables teachers to make quick comparisons from year to year.

Standard Deviations

A **standard deviation** indicates the average amount that a set of scores varies from its mean and, as such, serves many purposes in testing and measurement. The formula for finding the standard deviation is:

$$
\sigma = \sqrt{\frac{\Sigma (X_i - \mu)^2}{N}}
$$

where

σ (sigma) = standard deviation
Σ = sum of
X_i = individual score
μ = mean
N = total number of scores

Thus, to find the standard deviation of the scores 1, 2, 3, 4, and 5:

1. Compute the mean (μ):

$$1 + 2 + 3 + 4 + 5 = \frac{15}{5} = 3 = \mu$$

2. Subtract the mean from each score ($X_i - \mu$):

$$1 - 3 = -2$$
$$2 - 3 = -1$$
$$3 - 3 = 0$$
$$4 - 3 = 1$$
$$5 - 3 = 2$$

3. Square each difference and find their sum (Σ):

$$(-2)^2 = 4$$
$$(-1)^2 = 1$$
$$(0)^2 = 0$$
$$(1)^2 = 1$$
$$(2)^2 = \underline{4}$$
$$10$$

4. Divide the sum by the total number of scores (N) to determine the **variance** (σ^2):

$$\frac{10}{5} = 2 = \sigma^2$$

5. Find the square root of the variance ($\sqrt{\sigma^2}$):

$$\sqrt{2} = 1.414$$

Thus, the standard deviation is the average amount that a set of scores deviates from this mean. Since it takes into account the amount that each score deviates, it provides a stable measurement of variability. If any one score were changed, the standard deviation would also change, albeit only slightly in some cases. Statistically, the mean and the standard deviation are in the same family, because they both take into account the value of every score. The standard deviation is generally preferable to the range and interquartile range unless there are extreme scores. Table 22.1 may be used as a handy reference when working with standard deviations.

Table 22.1 Commonly Used Standard Deviations

Number of Scores	Approximate Standard Deviation	Number of Scores	Approximate Standard Deviation
10	3.1	100	5.0
20	3.7	150	5.3
30	4.0	200	5.5
40	4.3	200+	(1/16 of
50	4.5		the range of scores)

The concept of standard deviation is especially important to understanding the normal curve and standardized test scores, which will be discussed in the next chapter.

Summary

The most common and, for most purposes, the most accurate measure of central tendency is the mean. Its main disadvantage is that extreme values will distort the data. The median or counting average is a statistic that is not influenced by extreme scores. The main disadvantage of medians is that there are problems using them with most other statistics. The mode is the most frequently occurring number in a set of data. Like a median, a mode is not affected by extreme scores, but there are difficulties in using them with most other statistics. When analyzing data, one must be careful to use the measure of central tendency that is most appropriate. Measures of dispersion show the spread of scores. The simplest is the range, which is equal to the highest score minus the lowest score + 1. Interquartile, semi-interquartile, and Kelly's ranges help to minimize or eliminate the effects of extreme scores. A standard deviation indicates the average amount that a set of scores varies from its mean. It is generally preferable to the range unless there are extreme scores.

Suggested Readings

Karmel, Louis J. and Marylin O. Karmel. *Measurement and Evaluation in the Schools*. 2d. rev. ed. New York: Macmillan, 1978. Chapter 3.

Lindvall C. Mauritz and Anthony J. Nitko. *Measuring Pupil Achievement and Aptitude*. 2d rev. ed. New York: Harcourt Brace Jovanovich, 1975. Chapter 5.

Sax, Gilbert. *Principles of Educational Measurement and Evaluation*. Belmont, Calif.: Wadsworth Publishing Company, 1974. Chapter 8.

23 The Normal Curve, Standard Scores, and Correlation Coefficients

When large amounts of data pertaining to a quality or an event are separately graphed, they form what is known as a **normal curve**. A normal curve is usually unimodal—that is, it has one peak—and is symmetrical, as shown in Figure 23.1. Most of the cases are grouped around the mean, or center.

The farther one gets away from the center, the *fewer* cases there are. Because of its shape, the normal curve is sometimes called a **bell-shaped curve**.

The Normal Curve

In order to produce a normal curve, a large number of observations are necessary. The more observations one has, the closer their distribution will approximate a normal curve. Almost all characteristics, such as height, weight, running speed, I.Q., and the like, are normally distributed. When the data are not normal, (lopsided or skewed) an

Figure 23.1 The Normal Curve

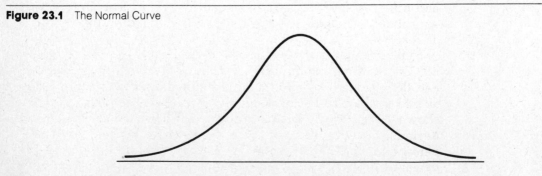

artificially caused factor has usually forced their skewedness. An excellent example of distortion of the normal curve could be found by graphing the I.Q.'s of college students. A normal curve would not result because selection into college is based indirectly on I.Q. Thus, very few individuals of low I.Q. would be found in college. If one looked at the I.Q.'s of the entire population, they would be distributed in the form of a normal curve. But when looking at a select group, one finds distortions. In a positively skewed group, distribution of most of the scores would fall at the low end of the distribution, and the median score would be closer to the lowest score than to the highest. This might indicate that a test was extremely difficult. In a negatively skewed distribution, most of the scores fall at the high end of the distribution and the median is closer to the highest score than it is to the lowest. This kind of distribution might be expected for scores on a mastery test or when a test is quite simple. The distribution of cases along a normal curve is predictable.

A specific percent of cases tend to fall within certain points, as shown in Figure 23.2. These points are measured in standard deviations. For example, between the mean and one standard deviation on each side of the mean, we usually find about 34 percent of all cases. This is an *average*, but with a sufficiently large number of scores, this average tends to be accurate. Scores that fall between one and two standard deviations tend to account for 14 percent of all cases. Between two and three standard deviations we usually find 2 percent of all cases. And above four standard deviations, we find only about .13 percent of all cases.

To illustrate the usefulness of the normal curve, let us assume that Mr. Gomez has given his class a test on which the average score is 50 and the standard deviation is 10. Based on this information, we are able to compare and evaluate students' performances using the curve shown in Figure 23.3. For example, a score of 60 would be one standard deviation above the mean. It would also be above 50 percent + 34, or 84 percent, of all the other scores. A score of 70 would have a standard deviation of 2 and would be above 84 percent + 14 percent, or 98 per-

Figure 23.2 Approximate Percentage of Cases within Each Standard Deviation

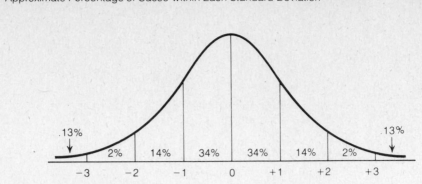

cent of all other scores. On the other hand, a student with a score of 40 would be one standard deviation *below* the mean and would thus be *above* 14 percent + 2 percent + .13 percent of the cases, or a total of about 16.13 percent. I.Q. scores are also distributed normally. The mean of all I.Q. scores is 100 and the standard deviation of most tests is either 15 or 16. Figure 23.4 illustrates the normal distribution of I.Q. scores. One standard deviation above the mean would equal an I.Q. of 115, two standard deviations above would equal an I.Q. of 130 and so forth.

Figure 23.3 Normal Curve for a Test with Mean = 50 and S.D. = 10

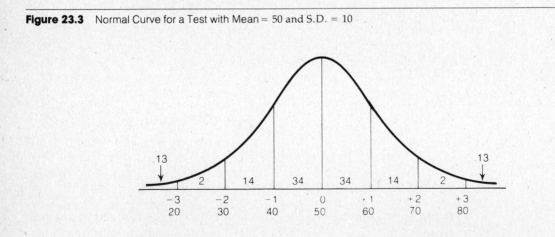

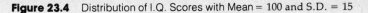

Figure 23.4 Distribution of I.Q. Scores with Mean = 100 and S.D. = 15

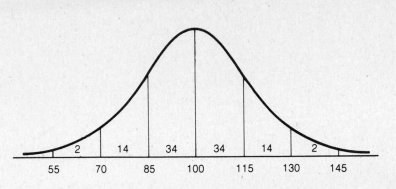

	2	14	34	34	14	2	
55	70	85	100	115	130	145	

Standard Scores

z-Scores

Unfortunately, I.Q.'s of exactly 115 or 130 are not that common. A typical score is more likely to be 124, 102, or some other number that is not exactly one or two standard deviations above or below the mean. To convert a raw score into its equivalent standard deviation from the mean, called a **z-score**, the following formula is used:

$$\text{z-score} = \frac{\text{raw score} - \text{mean}}{\text{standard deviation}}$$

or

$$z = \frac{X - \mu}{\sigma}$$

Thus, if a student has an I.Q. of 121, if the mean (μ) is 100 and the standard deviation (σ) is 15, her z-score would be calculated as follows:

$$z = \frac{121 - 100}{15} = \frac{21}{15} = +1.40$$

and her I.Q. would be 1.4 standard deviations above average.

The Meaning of z-Scores A z-score of $+1.0$ indicates that the individual score is exactly one standard deviation above the mean, while a z-score of -1.00 indicates that the score is exactly one standard deviation below the mean. Negative z-scores always indicate scores below the mean. Likewise, positive z-scores always indicate scores above the mean. The range of z-scores usually runs from −4.00 to +4.00. Their mean is zero (0) and their standard deviation is 1.

When compiling test results, many teachers find it convenient to convert each student's raw score into a z-score. By doing this it is easy to compare one person's score with any *other* person's score on the same or another test or one person's score in one subject with his or her score in a different subject. For example, note how z-scores make it possible to compare Henry's scores on two different tests:

Test 1: Mean = 62
Standard deviation = 8
Henry's raw score = 67
$$z = \frac{67 - 62}{8} = \frac{5}{8} = .625$$

Test 2: Mean = 34
Standard deviation = 4
Henry's raw score = 34
$$z = \frac{36 - 34}{4} = \frac{2}{4} = .50$$

Henry's performance was above average on both tests, but he definitely did better on the first.

T-Scores

A **T-score** is a standard score very similar to a z-score except that it eliminates the problems of negative numbers and decimals. One-half of all z-scores are negative, and most contain decimals, but T-scores are always positive whole numbers. The formula for transforming a z-score into a T-score is:

$$T = 10z + 50$$

When the student's z-score is known, it is multiplied by 10 and 50 is added. This eliminates decimals to the tenth place as well as negative numbers. T-scores have a mean of 50 and a standard deviation of 10. For example, if a student's z-score is 2.0, her T-score would be:

$$10\,(2.00) + 50 = 20.0 + 50 = 70$$

Similarly, if her z-score were −2.0, her T-score would be:

$$10\,(-2.00) = 50 = -20.0 + 50 = 30$$

I.Q. Scores

Another score that is derived in much the same way as a T-score is an I.Q. score. I.Q. scores have a standard deviation of 15 or 16 and a mean of 100. Given these constraints, we can change a z-score into an I.Q. score with either one of the following formulas:

$$I.Q. = 15\,(z) + 100$$

$$I.Q. = 16\,(z) + 100$$

Thus, using the first formula, if a student has a z-score of 2.0, his I.Q. score would be:

$$15\,(z) + 100 = 30 + 100 = 130$$

College Board Scores

The scores for Graduate Record Examinations and College Entrance Examination Boards are also based on z-scores and are designed to improve precision by maintaining as much data as possible. For this reason they use a higher mean and standard deviation. Their formula is:

$$100\,(z) + 500$$

A z-score of 2.00 would therefore yield a CEEB or GRE score of:

$$100\,(2) + 500 = 200 + 500 = 700$$

This number corresponds to a T-score with the decimal point moved one place to the right.

Thus, standard scores such as T-scores, CEEB scores, and I.Q. scores are merely variations of z-scores. These variations are used primarily because of convenience and tradition. Whole (without fractions), positive numbers are easier to work with and lead to fewer clerical errors.

Stanines

Stanines are single-digit standard scores with a mean of 5 and a standard deviation of 2. The word *stanine* score comes from the expression *standard nine-point scale,* because the distribution is divided into nine sections. The following formula is used to obtain stanine scores:

$$2\,(z) + 5$$

Thus, a z-score of 2 would yield a stanine of 9:

$$2\,(z) + 5 = 4 + 5 = 9$$

Stanine scores divide a normal curve as illustrated in Figure 23.5.

Figure 23.5   Stanine Scores Divide a Normal Curve

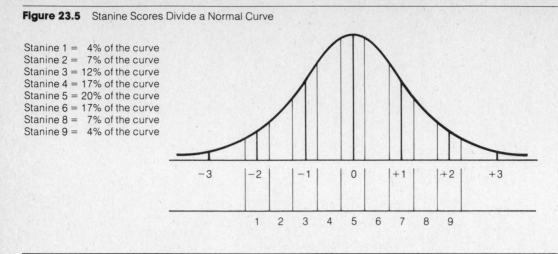

Stanine 1 =   4% of the curve
Stanine 2 =   7% of the curve
Stanine 3 = 12% of the curve
Stanine 4 = 17% of the curve
Stanine 5 = 20% of the curve
Stanine 6 = 17% of the curve
Stanine 8 =   7% of the curve
Stanine 9 =   4% of the curve

Correlation Coefficients

A correlation coefficient describes the relationship between two sets of data pertaining to the same person or group. For example, one might be interested in the correlation between performance on a reading readiness test and performance on a later reading comprehension test. If the correlation between the two test scores is high, students who do well on the readiness test could be expected to do well on the comprehension test; likewise, students who do poorly on the first test would probably do poorly on the second.

Correlation coefficients can convey useful information about many educational situations. But to determine a correlation coefficient, one must have *two* scores for *each* person. For example, suppose that we wanted to find out the relationship (correlation) between the number of pages in a term paper and the grade it receives. Do longer papers receive higher grades? Or is the length of the paper irrelevant? The information we need to do a correlation is the *grade* and the *number of pages* of each paper. And it is important that we know which grade goes with which paper. Assume we have collected and graphed the data shown in Figure 23.6.

If, as one factor (number of pages) increases, the other factor (grade) increases, the two show a positive correlation. In this case, as the number of pages increases, the grade goes up. On the other hand, when some papers with only a few pages also receive high grades, while others with many pages receive low grades, there may be *little* or *no correlation*, as illustrated in Figure 23.7. Finally, when one variable *goes up* and the other *goes down*, there is the negative correlation shown in Figure 23.8.

Figure 23.6 Positive Correlation between Term Paper Grades and Lengths

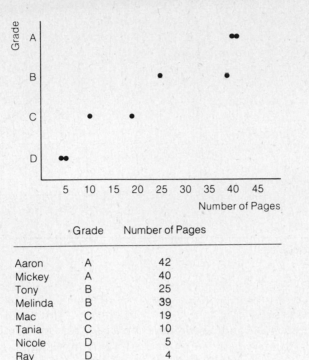

	Grade	Number of Pages
Aaron	A	42
Mickey	A	40
Tony	B	25
Melinda	B	39
Mac	C	19
Tania	C	10
Nicole	D	5
Ray	D	4

Correlations Do Not Prove Causation

It is important to stress that correlations show only *relationship*, they do *not* show *causation*. For example, the fact that longer papers receive higher grades does not mean that longer papers *produce* higher grades. The real explanation could be that better students typically write longer papers, or there may be no explanation at all. A correlation coefficient can tell us the extent of a relationship, but only reason, logic, and understanding of all factors involved can lead to a conclusion that one factor *causes* another.

Negative Versus Positive Correlations

The usefulness of a correlation coefficient depends upon the factors being correlated and the relationships in which we are interested. Most of the time the degree of correlation is the most important consideration. For example, the correlations −.90 and +.90 are equally high, even though one is a negative number and the other is a positive one. In fact, sometimes a negative correlation is desirable. For example, we would expect to find that as the compatibility between two people goes up, the number of fights and disagreements they have goes down.

There are several ways of determining correlation coefficients, but we will discuss only the most common one. No matter which method is used, a number within the range of -1.00 (perfect negative) to $+1.00$ (perfect positive) is obtained. The slope of a perfect negative correlation is illustrated in Figure 23.9, while the slope of a perfect positive correlation is shown in Figure 23.10. Note that in this case the slope of the dots is the *opposite* of the slope in Figure 23.9.

Figure 23.7 No Correlation between Term Paper Grades and Lengths

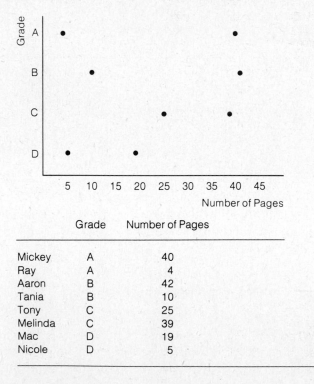

	Grade	Number of Pages
Mickey	A	40
Ray	A	4
Aaron	B	42
Tania	B	10
Tony	C	25
Melinda	C	39
Mac	D	19
Nicole	D	5

Figure 23.8 Negative Correlation between Term Paper Grades and Lengths

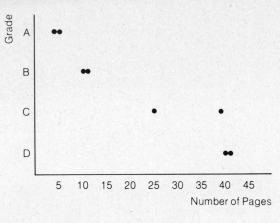

	Grade	Number of Pages
Ray	A	4
Nicole	A	5
Tania	B	10
Mac	B	19
Tony	C	25
Melinda	C	39
Mickey	D	40
Aaron	D	42

Figure 23.9 Perfect Negative Correlation

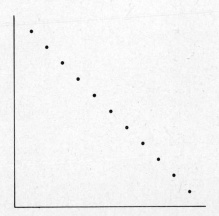

When a perfect correlation occurs, there are no exceptions. In every case, if *one* score is known, its corresponding score can be accurately predicted. A perfect correlation is linear and has no exceptions, thus

every point would fall in a straight line and there would be no deviation. Two sets of data that had 0 correlation, when graphed, would produce a series of points equally spread out on the entire correlational matrix, as in Figure 23.11. In every case, it would be impossible to predict one score on the basis of knowledge of another score. Perfect correlations, whether positive, negative, or even zero, are very rare. Most correlations fall somewhere between these extremes.

Figure 23.10   Perfect Positive Correlation

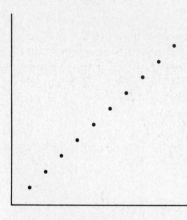

Figure 23.11   Zero Correlation

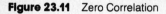

Calculating Correlation Coefficients

When working with raw scores, the correlation coefficient may be obtained by using the formula:

$$r_{xy} = \frac{\Sigma xy}{\sqrt{\Sigma x^2 y^2}}$$

where

r_{xy} = correlation coefficient
Σ = sum of
$x = X - \mu_x$
$y = Y - \mu_y$

Table 23.1 shows the calculation of the correlation between scores on two kinds of German tests—one on vocabulary (X) and one on grammar (Y). First the mean score is found for each test (μ_x and μ_y). Then the amount that each score deviates from the mean is calculated (X − μ_x = x and Y − μ_y = y). Note that for each test, the sum of the deviations (x and y) is zero. Working pair by pair, the deviation on Test X is multiplied by the deviation on Test Y (xy). Next, each deviation is squared (x^2 and y^2). Finally, the numbers in each column of the table are totaled and substituted into the formula to obtain the correlation coefficient, also known as **Pearson's r**.

Table 23.1 Calculation of Correlation for Two Tests

X	Y	x	y	xy	x^2	ay^2
95	80	15	5	75	225	25
90	85	10	10	100	100	100
85	80	5	5	25	25	25
80	70	0	− 5	0	0	25
75	80	− 5	5	− 25	25	25
75	75	− 5	0	0	25	0
60	55	− 20	− 20	400	400	400
Σ 560	525	0	0	575	800	600

$\mu_x = 80$
$\mu_y = 75$
$\mu_{xy} = \dfrac{575}{\sqrt{(800)(600)}} = \dfrac{575}{692.82} = .83$

Interpreting Correlation Coefficients

Table 23.2 can serve as a basic guide to the meaning of most correlation coefficients. The extent of correlation remains the same regardless of whether the coefficient is positive or negative.

Table 23.2 Interpreting the Size of a Correlation Coefficient

Range	Extent of Correlation
± .90 – 1.00	Very high correlation
± .70 – .89	High correlation
± .50 – .69	Moderate correlation
± .30 – .49	Medium correlation
± .00 – .29	Little, if any

Squaring the correlation coefficient yields a quick estimate of the level of relationship between two sets of data. For example, .50 squared equals .25. This would indicate that 25 percent of the variation in factor X is directly associated with variable Y. The closer the number comes to 1.00 in either a positive or a negative direction, the higher the correlation is. A correlation coefficient of .40 tells us that 16 percent of factor A is directly related to factor B; a correlation of .80 shows a 64 percent relationship, and so forth.

Although a correlation coefficient of 1.0 indicates a perfect relationship between two factors, a coefficient of .50 does *not* indicate a 50 percent perfect relationship, nor is a correlation of .50 twice the relationship of one that is .25. Actually a correlation of .50 is four times as powerful as a correlation of .25. The closer a correlation approaches +1.00 or −1.00, the more **significant** it is. The more significant a correlation is, the more likely it is that the relationship would not occur by chance.

Summary

When large amounts of data pertaining to a quality or event are separately graphed, they form a normal or bell-curve. It is usually unimodal and symmetrical. A z-score is the conversion of a raw score into its equivalent standard deviation from the mean. A T-score is a standard score similar to a z-score except that it eliminates the problems of negative numbers and decimals. An I.Q. score is derived in much the same way as a T-score, while GRE and CEEB scores are based on z-scores. Stanines are single-digit standard scores in which the distribution is divided into nine sections. A correlation coefficient describes the relationship between two sets of data pertaining to the same person or group. Correlations show relationship, but not causation. Their usefulness depends upon the factors being correlated and the relationships in which we are interested.

Suggested Readings

Karmel, Louis J. and Marylin O. Karmel. *Measurement and Evaluation in the Schools.* 2d. rev. ed. New York: Macmillan, 1978. Chapter 3.

Lindvall C. Mauritz and Anthony J. Nitko. *Measuring Pupil Achievement and Aptitude.* 2d. rev. ed. New York: Harcourt Brace Jovanovich, 1975. Chapter 5.

Sax, Gilbert. *Principles of Educational Measurement and Evaluation.* Belmont, Calif.: Wadsworth Publishing Company, 1974. Chapter 8.

References

Ahmann, Stanley, and Glock, Marvin. *Evaluating Pupil Growth: Principles of Tests and Measurements.* 5th rev. ed. Boston: Allyn and Bacon, 1975.

Aiken, Lewis R. *Psychological Testing and Assessment.* 3d rev. ed. Boston: Allyn and Bacon, 1979.

Asher, J. William. *Educational Research and Evaluation Methods.* Boston: Little, Brown, 1976.

Beggs, Donald L. and Lewis, Ernst L. *Measurement and Evaluation in the Schools.* Boston: Houghton Mifflin, 1975.

Beggs, Donald L. and Lewis, Ernst L. *Instructor's Manual for Measurement and Evaluation in the Schools.* Boston: Houghton Mifflin, 1975.

Bergman, Jerry. "A Study of Accuracy of Handscoring of Standardized Tests." Unpublished paper. Detroit, Mich.: Wayne State University, 1970.

_____ . "A Study of an Innovative Student Input Report Card System." Unpublished paper. Madison Heights, Mich.: Lamphere Schools, 1971.

_____ . "A Study of Student Attitudes Toward Tests Among College Students." Unpublished paper. Bowling Green, Ohio: Bowling Green State University, 1976b.

_____ . "C.A.T.—Cross Age Tutoring. Is it the Answer?" *American Secondary Education,* vol. 8, September 1978.

_____ . "Evaluation of an Experimental Program Designed to Reduce Recidivism Among Second Felony Criminal Offenders." Ph.D. Dissertation. Detroit, Mich.: Wayne State University, 1976a.

_____ . "The Relationship Between Personality and Ratings Focusing on the Personality of the Rater and Generosity, Severity, and Central Tendency Error." Bowling Green, Ohio: Bowling Green State University, 1980.

Blumberg, Phyllis. *Instructor's Manual for Psychology for the Classroom/Gibson.* Englewood Cliffs, N. J.: Prentice-Hall, 1976.

Borg, Walter R. and Gall, Meredith D. *Educational Research: An Introduction.* 2d rev. ed. New York: David McKay, 1971.

Campbell, Stephen K. *Flows and Fallacies in Statistical Thinking.* Englewood Cliffs, N.J.: Prentice-Hall, 1974.

Chase, Clinton I. *Measurement for Educational Evaluation.* Reading, Mass.: Addison-Wesley, 1978.

Cleary, T. Anne et al. "Educational Uses of Tests with Disadvantaged Students." *American Psychologist,* January 1975, 15–40.

Cleary, T. Anne and Thomas L. Hilton. "An Investigation of Item Bias." *Educational and Psychological Measurement,* vol. 28 (1968), 61–75.

Coffman, W.E. "Essay Examinations." In Thorndike, Robert L., ed. *Educational Measurement.* Washington, D.C.: American Council on Education, 1971.

Colwell, Richard. *The Evaluation of Music Teaching and Learning.* Englewood Cliffs, N.J.: Prentice-Hall. 1965.

Cronbach, Lee J. "Equity in Education—Where Psychometrics and Political Philosophy Meet." *Journal of Educational Measurement,* vol. 13 (1976), 31–41.

Cronbach, Lee J. *Essentials of Psychological Testing.* 3d rev. ed. New York: Harper and Row, 1970.

Cross, Aleene. *Home Economics Evaluation.* Columbus, Ohio: Charles E. Merrill, 1973.

Darlington, Richard B. "Another Look at 'Cultural Fairness'." *Journal of Educational Measurement,* vol. 8 (1971), 71–82.

Downie, N.M. and Heath, R.W. *Basic Statistical Methods.* 4th rev. ed. New York: Harper and Row, 1974.

Eagle, Norman and Harris, Anna S. "Interaction of Race and Test on Reading Performance Scores." *Journal of Educational Measurement,* vol. 34 (1974), 131–35.

Ebel, Robert L. *Measuring Educational Achievement.* Englewood Cliffs, N.J.: Prentice-Hall, 1965.

Echternacht, Gary. "A Quick Method for Determining Test Bias." *Educational and Psychological Measurement,* vol. 34 (1974), 271–80.

Feldmesser, Robert A. "The Positive Functions of Grades." In *Readings in Measurement and Evaluation in Education and Psychology,* William A. Mehrens, ed. New York: Holt Rinehart and Winston, 1976.

Fine, Benjamin. *The Stranglehold of the I.Q.* Garden City, N.Y.: Doubleday, 1975.

Flanders, Ned A. *Analyzing Teachers' Behavior*. Reading, Mass.: Addison-Wesley, 1970.

Furst, Edward J. *Constructing Evaluation Instruments*. New York: Longmans, Green, 1958.

Galfo, Armand J. *Interpreting Educational Research*. 3d rev. ed. Dubuque, Iowa: W.C. Brown, 1975.

Gerberich, J. Raymond, Greene, Harry A., and Jorgensen, Albert N. *Measurement and Evaluation in the Modern School*. New York: David McKay, 1962.

Goertzel, Victor and Goertzel, Mildred. *Cradles of Eminence*. Boston: Little, Brown, 1962.

Greene, Harry A., Jorgensen, Albert N., and Gerberich, J. Raymond. *Measurement and Evaluation in the Elementary School*. 2d rev. ed. New York: Longmans, Green, 1953.

Gronlund, Norman E. *Measurement and Evaluation in Teaching*. 2d rev. ed. New York: Macmillan, 1971.

_____ . *Measurement and Evaluation in Teaching*. 3d. rev. ed. New York: Macmillan, 1976.

_____ . *Readings in Measurement and Evaluation*. New York: Macmillan, 1968.

Gross, Martin L. *The Brain Watchers*. New York: Random House, 1962.

Hardaway, Mathilde. *Testing and Evaluation in Business Education*. Cincinnati, Ohio: Southwestern, 1966.

Hill, Joseph E. and Kerber, August. *Models, Methods, and Analytical Procedures in Education Research*. Detroit, Mich.: Wayne State University Press, 1967.

Hills, John R. *Exercises in Classroom Measurement*. Columbus, Ohio: Charles E. Merrill, 1976.

_____ . *Measurement and Evaluation in the Classroom*. Columbus, Ohio: Charles E. Merrill, 1976.

_____ . *Instructor's Guide for Measurement and Evaluation in the Classroom*. Columbus, Ohio: Charles E. Merrill, 1976.

Hoffman, Banesh. *The Tyranny of Testing*. New York: Crowell-Collier, 1964.

Hopkins, Charles D. and Antes, Richard L. *Classroom Measurement and Evaluation*. Itasca, Ill.: F.E. Peacock, 1978.

_____ . *Instructor's Manual for Classroom Measurement and Evaluation*. Itasca, Ill.: F.E. Peacock, 1978.

Kallingal, Anthony. "The Prediction of Grades for Black and White Students at Michigan State University." *Journal of Educational Measurement*, vol. 8 (1971), 263–65.

Karmel, Louis J. *Measurement and Evaluation in the Schools.* New York: Macmillan, 1970.

Karmel, Louis J. and Karmel, Marylin O. *Measurement and Evaluation in the Schools.* 2d rev. ed. New York: Macmillan, 1978.

——————. *Instructor's Supplement for Measurement and Evaluation in the Schools.* 2d rev. ed. New York: Macmillan, 1978.

Kellogg, Rhoda. *Analyzing Children's Art.* Palo Alto, Calif.: National Press Books, 1970.

Lehman, Paul R. *Tests and Measurements in Music.* Foundations of Music Education Series. Englewood Cliffs, N.J.: Prentice-Hall, 1968.

Lien, Arnold J. *Measurements and Evaluation of Learning.* 3d rev. ed. Dubuque, Iowa: W.C. Brown, 1976.

Lindeman, Richard H. and Peter F. Merenda. *Educational Measurement.* Glenview, Ill.: Scott Foresman, 1979.

Lindvall, C. Mauritz and Nitko, Anthony J. *Measuring Pupil Achievement and Aptitude.* 2d rev. ed. New York: Harcourt Brace Jovanovich, 1975.

Lyman, Howard B. *Test Scores and What They Mean.* 2d rev. ed. Englewood Cliffs, N.J.: Prentice-Hall, 1971.

Marshall, Hales. *Classroom Test Construction.* Reading, Mass.: Addison-Wesley, 1971.

Mehrens, William A. and Lehmann, Irvin, J. *Measurement and Evaluation in Education and Psychology.* 2d rev. ed. New York: Holt Rinehart and Winston, 1978.

Mehrens, William A. and Lehmann, Irvin J. *Standardized Tests in Education.* 2d rev. ed. New York: Holt Rinehart and Winston, 1973.

Mehrens, William A. and Ebel, Robert L., eds. *Principles of Educational and Psychological Measurement.* Chicago: Rand McNally, 1967.

Meyer, G. "An Experimental Study of the Old and New Types of Examination: The Effect of the Examination Set on Memory." *Journal of Educational Psychology,* vol. 25 (1934), 64.

Miller, David Monroe. *Interpreting Test Scores.* New York: John Wiley and Sons, 1972.

Noll, Victor H., Scannell, Dale P. and Craig, Robert C. *Introduction to Educational Measurement.* 4th rev. ed. Boston: Houghton Mifflin, 1979.

Payne, David A. *The Assessment of Learning, Cognitive and Affective.* Lexington, Mass.: D.C. Heath, 1974.

Ross, Clay Campbell and Stanley, Julian C. *Measurement in Today's Schools.* 3d rev. ed. Englewood Cliffs, N.J.: Prentice-Hall, 1954.

Rugg, Earle. "Who Shall Be Educated for Teaching?" *Journal of Teacher Education*, June, 1965.

Sax, Gilbert. *Principles of Educational Measurement and Evaluation*. Belmont, Calif.: Wadsworth, 1974.

Starch, D. and Elliot, E.C. "Reliability of Grading of High School Work in English." *School Review*, vol. 20 (1912), 442–57.

Tarczan, Constance. *An Educator's Guide to Psychological Tests*. Springfield, Ill.: Charles C. Thomas, 1975.

TenBrink, Terry D. *Evaluation: A Practical Guide for Teachers*. New York: McGraw-Hill, 1974.

Thomas, Murray R. *Judging Student Progress*. 2d. rev. ed. New York: David McKay, 1960.

Thorndike, Robert L. *Educational Measurement*. Washington, D.C.: American Council on Education, 1971.

Thorndike, Robert L. and Hagen, Elizabeth. *Measurement and Evaluation in Psychology and Education*. 4th rev. ed. New York: John Wiley and Sons, 1977.

Torrance, E. Paul. *Guiding Creative Talent*. Englewood Cliffs, N.J.: Prentice-Hall, 1962.

Tuckman, Bruce W. *Measuring Educational Outcomes: Fundamentals of Testing*. New York: Harcourt Brace Jovanovich, 1975.

Van Allen, Edward. *The Branded Child*. Mineola, N.Y.: Reportorial Press, 1964.

Valette, Rebecca M. *Modern Language Testing*. 2d rev. ed. New York: Harcourt Brace Jovanovich, 1977.

Watson, Goodwin, "The Specific Techniques of Investigation: Testing Intelligence, Aptitudes, and Personality." *The Scientific Movement in Education. Thirty-Seventh Yearbook of the National Society for the Study of Education, Part II*. Chapter 30. Bloomington, Ill.: Public School Publishing, 1938.

Webb, Eugene J., Campbell, Donald T., Schwartz, Richard D., and Sechrest, Lee. *Unobtrusive Measures: Nonreactive Research in the Social Sciences*. Chicago: Rand McNally, 1966.

Woodruff, Asahel and Pritchard, Maralyn W. "Some Trends in the Development of Psychological Tests." *Education and Psychological Measurement*, vol. 9 (1949), 105–108.

Index

WESTMAR COLLEGE LIBRARY

LB 3051 .B42   (89-452)
Bergman, Jerry.
Understanding educational
  measurement and evaluation

≠ DEMCO ≡